The Religious Press in Britain, 1760–1900

Recent Titles in
Contributions to the Study of Religion

Marchin' the Pilgrims Home: Leadership and Decision-Making in an Afro-Caribbean Faith
Stephen D. Glazier

Exorcising the Trouble Makers: Magic, Science, and Culture
Francis L. K. Hsu

The Cross, The Flag, and The Bomb: American Catholics Debate War and Peace, 1960–1983
William A. Au

Religious Conflict in Social Context: The Resurgence of Orthodox Judaism in Frankfurt Am Main, 1838–1877
Robert Liberles

Triumph over Silence: Women in Protestant History
Richard L. Greaves, editor

Neighbors, Friends, or Madmen: The Puritan Adjustment to Quakerism in Seventeenth-Century Massachusetts Bay
Jonathan M. Chu

Cities of Gods: Faith, Politics and Pluralism in Judaism, Christianity and Islam
Nigel Biggar, Jamie S. Scott, William Schweiker, editors

Theodicies in Conflict: A Dilemma in Puritan Ethics and Nineteenth-Century American Literature
Richard Forrer

Gilbert Tennent, Son of Thunder: A Case Study of Continental Pietism's Impact on the First Great Awakening in the Middle Colonies
Milton J Coalter, Jr.

Lighten Their Darkness: The Evangelical Mission to Working-Class London, 1828–1860
Donald M. Lewis

The United Synod of the South: The Southern New School Presbyterian Church
Harold M. Parker, Jr.

Covenant and Community in Modern Judaism
S. Daniel Breslauer

The Religious Press in Britain, 1760–1900

Josef L. Altholz

CONTRIBUTIONS TO THE STUDY OF RELIGION,
NUMBER 22

Henry Warner Bowden, Series Editor

Greenwood Press
New York • Westport, Connecticut • London

Library of Congress Cataloging-in-Publication Data

Altholz, Josef Lewis
The religious press in Britain, 1760-1900 / Josef L. Altholz.
p. cm. – (Contributions to the study of religion, ISSN 0196-7053 ; no. 22)
Bibliography: p.
Includes index.
ISBN 0-313-25738-8 (lib. bdg. : alk. paper)
1. Journalism, Religious–Great Britain–History. 2. Religious literature–Publication and distribution–History. I. Title. II. Series.
PN5124.R45A48 1989
070.4'49291'0941–dc 19 89-1956

British Library Cataloguing in Publication Data is available.

Library of Congress Catalog Card Number: 89-1956
ISBN: 0-313-25738-8
ISSN: 0196-7053

First published in 1989

Greenwood Press, Inc.
88 Post Road West, Westport, Connecticut 06881

Printed in the United States of America

The paper used in this book complies with the Permanent Paper Standard issued by the National Information Standards Organization (Z39.48-1984).

10 9 8 7 6 5 4 3 2 1

Contents

Series Foreword by Henry Warner Bowden vii

Preface ix

1. Introduction 1
2. The Development of the Religious Press 7
3. Anglican Evangelicals 15
4. The High Church 23
5. Not Angels, But Anglicans 33
6. Evangelicals 45
7. Nonconformity 57
8. The Old Dissent 67
9. The New Dissent 79
10. Presbyterians 89
11. Roman Catholics 97
12. Others 109
13. Freethought 117
14. Movements 123
15. Specialities 131

16. Conclusion: Heralds and Witnesses 141

Appendix 145

Notes 147

Selected Bibliography 177

Index of Religious Periodicals, 1760–1900 181

General Index 203

Series Foreword

It has long been a stock in trade for religious institutions to disseminate their ideas to both adherents and those not yet converted. Preaching and other forms of oral communication have usually predominated. When printing superseded hand-copied manuscripts, religious writings tended to cluster around theological treatises and biblical commentaries. Such publications, together with printed sermons and tracts, constitute a large segment of the history of early printing. By the late eighteenth century, though, cheaper production methods and a better-educated reading public inaugurated a new era. Periodicals of all sorts began to expand in unprecedented variety and extent. Journals of religious opinion flourished most noticeably in the British Isles, totaling as many as three thousand between 1760 and 1900. This book makes the first attempt to classify the unruly proliferation spawned by the religious press.

From one perspective this volume has a simple, straightforward purpose: to correlate religious magazines, reviews, and newspapers with their provenance. Those periodicals are essential primary sources for students of religion in popular culture. A guide to those sources is a crucial aid to investigation, orienting researchers in the milieu they hope to fathom. No other publication exists that performs this service for the time period and subject matter it covers.

From another perspective this volume goes far beyond furnishing bibliographical data. It is a historical overview of this branch of journalism, and in its coverage makes judgments as to which periodicals were worth including. This selectivity required Josef Altholz to be as open-minded as possible in perceiving which publications had "religious" content. Further, it demanded that he treat materials in a discriminating way in order to assess their relative importance as historical factors. All this Altholz has done while informing researchers of each periodical's dates of existence, frequency of appearance, denominational affiliation and stance on specific controversial topics. The index of this volume provides quick information. The text itself yields details in greater length regarding the extent of each periodical's historical significance and its value as a resource for investigators. These sorts of judgments and descriptions make Altholz's work indispensable to those trying to probe the popular mind of Victorian England. Those wishing to understand the massive output of religious ideas related to parochial and social issues now have an invaluable guide and research tool to help them.

Henry Warner Bowden

Preface

In the springtide of periodicals research, about 1970, when we were "a society of projectors," Michael Wolff, who was projector-in-chief, proposed that I write a volume on the religious press as part of what might become a general history of Victorian periodicals. I declined, thinking that no single scholar could manage all the different denominations and movements; I might do the Roman Catholics, but a team of specialists must be assembled for all the rest. In 1981, after I had converted academically to the study of Anglicanism, the work on the religious press appeared to me in a new light. It could only be done by one person, for there was no prospect of a team of authoritative specialists of uniform quality in all subjects (especially the intractable Anglican press); and, as a scholar who had worked extensively in the fields of Victorian religion and of Victorian periodicals, I had to undertake this work, for no one else would.

The completion of this project would not have been possible without financial support from the Graduate School of the University of Minnesota, specifically a Bush Fellowship to supplement my sabbatical in Britain in 1983–84, a single-quarter leave for writing, and a grant-in-aid for a research assistant for indexing in 1988. Research was largely done in the holdings of the British Library and its Newspaper Library at Colindale, supplemented by resources at the Institute of Historical Research and the University of London Library and a trip to the University of Edinburgh and New College, Edinburgh; I wish to express my thanks to the authorities and staffs of these libraries and those of my own university. I thank Greenwood

Press for offering me a contract when my project was still being formulated and for imposing on me an end-of-1988 deadline, which concentrated my mind wonderfully. To my editor, Cynthia Harris, I must express my thanks for reconciling the imperious demands of house style and format with my own whim of iron.

For advice and assistance, I am indebted to many scholars, not all of whom may have been aware that they were assisting this project: Professors James C. Holland, John Kent, Emmet Larkin, Patrick Scott, and Michael Wolff; the late Professor Walter E. Houghton and Esther Rhoads Houghton; Jean Slingerland of the Wellesley Index to Victorian Periodicals; Leanna Langley of the University of Notre Dame London Program; A. Lawrence Marshburn, director of the Biola Library; and former or present students Deng Shih-An, David Heughins, P. J. Kulisheck, Shirley A. Mullen, and Paula Reed Nancarrow.

Some passages in chapters 1 and 2 were first used in an article, "The Religious Press," in *Victorian Periodicals II*, edited by J. Don Vann and Rosemary T. VanArsdel, being published by the Modern Language Association of America. Many passages in chapter 11 were published in my article, "The Redaction of Catholic Periodicals," in *Innovators and Preachers: The Role of the Editor in Victorian England*, edited by Joel H. Wiener (Westport, Conn.: Greenwood Press, 1985), 143–60.

I should like to call readers' attention to the first of the two indexes, an Index of Religious Periodicals, 1760–1900, which is designed as a reference tool providing dates, sponsor or category, frequency, type, and related titles. The list is not intended to be complete but includes every religious periodical that is mentioned in this book and that, I trust, is every one of any significance (and some of none).

The Religious Press in Britain, 1760–1900

1

Introduction

Why do we study religion in nineteenth-century Britain? Because it was there. "Victorian England was religious" is the simple and sufficient opening of Owen Chadwick's magisterial *Victorian Church.*[1] "Probably in no other century," said Kitson Clark, "except the seventeenth . . . did the claims of religion occupy so large a part in the nation's life, or did men speaking in the name of religion contrive to exercise so much power."[2]

Just how did men speak in the name of religion? That issue is the peculiar concern of this study: neither the extent nor the content of nineteenth-century religion, but the media by which it was propagated. Specifically, this study is concerned with the medium that was to become the most extensive and important, the periodical press.

The nineteenth century saw the establishment of the periodical press as the preeminent medium of communication on all subjects, secular and religious. It became the rule that every movement, every school of thought, every sect, and every party had to have at least one periodical organ of expression. These periodical organs provide the best means of entry into the minds and histories of those for whom they spoke. This fact is as true for the religious press as for any other. Once the medium had been established, periodical publication became obligatory. The classic instance is the Mormon missionary to England, Parley Pratt, who landed in Liverpool on April 6, 1840, and published the first number of the *Latter Day Saints Millennial Star* on May 1. It is fair to say that the press in all its forms, newspaper, magazine, review, and annual, is the indispensable primary source for the study of nineteenth-century religion.

It must be acknowledged that the press was never the exclusive nor always the most prominent form of religious propaganda. There was the oral competition of the sermon, the time-honored form once dominant in the age of mass illiteracy, still vital as literacy advanced, and capable of further dissemination in print. There was also the written competition of the religious tract, the favorite medium of the evangelical revival, published in the hundreds of thousands, cheaply disseminated or freely given to the poor. The periodical press gradually encroached on these competitors. From the beginning, periodicals published sermons; later there appeared sermon-periodicals such as Spurgeon's *Metropolitan Tabernacle Pulpit* or Pitman's shorthand *Phonographic Pulpit*; eventually the separate publication of sermons declined as their reuse by other preachers became unacceptable.[3] Similarly, periodicals first supplemented and then supplanted tracts: the Religious Tract Society began to issue periodicals in the 1820s, widened their scope from the 1850s, and attained best-seller status with the *Boy's Own Paper* in 1879.

The study of the religious press is beset by difficulties, the most obvious of which is the immensity of the task. *The Waterloo Directory of Victorian Periodicals*, a conflation of the leading catalogues, lists some 29,000 periodical titles for the period 1824–1900;[4] allowing for errors, duplications and changes of title, this list represents between twenty and twenty-five thousand actual periodicals; and many more have eluded the cataloguers. My own combing of the *Waterloo Directory* for periodicals that may be described as religious has yielded some 4,000 entries, representing some 3,000 actual periodicals. A narrower survey indicates the proportionate scale of the religious press: from 1841 to 1851, 845 periodicals other than newspapers were published in the London area, of which 149 (17.6%) were religious.[5] A mere list of the entire religious press would be a major project; yet such a list, including as it would many ephemeral, local, or unimportant periodicals, would be of rather little value. What is being attempted here is a general historical study of this class of journalism, identifying the more important or representative periodicals and assigning them to their appropriate denominations or movements.

A second problem is that of definition. What may be included (and what may be excluded) under the heading of religious periodicals? There is no universally accepted definition of religion, though there is an entire discipline devoted to the subject. As a true historian, I shall not attempt to define my term. Let it suffice to say that this study will employ the broadest possible usage of the term so as not to exclude any reasonable possibility. All denominations of any kind and all movements whose motivation was prominently religious will be covered. This working definition does not omit freethought and atheism: though they opposed religion, they were responding to it. Even a mimic of religion such as the British Israel movement must be included, if only to prevent it from confusing the issue.

The next problem is to identify the religious periodicals. Existing catalogues generally do not separate them out.[6] Reliance on titles can be dangerous—who without foreknowledge would recognize that titles such as *Patriot* or *Rambler* conceal religious journals or would know that the *Banner of Israel* was *not* Jewish? This difficulty is a main reason why a merely bibliographical approach to this subject would be inadequate: no list could be certain of being complete unless all 29,000 titles were individually checked for content and character. A workable study of the religious press requires the peculiar skills, experience, and limitations of a historian of British religion.

Closely connected with the problem of identification is that of classification or categorization, which is, in fact, the most important task of the student of the religious press. The greatest need of historians and other scholars is to have the significant periodicals identified and placed in their appropriate categories (denomination, movement, or tendency). "You can't tell the players without a scorecard." This volume, with its appended index of religious periodicals, is intended to provide such a scorecard within the framework of a general history of the religious press.

The most difficult problem is to determine the appropriate categories for the classification of religious periodicals. It might seem obvious to classify periodicals by denomination, but this method is neither entirely satisfactory nor quite adequate. One denomination, the established Church of England, contained movements or tendencies within itself which would be denominations in any other context; the Low and the High Church will each require its own chapter. There are also periodicals that linked evangelicals within the establishment with evangelical nonconformists or that served several groups of nonconformist denominations or Nonconformity as a whole. Aside from these movements, there were movements that were not denominational but were clearly religious in their origin or character, most notably the immense temperance press. Separate categories must also be set up for specialized types of periodicals, such as family or children's magazines, whose motivation was evidently (though often vaguely) religious. (The appendix illustrates a Victorian effort to cope with these categories.)

How does one assign a periodical to its appropriate category? Affiliation was rarely proclaimed, except for officially sponsored publications. Prospectuses or manifestoes were as likely to disavow as to acknowledge a specific religious connection. The ordinary skills and techniques of historical research are required to get behind the conventional reticence of Victorian editors. Secondary works, in the form of histories of denominations, movements, or (rarely) individual periodicals, are helpful when available. Biographies of proprietors, editors, or contributors would be useful, but it is usually harder to identify such personalities because of the convention of anonymity than it is to identify the periodicals. Even then one must ask in what capacity the person was involved, for example, did Edward Miall edit the *Nonconformist* as a Congregational minister or as a nondenominational voluntaryist? Often there is nothing to do but to study the periodical itself, looking for clues either in the positions it takes on issues or in the language it employs. This kind of stylistic analysis, especially the recognition of key words, may be the most fruitful: by their clichés ye shall know them. A term such as *serious* is a code word for evangelicals; *Protestant* almost always means anti-Catholic; *Catholic* means Roman Catholic when capitalized but frequently indicates High Anglican in lowercase. (The most misleading word is *true.*)

All this is great fun as well as serious history, but it only scratches the surface of periodicals. One would wish to penetrate the fiction of the corporate identity of most nineteenth-century periodicals, with their unsigned articles, so as to identify the specific writers and their specific contributions; how much better it would be to say "Macaulay said this" rather than "the *Edinburgh Review* said this." Thanks to Walter Houghton's *Wellesley Index to Victorian Periodicals*,[7] it is possible to be specific for a select list of the "higher journalism"; but only a few periodicals are amenable to such analysis. There are simply too many articles to be studied. For the most part, we must content ourselves with an overview of periodicals, each of which might be the subject of a monograph or an article. Another generation of scholars may build on this foundation.

The unit of study for this work is the largest possible one: the British Isles. Although the British religious press had important relations with the presses of the colonies, India, and the United States, the English-speaking world is too large a unit for study at this time, and its components have distinct histories and literatures of their own. On the other hand, literary and historical scholars have too often limited the scope of their study to England proper. In the century of the Union, the British Isles were an intellectual common market. To be sure, Scotland is an ecclesiastical world of its own, difficult of entry for the Southron scholar; but it must be entered, for its press was important, often impacted on England, and served to mediate German scholarship to the English-speaking world. Ireland, for all its peculiarities, proved manageable for this study; and Irish scholars may forgive its inclusion in "Britain" in a necessarily terse title. The most difficult part of the British Isles is Wales, where a major part of the religious press is in the Welsh language; in this case I am entirely dependent on secondary literature.

The temporal scope of this study was originally intended to be simply the nineteenth century. Research into the prehistory of the religious press revealed that the natural starting point for this study should be 1760, in which year the religious magazine appeared on the scene and immediately established itself as the dominant type of publication for over a century. There is no particular significance to the year 1900, but one must stop somewhere. Several bibliographic sources use that as a terminal date.

More than half a century ago, a historian of the Congregationalists lamented that "there is nothing more difficult to discover than the exact facts in regard to the periodical literature of the nineteenth century."[8] Since he wrote those words, the religious press has been the subject of chapters and articles,[9] but no book has been devoted to the subject. A booklength study would not have been possible without the development in the last thirty years of an interdisciplinary field of periodicals research dealing with Victorian Britain, a development that has indicated both the possibilities and the limitations of a study of the religious press and has supplied some of the basic tools and concepts with which the study may be done. This work is a direct outgrowth of this professional development and a test of the state of its art.

2

The Development of the Religious Press

The religious press is a subcategory of what the Victorians called "class journalism," that is, journalism directed to a particular class of readers rather than the public at large. Like most other types of class journalism, religious journalism was entirely derivative in form and contributed little of its own to the technical advancement of the press. The various types of periodicals were innovated by the general press in the seventeenth century and the first third of the eighteenth and were later adopted for religious use, often with some reluctance.

The reticence of the religious press should not be surprising. In the Protestant traditions that predominated in Britain, there was little sense of timeliness or periodicity. The "good news" had been once delivered to the saints and was timeless; a concern for current information smacked of worldliness. The one periodical event that mattered to the devout was that fearsome institution, the British Sabbath, whose organ was the sermon. It is significant that the newspaper, one of the earliest types of general periodical, was one of the last to be adopted by the religious press. A sense of urgency, and hence a need for periodicals, was at first the province of politics. But so much of the politics of the seventeenth century was religious that, although there were no religious periodicals as such, religious news and, still more, religious polemics were frequent features of periodicals, whose titles, moreover, have a deceptive appearance of religion, *Protestant* being a favorite synonym for *Whig.*[1] At a time when politics revolved around the Catholic issue, some periodicals were devoted entirely to anti-Catholic polemics, notably Henry Care's *A Pacquet of Advice From Rome* (1678ff.), continued as *The Anti-Roman Pacquet.*[2]

The pioneer of religious journalism and of much else in the history of literary periodicals was an enterprising printer and publisher, John Dunton.[3] His *Athenian Mercury* (1690–97) was a forerunner of *Notes & Queries* with its questions and answers; and his *Compleat Library* (1692–94) anticipated modern learned journals in combining original articles (on religious subjects) with abstracts and criticism. His monthly *Post-Angel* (1701–02) was the first religious miscellany, though perhaps the word *farrago* would describe it better. Its first and largest section recounted marvelous "providences"; other sections dealt with the deaths of eminent persons, questions and answers, the news ("improved" by the comments of a "spiritual observator"), a catalogue of new books, and sometimes poetry and essays.

The usual religious periodical in the first half of the eighteenth century was a type generally popular at that time and never since, the essay-periodical, consisting of a single essay in each issue, Steele and Addison's *Tatler* and *Spectator* being the great exemplars. The first of this type was the *Mercurius Theologicus; or, the Monthly Instructor* (1700–01), "briefly explaining and applying all the doctrines and duties of the Christian religion that are necessary to be believ'd and practis'd in order to Salvation," by "a divine of the Church of England." The subtitle (as was often the case) said it all. Closely related to the essay-periodical, but outliving it into the nineteenth century, was the tract-periodical, a tract complete in each issue or continued through several issues, differing from tracts properly so-called only in being published at regular intervals.

An important exception to these essay-periodicals was the *Weekly Miscellany* (1732–41), "giving an account of the religion, morality, and learning of the present times, with occurrences both foreign and domestic," written pseudonymously by William Webster, D.D. This was a true weekly magazine, consisting of orthodox Anglican essays on religion, morality and government (some in the form of letters), notices of foreign books, and snippets of general news (probably culled from the *Gazette*). This remarkable production lasted over eight years, longer than any other religious periodical of the time, and probably served as a model for the typical magazine when that was established on a monthly basis after 1760.[4]

The other notable religious periodical of this early period was the first fruit of the evangelical revival. The *Christian's Amusement* or *Weekly History* (1741–48), "an account of the most remarkable passages relating to the present progress of the Gospel," was published under the control of George Whitefield to recount his evangelistic triumphs in Britain and America.

By 1760, the essay-periodical had been superseded as the commonest type of periodical (other than the newspaper) by the magazine, a genre pioneered in 1731 by the *Gentleman's Magazine.* The magazine (the name was taken from military storehouses) is, unlike most of its predecessors, a miscellany containing several different types of contributions, essays of various kinds, reviews, and poetry. It could appear at various intervals, but monthly publication was preferred. The *Weekly Miscellany* had been a magazine without the name; the name had occasionally been used by religious periodicals without the substance; but the first religious journal to be a magazine and call itself such was the *Christian's Magazine*, which appeared in 1760 and immediately fixed the type.

The *Christian's Magazine* (1760–67) was edited by the celebrated Dr. William Dodd, chaplain to the king. Dr. Dodd is celebrated for another reason: he is the only editor of a religious periodical to be hanged (for forgery, in 1777). His periodical was one of his happier enterprises (although it ominously included his "Reflections on Death"). It was systematically departmentalized, providing a model for its successors, and decently illustrated with engravings. The departments are curious: "Systematical Divinity" drawn from the writings of leading divines; "Historical Divinity" or biographies of Reformers and divines; "Physico-Theology" or "the Wonders of GOD in Creation"; "Antiquities of the Jewish or Christian Church"; "Occasional or Miscellaneous Divinity" or "Critical, Controversial, or Practical Pieces"; "Poetical Divinity," including a hymn with music (Christopher Smart was a contributor); "Literary Divinity," a list of all recent religious books, occasionally with extracts; and a "Brief Diary" of current news and notable births, deaths, and church preferments. It was soundly Anglican ("Printed pursuant to his Majesty's Royal Licence"). John Wesley praised it as "of great use to mankind";[5] what he meant was that it was not Calvinist. Wesley used it as the model for his own *Arminian Magazine*; so too did its two immediate successors.

The other monthly magazines of the 1760s were of the Calvinistic side of Anglicanism. The *Spiritual Magazine* (1761ff.) was produced by Mrs. Ann Dutton. Its first numbers contained general news and secular matters, but thereafter it confined itself to "pious thoughts" and poetry. It certainly continued to 1763, probably to Mrs. Dutton's death in 1765 and possibly to 1784.[6] The *Gospel Magazine* (1766-84) was not only Calvinist ("The articles of the church of England . . . are according to *Calvin*'s doctrines")[7] but evangelical; its second editor was Augustus Toplady, author of the hymn "Rock of Ages," which first appeared in its pages. Its departmental structure included divinity, biography, dialogues to illustrate Scripture, "Casuistical Divinity" or questions and answers, miscellaneous letters, essays and reviews, and hymns and poetry.

These three miscellanies established the magazine in its monthly form (convenient for part-time editors such as clergymen) as the normal form of religious periodical. This was true even though the other major periodical of the 1760s, Joseph Priestley's *Theological Repository* (1769–71, 1784–88), was quite different in kind, a learned journal, irregularly published, and inviting open debate in its pages (though only Arians and Unitarians actually participated). Wesley confirmed the triumph of the monthly magazine by adopting the type for his own belated entry into journalism, the *Arminian Magazine* in 1778. The unusual name reflects his hostility to Calvinism; he saw his magazine as a corrective to the *Spiritual* and *Gospel Magazines.* Wesley's successors changed the name to the *Methodist Magazine* in 1798; after further changes it reverted to that name, under which it continues, boasting itself "The Oldest Religious Periodical in the World."[8] Other religious magazines followed in the 1780s, the only one of note being Mrs. Sarah Trimmer's *Family Magazine* (1788-89), an early Anglican effort to reach the lower classes, servants, and laborers.

From the 1790s on, the number of religious periodicals burgeoned. The reaction to the French Revolution was part of this growth, as Anglicans and Methodists consciously sought to head off revolution by presenting religion as the opiate of the people. More importantly, it was in this period that each party or tendency in politics or thought (and hence each religious denomination or movement) came to feel a necessity to express itself through a periodical organ. The religious press, whose numbers increased fourfold from 1790 to 1825, shared in this conventionalization of periodical partisanship; denominational monthlies were the best-selling magazines.[9] Still another factor was specific to the field of religion: this was the great age of the formation of organizations (generally evangelical) for religious, philanthropic, and missionary purposes. These societies came to publish official periodicals, sometimes simply giving organizational intelligence, sometimes combining this with other elements of a magazine. Eventually these movements spun off more specialized periodicals for juvenile readers or local branches. The missionary press was the most numerous element in the religious field until it was swamped by the temperance press in the mid-nineteenth century.

The early nineteenth century saw one new genre of periodical, the quarterly review. To be sure, the critical review had been pioneered in the seventeenth century, and the *Eclectic Review* (1805–68) was the first of several distinguished nonconformist monthly reviews. But the quarterly became the most pretentious species of periodical, large volumes of article-length reviews (often really articles appended to book titles) by anonymous but weighty authors. The genre was modeled on the *Edinburgh Review* of 1802 and the *Quarterly Review* of 1809, joined by the *Westminster Review* in 1824. The "big three" were general reviews, not religious, though the *Quarterly* was Tory in politics and therefore implicitly Anglican. The first religious quarterly review was the *Quarterly Theological Review* (1825–26), a brief spin-off from the High Church *British Critic* (1793–1843), which itself became a quarterly later in 1825. Religious quarterlies were slow to emerge, the only notable product of the 1830s being the Roman Catholic *Dublin Review* (1835–1969), until several appeared almost simultaneously in 1844–45. The publication of a quarterly was a sign that a denomination or movement had arrived intellectually, although none of the religious quarterlies—except the liberal Catholic *Home and Foreign Review* (1862–64) and some of the Unitarian reviews—matched the quality of the big three. Reaching a small elite audience, the quarterly reviews were perhaps more eminent than effective as vehicles of religious propaganda.

Potentially the most effective type of journalism was the newspaper, already established in political journalism. The religious press was hesitant to venture into this sphere. It lacked the sense of urgency or timeliness;[10] a daily paper was quite beyond its capabilities;[11] the most it could manage was thrice- or twice-weekly publication, and its normal frequency was weekly. Even this might require a paid editor or staff and therefore a circulation larger than most magazines; but circulation was limited by the requirement of a stamp tax, raised to four-pence in 1815. Ironically, a radical and often antireligious "unstamped" press might defy the tax, despite official prosecutions, while the religious press was dutifully inhibited. The first professed religious newspaper, the *Weekly Register*, appeared in 1798 and 1799, known only from a prospectus and one stray issue. No other appeared until 1817. The first of any significance was the nonconformist *World* (1827-32), later the *Patriot* (1832-66); it was followed shortly by the strong evangelical Anglican *Record* (1828-), published twice weekly. Typically, these early papers apologized for their existence by reflecting on the immorality of the general press and the need for "a Journal of passing events, which shall offer nothing offensive to the eye of decency, or derogatory to the sacred claims of morality and religion."[12] This was pretty tame stuff, although religious controversy could supply an alternative form of indecency. But Victorians (and pre-Victorians) preferred their reading to be safe, even if it was stodgy. It may be acknowledged that their religious press achieved a satisfactory stodginess. Fascinating as a class of literature, its individual exemplars are nearly always dull reading.

The reduction of the stamp tax to one penny in 1836 began to liberate the potential of the religious newspaper. There was an outburst of new titles in the latter 1830s and the 1840s. Religious newspapers were still generally unexciting, appealing to a safely middle-class audience; two-pence a week was too much for workers to pay, especially when an increasing number of magazines were now being published for them at a penny a month. The most effective editor under these circumstances (and probably the greatest of Victorian religious editors) was the ebullient and combative John Campbell, who edited two successful Congregationalist monthlies while simultaneously attempting to reach "the Millions!" with the weekly *British Banner* (1848-58) and later the *British Standard* (1857-67). His journals in fact reached the tens of thousands, while his penny monthly sold 100,000.[13] His career illustrated two key points: the importance of a strong (even controversial) editorial personality and the fact that the paid audience of the religious press was limited to the middle class, perhaps reinforced by some of the "aristocracy of labour." (One should note that there was a larger nonpaying audience: journals were passed around or read aloud, and many periodicals were sold in bulk for free distribution locally.)[14]

The possibility of reaching a mass audience was opened by the abolition of the stamp tax in 1855, part of a general repeal of the "taxes on knowledge" (the advertisement duty in 1853 and the paper duties in 1861). The general newspaper press began to increase its daily circulation on an unprecedented scale, and the "new journalism" of the 1880s and 1890s yielded circulations over a million. The response of the religious press (still mostly weekly) was more restrained, but a new class of popular religious newspapers emerged, capitalizing on the lower-middle-class audience (itself growing). The nonconformist *Christian World* (1857-), the Roman Catholic *Universe* (1860-) and the High Anglican *Church Times* (1863-) eventually reached audiences over 100,000. As the century ended, William Robertson Nicoll's *British Weekly* (1886-) and Hugh Price Hughes's *Methodist Times* (1885-1937) were powers in the land, building toward the greatest (and last) triumph of nonconformity, the Liberal victory of 1906. In the process, the religious editor emerged as a major force, in a manner foreshadowed by John Campbell. Religious newspapers challenged the dominance of the religious magazine.

Magazines themselves experienced a revolution in Darwin's year, 1859-60, with the creation of a new style of magazine, at once more interesting and higher in literary quality, pioneered by *Macmillan's* (1859) and the *Cornhill* (1860). The *Fortnightly Review* (1865) abandoned the rule of anonymity, an example followed by most magazines though not the old reviews, and the *Contemporary Review* (1866- ; at first largely religious) opened its pages to a variety of opposing viewpoints. These changes coincided with a growing realization within the religious press that there was a need for reading that was interesting as well as edifying (especially to fill those awkward hours at home on Sundays). Of the new magazines, the best was Norman Macleod's *Good Words* (1860-1911), which ventured to include serialized novels by well-known writers. The reinvigorated magazines ensured that the quarterly reviews would lose their preeminence, though they continued to be published.

In other fields, children's periodicals ceased to be intolerable and learned how to be interesting. Family periodicals became popular. The temperance movement perfected the art of forming local and related organizations with innumerable periodical organs. Local periodicals burgeoned with the greater ease of publishing. The religious press had completed its development.

3

ANGLICAN EVANGELICALS

A survey of the religious press should begin with the Church of England, which at the outset was not merely the established church, with a monopoly of political power, but was the largest single denomination, the nominal religion of the bulk of the population and certainly the faith of the classes that mattered, the social and intellectual elite. Indeed, most dissenting denominations had begun as secessions from the Establishment, and its fissiparous tendencies continued, though in our period they took the form of large-scale movements within the Church, each of which was to develop a press of its own sufficient for a full denomination.

We may start with the evangelical wing of the Church, often called the Low Church because of its relative indifference to forms and hierarchies, the representatives within the established Church of a larger movement, the evangelical revival, which succeeded in imposing upon England that distinctive seriousness and moralism that we think of as Victorian. That revival had begun in the 1730s; its most prominent figure had been John Wesley, whose direct heirs were the various forms of Methodism that eventually reinforced Nonconformity. But there was also an evangelicalism that remained within the Church of England, linking up with the survivals of seventeenth-century Puritanism and producing the most active Church movement in the new century.

As a movement, the Low Church was first in the field with periodicals. The second religious magazine, Mrs. Ann Dutton's *Spiritual Magazine* (1761ff.), was a quasi-Calvinist continuation of Puritanism; the third, the *Gospel Magazine* (1766–84), was clearly evangelical, its second editor, Augustus Toplady of "Rock of Ages" fame, being one of the great names of the party.[1] That these periodical initiatives were not immediately followed up was due to the evangelicals' early preference for the large-scale distribution of Bibles and especially of tracts, their favorite means of reaching the lower classes. Yet Hannah More's *Cheap Repository Tracts*, the first organized series, which sold two million copies between 1795 and 1797, "were periodicals in all but name,"[2] published regularly every month.

The 1790s, which saw the first nonconformist evangelical magazines, drew from the Anglican evangelicals only *Zion's Trumpet* (1798–1801), "a theological miscellany . . . by a society of clergymen," which became the *Christian Guardian* (1802–53). Despite its clerical authorship (and a writing style of which only clergymen were capable), this was intended to appeal to a popular audience: "we attempt to kindle up a spark of heavenly light in the abodes of inferior citizens."[3] Enlarged in 1809, the *Christian Guardian* continued its dismal style of evangelicalism until 1853, for much of the time under the editorship of William Carus Wilson,[4] Charlotte Brontë's unattractive "Mr. Brocklehurst." Carus Wilson was also the founder of a small penny monthly for humbler readers, the *Friendly Visitor* (1819–1912). Like the *Children's Friend* (1824–1930), an early children's magazine founded by him, "its pages reverberate with his evangelical hatred of popery, with horror of sin and with fearful warnings of hell-fire."[5] Carus Wilson's specialty was the edifying (or horrifying) death-bed scene.

The principal organ of the Anglican evangelicals was a monthly, the *Christian Observer* (1802–77). This was proposed by a group of London evangelical clergy, the Eclectic Society; but the magazine was managed by the leadership of the movement, principally laymen, many of whom had settled at Clapham, just south of London, and came to be known as the Clapham sect. The editor during the critical formative years was Zachary Macaulay, father of the historian Thomas, who first appeared in print in the *Christian Observer*.[6] Priced at a middle-class shilling a month, the magazine contained a variety of articles, some heavily theological and others as light as was compatible with seriousness, a review of reviews that allowed the *Christian Observer* to engage in controversy with major opponents such as the liberal *Edinburgh Review*, and a summary of the events of the month, which was often the best feature.[7] The Anglican evangelicals never produced a quarterly review, but the monthly *Christian Observer* served many of the same purposes and was close to the same quality, though the movement had few shining intellects or sparkling writers. The magazine was perhaps too dignified (or stodgy) for so ardent a movement; its circulation held at a modest one thousand, easily distanced by the partisan newspaper, the *Record*, after 1828: "the *Christian Observer* practiced charity and had few subscribers, the *Record* acted vituperative partisan and had many subscribers."[8] Not that the *Christian Guardian* was bland: it regularly attacked the Oxford Movement, Popery, and other opponents; but the decorum that befitted the acknowledged chief organ of the movement was bought at the price of liveliness. The need for such an organ kept the magazine alive until 1877, despite its modest circulation.

When the *Christian Observer* failed, a need was immediately felt for a replacement, which emerged as the *Churchman* (1879-), a monthly that claimed a larger circulation, perhaps because it largely abandoned the old-fashioned practice of anonymous writing.[9] The *Churchman* continued into the twentieth century.

The most effective (or at least notorious) organ of the Anglican evangelicals was not a respectable monthly but a newspaper, the *Record.* Despite the evangelical distaste for worldly news, serious people could not avoid noticing the impact of the newspaper press on public opinion and lamenting the offensive matter (such as crime news) that was published therein. They could not compete with the daily press, but perhaps they could produce a weekly

> journal of passing events, which shall offer nothing offensive to the eye of decency, or derogatory to the sacred claims of morality and religion . . . to exclude from its pages whatever would render it an objectionable question in that sanctuary of modesty and refined feeling—the bosom of a well-regulated English Family.[10]

This pre-Victorian Victorianism was evangelical code language for the paper's religious purpose, which was not explicitly professed. A committee of London lay evangelicals commenced the *Record* as a twice-weekly newspaper (then the greatest frequency of any religious paper) on January 1, 1828. It almost came to an end in July, when it exhausted its capital and was losing money; but the announcements of its approaching end in fact brought its salvation, evoking expressions of support and offers of help.[11] This stimulated the committee to reorganize the paper and to find a new editor.

Their eventual choice was Alexander Haldane, a young barrister from Scotland, son and nephew of major figures in the Scottish evangelical revival. Haldane brought to the *Record* not only vigor and ability but also an intolerance and harshness perhaps attributable to his origins. His ascendancy at the *Record* (he soon became a proprietor) symbolized the transformation of evangelicalism from a movement to a party within the Church. But partisanship paid: the *Record* was soon solvent, with a circulation rising to a respectable 4,000. It had the advantage of being the only Anglican newspaper until 1843 and the only non-High Church newspaper thereafter. Its supplements were the fullest record of the May meetings of religious societies. Many who took it because it was indispensable lamented its tone; moderate evangelicals, including the *Christian Observer*, expressed occasional disapproval; but they bought and read it. The *Record* was ever present in controversies and fomented them if necessary. It was the first to denounce the Tractarians in 1833 and continued to oppose all aspects of Anglo-Catholicism; of course, it attacked Roman Catholicism; sternly Sabbatarian, it secured the ending of Sunday Cabinet dinners; puritan in other regards, it failed to have nude statues removed from the Great Exhibition. "For many people Evangelicalism meant the *Record*";[12] it was largely responsible for the distaste with which evangelicals were viewed outside their own circle, and a hostile critic could speak of the "Recordite party"[13] as the reductio ad absurdum of evangelicalism.

In 1854, with the death of the most prominent of the original proprietors, Andrew Hamilton, Haldane became managing proprietor of the *Record*, and (though he continued to write) he found it convenient to employ a paid editor, Edward Garbett, a prominent London clergyman. In fact, they shared the direction. The additional hand at the helm proved useful from 1855, when, after the repeal of the stamp tax, the *Record* changed from a biweekly to a triweekly, the greatest frequency of any religious paper. Some new emphases may be traced to Garbett, particularly a shift of controversial attention from the High Church to the Broad and indeed to religious liberalism generally. The *Record* was the most vigorous and persistent opponent of *Essays and Reviews* in the early 1860s. Garbett, an eminent defender of biblicism, combined the editorship of the *Record* with that of the *Christian Advocate*, a monthly that he founded in 1861 for controversial purposes; its first year was almost entirely absorbed by criticism of the biblical critics. He edited the *Christian Advocate* until it merged with the *Christian Observer* in 1874. He had resigned the editorship of the *Record* in 1867, though he continued to write for it.

Although the *Record* maintained its virulently partisan tone, Garbett's defense of orthodoxy versus biblical criticism had drawn him closer to the equally orthodox High Church party. Significantly Pusey, himself often the target of the *Record*'s attacks, published his protest against the acquittal of the Essayists in the *Record*, as the staunchest upholder of orthodoxy.[14] Garbett also participated in the Church Congresses from 1862, though most evangelicals shunned them as devices of the High Church party. Extreme evangelicals began to fear that the *Record* was wavering in the purity of its partisanship (though it is hard to believe that anybody could be more extreme than the *Record*). The extremists started a weekly newspaper of their own, the *Rock* (1867–1905), priced at a penny.[15] Whether because of the competition, its higher price, or its now old-fashioned stodginess under clerical editors, the *Record*'s circulation declined to about three thousand. Facing rivals in and out of its party, it was no longer as much of a power. Nonetheless, it stayed the course as a tri-weekly until shortly before Haldane's death in 1882. The *Record* then became a conventional four-penny religious weekly, the moderate evangelical counterpart of the High Church *Guardian*. By that time even the *Rock* had become less militant, and the extremists were left without an organ until 1884, when they purchased the hitherto High Church *English Churchman*.[16]

SOCIETIES

Despite its substantial periodical press and its immense outpouring of tracts, the evangelical party within the Church of England was most influential in the affairs of the nation through the network of religious and philanthropic organizations and societies that it either founded or took over, using them to draw into collaboration important or wealthy persons not themselves professedly evangelical, controlling them through an "interlocking directorate"[17] drawn from the Clapham sect and their successors, and letting their light shine forth before men by the well-publicized usefulness and prominence of their work. Nearly all these societies came to issue periodical publications, if only annual *Reports* or *Proceedings*, and these too must be reckoned as parts of the periodical press of the evangelical movement. Some of these, such as the Bible or Religious Tract Societies, were common to evangelicals of all denominations; others were specific to the Church of England.

The first of the great societies, the Church Missionary Society (CMS), was founded in 1799 to rival the official but half-dormant Society for the Propagation of the Gospel and to compete with new nonconformist missionary bodies. The CMS began publication promptly but modestly with *Proceedings* (1800–1922), containing the annual report. In 1813 the secretary of the CMS, Rev. Josiah Pratt, "a man whose very instinct it was to think imperially,"[18] commenced the monthly *Missionary Register* (1813–55), nominally unofficial, reporting (usually in their own words) the activities of all the missionary and Bible societies. It was "undoubtedly a great power in its early days"[19] before being superseded by the various societies' individual publications. The CMS published its own *Quarterly Papers* (1816–49), later the *Church Missionary Paper*, for weekly and monthly contributors. It moved into the monthly field in 1830 with the *Church Missionary Record* (1830–90), in which each issue concentrated on one missionary field. This publication proved neither timely nor extensive enough, and it was supplemented in 1849 by a full-fledged magazine, the *Church Missionary Intelligencer* (1849–1906; other names to 1934). For other tastes there was the *Church Missionary Gleaner* (1841–70, 1874–1920?). Like other missionary societies, to raise up the next generation of contributors, the CMS published parallel periodicals for children, such as the *Church Missionary Juvenile Instructor* (1842–90), later *Children's World* (1891–1900). New periodicals were still being founded toward the end of the century, notably *Mercy and Truth* (1897–1921), a record of CMS medical missions. This pattern of publication was typical of the missionary societies' efforts to build up the home base of the missions; it also set the pattern for domestic societies.

Another work of the Anglican evangelicals, involving extensive effort but minuscule results, was the London Society for Promoting Christianity Amongst the Jews, founded in 1809 and promptly issuing an annual *Report*. In 1813 the "Jews' Society" started a monthly, the *Jewish Repository* (1813–15), renamed *Jewish Expositor and Friend of Israel* (1816–31). This was supplanted by *Monthly Intelligence* of the proceedings of the Society (1830–34), renamed *Jewish Intelligence* (1835–92; continuing under other names) and the *Jewish Herald* (later *Jewish Missionary Herald*, 1846–). Notwithstanding the word *Jewish* in their titles, these were not Jewish periodicals (somewhat to the confusion of bibliographers) nor were they even addressed to the Jews; like other publications of missionary societies, they were intended to keep up the enthusiasm of Christian contributors.

A product of the second generation of Anglican evangelicals was the Church Pastoral Aid Society, founded in 1836 to provide evangelical curates and lay scripture readers in overpopulated parishes. At first it published only an *Occasional Paper* (63 numbers, 1836-61, not quite periodical), later the *Quarterly Paper* (1862-87). From the 1880s, however, it published several journals for young people and children as well as the organ of its home missionary work, *Church and People* (1889-). An offshoot, the Church of England Scripture Readers' Association, published from 1853 the *Scripture Readers' Journal* (1853-1907; under other titles to 1930), intended for its workers rather than contributors.

All evangelicals were enthusiastically anti-Catholic; Anglican evangelicals were especially concerned with the Roman Catholics of Ireland, where their own Church, although established until 1869, had been rejected by the majority of the population. Irish Catholics seemed as appropriate objects of missionary endeavor as any colonial heathen. In the 1830s an individual missionary, Edward Nangle, had opened a uniquely successful mission on Achill Island, whose nominal Catholics had been neglected by their own Church. To provide employment for his converts on this desolate island off the west coast, Nangle started a press, which inevitably produced a monthly, the *Achill Missionary Herald* (1837-69). This publication, at first quite crude, grew in importance as it became the spearhead of a Protestant crusade in Ireland;[20] its larger interest is shown by changes of title to *Irish Church Advocate* (1870-79) and *Church Advocate* (1879-91). The Famine, with its opportunities to reach desperate people, stimulated an organized proselytizing effort, the Society for Irish Church Missions to Roman Catholics, founded by a militant English clergyman, Alexander Dallas. The Irish Church Missions soon published an official monthly, the *Banner of the Truth in Ireland* (1851-93), later *Banner of Truth* (1893-), edited by Dallas and published in London but effective in keeping up denominational strife in Ireland.[21]

Party militancy, characteristic of a later generation of evangelicals, was most completely exemplified by the Church Association, founded in 1865 to oppose the growth of the High Church movement and especially its ritualistic wing. The Association's main effort was the prosecution of ritualists; but it too published a periodical, the *Monthly Intelligencer* (1867-84), later the *Church Intelligencer* (1884-1938).

REFORMED SECESSIONS

A few evangelicals, disheartened by the advance of Anglo-Catholicism, which the Established Church seemed legally unable to repress, were attracted to the idea of a free episcopalian but reformed Church. Two such bodies were attempted. The Free Church of England published a *Circular* in 1863 but then combined its efforts, at least journalistically, with the Countess of Huntingdon's Connexion, a bridge between Anglican and nonconformist evangelicalism dating from the previous century. The Huntingdonian *Harbinger* (1852-66; predecessors dating back to 1824) for a while became the *Free Church of England Magazine and Harbinger* (1867-68) and then the *Magazine* of the two churches (1869-85). A somewhat more important body was the Reformed Episcopal Church, which grew out of secessions in the American Episcopal Church imported into England in the 1870s. After two unsuccessful efforts at periodicals in 1879 and 1880, this body published an official monthly, the *Reformed Church Record* (1881-91), and later another, *Work and Worship* (1897-1915).

4

The High Church

The Low Church, whether puritan or evangelical, had always been paralleled in the Church of England by a High Church party, stressing the authority and good order of the established Church and opposing Calvinistic tendencies. Largely dormant during the eighteenth century, the High Church was to burst forth after 1833 in the form of the Oxford Movement, which rested the Church not on state establishment but on Divine authority conveyed through the apostolic succession of the bishops. But there was a High Church before the Oxford Movement. One element in it was best described as the "high-and-dry" Church, the party of the well-endowed, Tory in politics, more concerned to defend Church establishment and property than to recognize religious duties. Dr. Dodd's *Christian's Magazine* (1760–67) had represented this position; but the high-and-dry element (it could not be called a movement) generally relied on the Tory press to uphold its cause, most notably *John Bull* (1820–92), a "Church newspaper" but too scurrilous and political to be called a religious newspaper. But there was another element that, though muted, deserved to be called the old High Church, whose regard for the authority and order of the institutional Church was based on a foundation of solid piety of a truly English, understated sort. Their counterpart to the Clapham sect was the Hackney phalanx, a group of actively pious laymen whose most eminent figure was the philanthropist Joshua Watson.[1]

The *British Critic* (1793–1843) was the organ of the old High Church. It was founded as a monthly by Archdeacon Robert Nares to combat revolutionary tendencies and defend the Church, rather a high-and-dry approach; but in 1814 it was purchased by Watson and the Reverend Henry Norris of the Hackney phalanx.[2] In 1825 the publisher, Rivington, sought to transform it into the *Quarterly Theological Review*; but the Hackneyites kept the *British Critic* in their hands, making it also a quarterly in 1825. The rivalry was disastrous, the two reviews dividing the same readership; they merged as of January, 1827, the *British Critic* continuing as a quarterly review mixing theological and general articles. It never paid its way, being sustained by Watson's generosity. A new editor from 1834, J. S. Boone, attempted to make it more explicitly religious, but his views aroused much dissatisfaction.

At this point the *British Critic* was caught up in the Oxford Movement, which had been issuing the *Tracts for the Times* since 1833 but had been limited in its periodical expression by the conservatism of the *British Magazine.* In January 1836, John Henry Newman was able to effect an arrangement by which he and his friends would supply Boone with four sheets (sixty-four pages) out of fifteen each issue, gratis but exempt from the editor's control.[3] For the rest of 1836 and 1837, Newman served in effect as associate editor to Boone for the Tractarian share of the review, which sometimes contrasted with the remainder. Boone resigned late in 1837; S. R. Maitland, librarian of Lambeth Palace, replaced him but resigned in mid-1838, finding the editorship of a controversial journal incompatible with his duties to the archbishop of Canterbury. Newman was left in complete control; from July, 1838, the *British Critic* ceased to be an organ of the old High Church and became that of the Tractarians.

For three years Newman edited the *British Critic* as a partly theological, partly miscellaneous review, himself contributing some of its most important articles. He was simultaneously writing and editing *Tracts for the Times*: as long as they ran (to 1841), the Oxford Movement never depended on periodicals for its main outlet. Newman gave up the editorship in 1841 to his handpicked successor, his brother-in-law Thomas Mozley, just before Newman's crisis with Tract XC. Mozley was a bad choice, a most injudicious editor who attempted to replace the *Tracts* by the *British Critic* but allowed uncontrolled expression to younger extremists, W. G. Ward and Frederick Oakeley, who drew their inspiration not from antiquity but from the contemporary Roman Catholic Church, toward which they were moving. This drew criticism from more moderate Tractarians, notably William Palmer of Worcester College, whose *Narrative of Events Connected with the Publication of Tracts for the Times* (1843) contained scathing and explicit attacks on "certain recent tendencies to Romanism"[4] in the *British Critic.* Palmer and his friends persuaded Rivington, the publisher, "to suspend the publication of a periodical which had given such general offence . . . . virtually a Roman Catholic organ under Church of England colours."[5] Though Ward, Oakeley, and even Newman did eventually drift to Rome, the several efforts that were quickly made to replace the *British Critic* showed that the impulse of the Oxford Movement was still alive and required more, not less, periodical expression.

Well before the *British Critic* passed out of its hands, the old High Church had provided itself with other organs. The *Christian Remembrancer* (1819–68) was another product of the Hackney phalanx, dominated by the Reverend Henry Norris; a monthly, it seems to have originally been differentiated from the *British Critic* by an attempt to reach a wider audience, "to maintain the character and pretensions of the Establishment, upon popular arguments."[6] It remained a monthly when the *British Critic* went quarterly and continued as such, with no great distinction, until 1844. In that year the editor, William Scott, was joined by a coeditor, J. B. Mozley, perhaps the finest theological mind of the Oxford Movement; and at the beginning of 1845 the *Christian Remembrancer* was transformed into a quarterly review, evidently with the intention of succeeding the failed *British Critic.* By this time the old High Church had grown very old, and the *Christian Remembrancer* came to serve as the quarterly organ of the High Church in general except for the extremists. Distinguished, rather heavy, and "conservatively orthodox,"[7] it appealed to a limited clerical audience; its circulation declined in the 1860s until it ceased in 1868.

A link between the old High Church and the new was the *British Magazine* (1832–49), founded by Hugh James Rose, an eminent clergyman who was himself a link between the two, a Cambridge man who helped start the Oxford Movement. In an 1831 edition of Bishop Middleton's works, Rose noted the need for a sound church monthly; Rivington, publisher of the *British Critic*, thereupon offered Rose the editorship.[8] The prospectus indicated that the magazine was intended primarily as a professional journal for the clergy, not exclusively theological but including all areas of public improvement that might concern clergymen;[9] in fact, it became a journal of conservative High Church opinion. It provided an outlet for the poetry of the early leaders of the Oxford Movement, Newman, Hurrell Froude, and John Keble, whose *Lyra Apostolica* appeared in the *British Magazine* from 1833. But the Oxford men found Rose too conservative, restrained by his obligations as chaplain to the archbishop. Only in the *Tracts for the Times* could they express themselves fully and freely; they would have issued the *Tracts* at periodical intervals if they could have secured regular contributions, hence their quest for a periodical organ of their own, which eventually brought them to the *British Critic.*[10] Rose himself was in poor health and died prematurely in 1838; although S. R. Maitland edited the *British Magazine* for a decade from 1839, it never regained the distinction that Rose had brought and eventually became superfluous.

The next High Church periodical, the *Church of England Quarterly Review* (1837–58), was a throwback to the pre-Tractarian age. Defending all established institutions, it took its stand on "*Church and State*," crusading against "infidelity, liberalism and popery."[11] This is the old high-and-dry spirit, which was not yet dead, for the review lasted over twenty undistinguished years.

When the *British Critic* was suppressed, its publisher, Rivington, sought to establish a new quarterly to represent the old High Church, and this appeared in April, 1844 as the *English Review* (1844–53).[12] It was evidently intended to counteract the Romanizing tendencies of the late *British Critic.* A review in its second issue criticized both the *British Critic* and Newman, himself moving Romeward: "with grief . . . we avow our conviction that Mr. Newman's views *have changed.*"[13] Despite the correctness of this appreciation, the old High Church could no longer command lasting support for a quarterly review, which struggled for nine years.

A periodical of a quite different order, the product of an unrelated movement that must nonetheless be called High Church, was the *Ecclesiologist* (1841–68), originally the organ of the Cambridge Camden Society founded by John Mason Neale. The primary object of this society was to restore correct (that is, Gothic) principles of church architecture and decoration. In fact the society represented the first stirrings of the tendency that was to produce High Church ritualism: "to make taste subservient . . . to the promotion of sound religion."[14] This tendency soon produced controversy that led to the loss of the society's initially broad sponsorship, and a challenge to its use of a stone altar in the restoration of St. Sepulchre's, Cambridge, brought about the dissolution of the society in 1845. Neale reconstituted it in London as the Ecclesiological Society, which continued the *Ecclesiologist* as its organ.

The High Church (no longer "old") acquired its first newspaper with the *English Churchman* (1843-). This weekly included general news and literature but was mainly concerned with Church matters. An evangelical considered it "the organ of the extreme Tractarians,"[15] a statement that is probably an exaggeration. This journal appealed to "Tory High Church clergy,"[16] who kept it barely going with a rather poor circulation. This fact may explain its purchase and sudden transformation, on November 27, 1884, into an organ of the most extreme evangelicals, driven from the *Record* and the *Rock*.[17]

In 1846 the heirs of the Oxford Movement, recovering from the loss of the *British Critic* and Newman's secession, acquired proper organs of their own. The first was the *Ecclesiastic* (1846–68), a monthly directed specifically to the parish clergy. This was a narrow base to start with, and eventually they did not give the monthly enough support.[18]

The best and most enduring periodical produced by the successors of the Tractarians was a weekly newspaper, the *Guardian* (1846-), founded on January 21, 1846, by "a combination of young Oxford men,"[19] Frederic Rogers (later Lord Blatchford), T. H. Haddan, Montague Bernard, R. W. Church (later Dean of St. Paul's), and J. B. Mozley. These barristers and clergymen, journalistic amateurs working at first out of Haddan's chambers, provided both capital and literary staff. The literary quality was the highest of any religious newspaper (especially Church's weekly book reviews); but editorship by a committee of busy men, several of them not resident in London, was not really practical, and the *Guardian* had a slow start. The management improved when a working journalist, Martin R. Sharp, was employed in July, 1846, originally as publisher but soon taking a part in the editorial direction "until at last . . . the publisher became the editor."[20] The *Guardian* established itself in 1847 when the controversial liberal R. D. Hampden was appointed a bishop; swiftly organizing an opposition, the paper "seized the occasion to become the organ of high churchmen."[21]

The *Guardian* was the effective High Church alternative to the evangelical *Record*, a general newspaper with a religious point of view but with a much higher literary tone than Haldane's venom.[22] The *Guardian*'s politics were "generally Conservative, but without involving an unqualified adherence to any existing political party."[23] This position meant that the newspaper followed the High Churchman W. E. Gladstone, to whom Rogers and Church were devoted, in his journey from Tory to Peelite to Liberal; this final development (after 1859) cost the *Guardian* some support among Churchmen, most of whom remained committed to the Tories. Where Church parties were not concerned, the *Guardian* could be quite broad-minded, keeping (for instance) an open mind towards Darwinism and a generous feeling towards the Roman Catholic Newman.[24] The *Guardian* was perhaps too high-class, too judicious; it never sought the mass audience reached after 1863 by the *Church Times*, more popular and more partisan. But as a high-class religious journal, it was matched only by the *Spectator* in its heyday under R. H. Hutton.

In 1874 Church withdrew from the *Guardian* because Rogers, always the leading spirit, did not sufficiently condemn the legislation against ritualism. Sharp continued as editor until his death in 1883. The only suitable replacement was D. C. Lathbury, a more extreme Anglo-Catholic, who had served his literary apprenticeship on liberal Roman Catholic journals and then been joint editor of the *Economist* from 1878 to 1881. A devotee of Dean Church, Lathbury insisted on his return to the *Guardian*'s management.[25] Lathbury continued as editor till the end of the century, resigning in 1899 to found his own journal, the *Pilot*.

While the High Church periodicals now ran the gamut from newspaper to review, they produced little, compared to the evangelicals, in the way of magazines designed for particular classes of readers, such as children. A notable exception was the *Monthly Packet* (1851-99) of "evening readings for younger members of the English Church," not children but adolescents and young women. This was the product of Charlotte Yonge, "the novelist par excellence of the country parish,"[26] a friend and disciple of Keble, the Tractarian model parish priest. The *Monthly Packet* was the periodical expression of "the world we have lost," the old-fashioned churchgoing village presided over by squire and parson. It did not long survive the death of its ideal.

Another specialized publication was the *Literary Churchman* (1855-1892), a fortnightly review devoted solely to notices of religious books and lists of general literature. Its object, "to afford such information, with regard to Religious Literature, as the 'Athenaeum,' 'Literary Gazette,' etc., supply with regard to secular Literature,"[27] was valuable to clergymen of all persuasions, who sought to keep up with the outpouring of books and pamphlets without actually reading them. There was a distinct High Church bias in the reviews, some of which were signed; the most notable reviewer was the ritualist T. T. Carter.[28]

The most extreme wing of the High Church, dissatisfied with the *Guardian*'s drift from Conservatism to Gladstonianism, purchased the neutral *Church and State Gazette* (1842–56) and transformed it into their own newspaper, the *Union*, in 1857. Ecclesiastically, these Anglo-Catholics sought the corporate reunion of the Church of England with the Roman Catholic Church, for which end they organized the Association for the Promotion of the Unity of Christendom (APUC) in the same year. In 1862 the *Union*, now officially the organ of the APUC, became a monthly. In 1863 it was transformed into a bimonthly review, the *Union Review* (1863–75). The *Union* and the *Union Review* claimed to have "succeeded the *Guardian* in the 'extreme right' of the Church movement."[29] The APUC was far enough to the right to attract some Roman Catholic support; but that Church deprecated corporate reunion in favor of individual submissions to Rome; the principles of the APUC were condemned by the Inquisition, and the Roman Catholic members fell away. The *Union Review*, edited by a fascinating eccentric, F. G. Lee, remained in the hands of what may be termed the lunatic fringe of Anglo-Catholicism until its demise a decade later.[30]

To protect the political and legal interests of the High Church party (especially its ritualist element), the English Church Union (ECU) was founded in 1860, soon evoking the Church Association as its evangelical counterpart. In 1861 the ECU started "a popular periodical . . . to defend the English Church,"[31] the *Church Review* (1861–1902). In 1862 the *Church Review* was transformed into a weekly with more coverage of general topics. It did not compete with the weekly newspapers but remained the house organ of the ECU.

A remarkable journal of idiosyncratic character was the *Church and State Review* (1862–67), the personal periodical of Archdeacon G. A. Denison, the most adamant of High Churchmen, who was proprietor, editor, and major contributor. His goal was to assert the rights and doctrines of the Church, its establishment and its self-government through Convocation, whose Lower House was dominated by Denison. He promoted "the revival of spiritual discipline within the Church,"[32] that discipline being directed particularly at the authors of *Essays and Reviews*, whose "synodical condemnation" by Convocation was the principal reason for the *Church and State Review*. The condemnation of the Essayists in 1864 was Denison's triumph both as parliamentarian and as editor, but it rendered the *Church and State Review* somewhat otiose.

When the *Union* ceased to be a newspaper in 1862, the printer, George Josiah Palmer, took the advice of a noted clergyman, Richard F. Littledale, and began a weekly newspaper of his own, the *Church Times* (1863-). Unabashedly Anglo-Catholic and Conservative, the *Church Times* was the first (and for a long time the only) Anglican paper to take full advantage of the repeal of the newspaper taxes and publish at the popular price of a penny. More, however, was needed to establish this shoestring venture. The opportunity came when, at the marriage of the Prince of Wales, stands were erected in the churchyard of St. Martin's-in-the-Fields to view the procession; the new paper denounced this desecration, and "from that moment the reputation of the *Church Times* was made."[33] Advertisements, indispensable for the success of a newspaper, flowed in to the extent of two out of eight pages per issue, and the *Church Times* soon claimed "the largest sale of any Church paper in the kingdom." Where the elite *Guardian* slew its thousands, the *Church Times* slew its tens of thousands by 1870, rising to a circulation of 45,000 in 1900.

Popularity was something to which the High Church party was unaccustomed. The *Church Times* was the only Church of England entry into the new mass market, comparable to the nonconformist *Christian World* and the Roman Catholic *Universe*, founded at about the same time, reflecting a new stage of professionalism in religious journalism.[34] Palmer mixed lay journalists with clerical contributors such as Littledale (whose "great achievement . . . was to popularise ceremonial"[35]) and James Edward Vaux, who had the inspiration for the St. Martin's affair. Palmer kept the direction in his own hands (after 1887 his sons') and introduced popular features such as a weekly sermon and answers to correspondents. Much of the growth of Anglo-Catholicism in the latter decades of the century was a growth of lay support for an originally clerical movement, and the *Church Times* contributed significantly to this support. No other Church newspaper compared to it; the *Rock* was the nearest thing to an evangelical counterpart. A Church daily (the greatest frequency of any religious paper) was attempted in 1877 with the *Daily Express*, but it quickly failed. The *Church Times* bore the banner both of the Church and of its own party.

With the failure of the *Christian Remembrancer* in 1868, the High Church party lacked a quarterly review; and in 1874 Dean Church, who had just broken from the *Guardian* over its inadequate support for ritualism, summoned a meeting to propose a new quarterly. This appeared in 1875 as the *Church Quarterly Review* (1875–1968). The first article was by Gladstone, and eventually everybody who was anybody in the High Church wrote for the new review.[36] It was less fortunate in its editors. The first, Canon A. R. Ashwell, required several months before he could disengage himself from the *Literary Churchman*, which he had been editing since 1864; and he died prematurely in 1879. The editor from 1885 to 1900, a layman, Christopher Knight Watson, made matters worse by an "intolerant and reactionary"[37] editorial policy that rejected even the degree of biblical criticism that the younger Anglo-Catholics now found acceptable. With the appointment of Arthur C. Headlam (later bishop of Gloucester) as editor in 1901, the *Church Quarterly Review* entered the modern theological world and became somewhat less stodgy, though still firmly High Church.

The least stodgy High Church periodical was the *Newbery House Magazine* (1889–94), which was named after John Newbery, publisher of the original *Christian's Magazine*, and which intended "to fill the place in periodical literature which the *Guardian* and *Church Times* fill in newspaper literature."[38] This "monthly review for churchmen and churchwomen" offered more variety than the usual Anglican magazine, including serialized novels. Perhaps the High Church public was not ready for such liveliness; the magazine lasted little over five years.

When D. C. Lathbury left the editorship of the *Guardian*, his friends raised money for him to start a weekly review of his own, the *Pilot* (1900–04). This was a high-class journal with a distinguished list of signed contributors.[39] Lathbury had (though firmly Anglican himself) maintained an interest in Roman Catholicism, and the *Pilot*'s most original role was to provide an outlet for liberal or modernist Roman Catholics denied periodical expression in their own communion. For all its merits, the *Pilot* was a financial failure. This has been attributed to the fact that "the editor would not read manuscript. He had every article submitted to him set up in type."[40]

Lathbury was no longer young, and perhaps his eyes were failing; at any rate, his journal was.

5

Not Angels, But Anglicans

BROAD CHURCH

The great phalanxes of High and Low Churchmen did not exhaust the party tendencies in the Church of England. There was a third element, hardly cohesive enough to be called a movement, composed of individuals who rejected the doctrinal quarrels of High and Low and stressed instead the tolerant, inclusive, and national character of the Church and its openness to new social and scholarly ideas. This Broad Church, spiritually descended from Coleridge or Thomas Arnold of Rugby, was small in numbers but included several constellations of talent: the group that gathered around the prophetic figure of F. D. Maurice, best known for Christian Socialism, unwilling to form a party but free in theology; biblical scholars such as Benjamin Jowett and the future Archbishop Frederick Temple, participants in the controversial volume *Essays and Reviews* (1860), and their friend A. P. Stanley, dean of Westminster. They had, indeed, more talent than any other party, but they were not a party; though they published much, they never had a periodical organ distinctively their own. This, the most striking fact about them, drew the attention of the *Edinburgh Reviewer* who coined the term *Broad Church*:

They are even destitute of that instrument, which every fractional subdivision of the smallest sects possesses, an organ in the periodical press. This is the more remarkable because among their ranks is comprehended almost every living clerical author whose name is distinguished in literature or science. . . . Yet this school of opinion, so rich in eminent writers, is unrepresented in the press, except by

> the isolated publications of individuals. The reason of this is not hard to find. It is always easier to keep together a body of partisans on a narrow than on a comprehensive basis. . . . A common hate is the cement to consolidate a party.[1]

This suggestion that the Broad Church died of a surfeit of love is not altogether wrong, but there were more concrete reasons for the failure of the Broad Church to establish a periodical organ. Many of its figures preferred to express themselves through books, tracts, or sermons rather than articles; others, such as the Mauricean novelists Charles Kingsley and Thomas Hughes and the colorful writer Stanley,[2] did not need an organ of their own in order to place their articles in the press. The most significant reason for the absence of a Broad Church periodical is the success of Broad Churchmen in capturing the use of periodicals not their own and not professedly religious, which, in fact, gave them an audience wider than any religious periodical could obtain.

Two future Essayists, Mark Pattison and H. B. Wilson, managed the philosophical and theological departments of the *Westminster Review* from 1854 to 1858. When a difference with the editor forced them to quit, they projected an annual review devoted solely to religious topics; this was the genesis of *Essays and Reviews*, a volume originally intended to be periodical, though the controversy aborted this plan.[3] Meanwhile, in 1859, a suggestion by the Mauricean J. M. Ludlow had led to the founding of *Macmillan's Magazine*, a serious general magazine that afforded the Maurice group all the advantages of an organ without the burden of management.[4] In 1866 the publisher Alexander Strahan added the *Contemporary Review* to his string of religious magazines. The *Contemporary* was unique among religious magazines in being genuinely open to all parties and sects; but it was particularly useful to Broad Churchmen to whom few other organs were open. It retained its religious character until 1882.[5] Its principle of the "open platform" was carried on by the *Nineteenth Century*, founded in 1877 by J. T. Knowles, formerly editor of the *Contemporary* and founder of the Metaphysical Society; but the emphasis of the *Nineteenth Century* was not primarily religious.

The most valuable capture by the Broad Church was the *Spectator*, already established since 1828 as a quality weekly, which between 1861 and 1886 came under the literary control of a singular Mauricean, Richard Holt Hutton. Originally a Unitarian and coeditor of the *Prospective* and *National Reviews*, Hutton was converted by

Maurice to a Broad Anglicanism that was at once deeply religious and open-minded, sympathetic to science and criticism and even doubt. Offered by Meredith Townsend the joint proprietorship and coeditorship of the *Spectator* in 1861, Hutton made its literary department an organ not of the Broad Church but of the best Broad Churchman until 1886. Hutton's sympathies extended beyond Broad Anglicanism:. he helped to shape the public success of Newman's *Apologia.* "It was said that Hutton did for Victorian journalism what Gladstone did for Victorian politics,"[6] raising it to a level above itself. Perhaps because it was not expressly a religious journal, Hutton's *Spectator* showed what Victorian religious journalism was capable of being— and what it almost never was.

CHRISTIAN SOCIALISTS

The Mauricean wing of the Broad Church first came to public notice in that year of revolution and Chartism, 1848. The initiative came from a French-educated barrister, John Malcolm Ludlow, who proposed to Maurice an effort to head off revolution by Christianizing the socialism of the working class and awakening the social conscience of rich "unsocial Christians."[7] Maurice boldly chose the name Christian Socialism for a movement that was strong in aspiration but somewhat cloudy in thought. The socialism consisted in both an appeal to cooperation or association as opposed to the profit motive and an effort to educate the workingman; the practical results were the cooperative movement and the Working Men's College. There was also a genuine desire to reach the workingman by sympathizing with his aspirations for self-improvement, infusing a Christian element into his efforts. Maurice preached, Kingsley wrote novels, everybody wrote tracts; but the first expression of the movement, befitting its sense of urgency, was a penny weekly, *Politics for the People*, beginning May 6, 1848. This was addressed to workingmen to teach them Christian nonrevolutionary politics; but its didacticism betrayed the educational level of its authors. Nonetheless it contained some of the finest writing of any religious journal, solid articles by Ludlow (coeditor with Maurice) and fiery pieces by Kingsley under the name of Parson Lot. *Politics for the People*, little read by the people, lasted only seventeen numbers.

Ludlow, the most coherent thinker in the group, published on his own another weekly, the *Christian Socialist*, beginning in November,

1850. His articles in the *Christian Socialist* constitute the fullest statement of a vision of a society at once Christian and socialist. But Ludlow was both more radical and more specifically Christian than many of his colleagues in the movement; unsupported by Maurice in a quarrel, he resigned at the end of 1851. Thomas Hughes took over the journal, changing the title to the former subtitle, *A Journal of Association*, and making it primarily the organ of the cooperatives.[8] On this basis it lasted only through the first half of 1852, though Ludlow replaced Hughes in April. The Christian Socialist movement as a whole fell apart in 1854.

There was a second Christian Socialist movement beginning in the 1870s, the product not of the Broad Church (by then defunct) but of advanced Anglo-Catholics. The oldest socialist body was the exclusively High Church Guild of St. Matthew, founded in 1877 by the headstrong Stewart Headlam. He provided it with an organ, the *Church Reformer* (1882–95); the title reflected his combination of Christian socialism with church reform, "the readaptation of the ecclesiastical machinery to the wants of the age."[9] The GSM was too narrow a body (200 members) to provide a foundation for the *Church Reformer*, hampered also by a lack of advertisements and small circulation.[10] It was really Headlam's personal organ. Nonetheless, the *Church Reformer* won praise from Shaw, Morley, and Ruskin.

The title *Christian Socialist* was revised in 1883 by J. L. Joynes, a former Eton master. Seeing the alternatives as social reform or social anarchy and regarding socialism and Christianity as "almost interchangeable terms,"[11] Joynes showed wide sympathy even to socialisms that were not Christian; for instance, the magazine printed a sensitive article on "The Death of Karl Marx" in July 1883. But the nascent socialist movement published its own organ, *Justice*, in 1884, and William Morris added his journal, *Commonweal*, in 1885, leaving little room for Joynes, who lacked the support of an organization. In 1887 the *Christian Socialist* passed from his Anglican hands to those of a nondenominational group, the Christian Socialist Society, which, though a High Churchman served as editor, was largely nonconformist.[12] The journal failed in 1891.

In 1889, Henry Scott Holland, canon of St. Paul's, founded the most serious and influential Anglican Christian socialist organization, the Christian Social Union (CSU). Himself an Anglo-Catholic, Holland drew into the CSU members of all parties within the Church, including dignitaries such as the first president, Bishop Westcott of Durham.

A few branches were formed, and the Oxford branch published the quarterly *Economic Review* (1891-1914), essentially a learned journal with an ethical emphasis. More outspoken was *Goodwill*, published from 1894 by the Hon. and Rev. James G. (Father Jimmy) Adderley, a novelist who was possibly the most effective Christian socialist writer of the day. With a diverse list of authors ranging from the surviving Mauriceans to ritualists[13] and a format that allowed it to be localized as a parish magazine, *Goodwill* published 30,000 copies and reached a larger audience than any other organ of the movement. It overlapped Holland's own periodical, *Commonwealth* (1896-), "a personal journal" that "contained some of the best writing" of the entire movement from an equally catholic and distinguished group of contributors.[14] As the century ended, the CSU had brought respectability to Christian socialism, and its trenchant periodicals contributed to that development.

GENERAL CHURCH PUBLICATIONS

We have hitherto considered the Church of England as if it were a collection of movements; but it was also an institution with a common organization and problems incident thereto. There were Church periodicals unattached to any party, serving the Church at large.

The first religious magazine, Dodd's *Christian's Magazine* (1760-67), was intended to reach a general Church audience. However, Dodd's tendency to Arminianism provoked a Calvinist evangelical response in the next two magazines, and for nearly seventy years Anglican periodicals belonged to one party or the other. The one exception, the *Clerical Guide* (1817, 1822, 1829, 1836), a simple directory of dignitaries and benefices, was not really periodical in its publication. It is noteworthy only as the forerunner of true annual directories, which began with the *Clergy List* (1841-1917).

A short-lived but distinguished quarterly that can be assigned to no recognized party was the *London Review* of 1829. This was the product of the noetics, a group associated with Oriel College, Oxford, critical minds but drawing orthodox conclusions. Richard Whately, later Archbishop of Dublin, and the economist Nassau Senior took the initiative and chose as editor Joseph Blanco White, a Spanish Catholic priest who had converted to Anglicanism. The young Newman was a contributor, as was the future Essayist Baden Powell and even the Utilitarian Edwin Chadwick, a wonderful mixture of distinguished authors writing heavy articles. All they lacked was readers; the review failed after two issues.[15]

The next periodical without a party took the Church itself as its party. This was the *Church of England Quarterly Review* (1837–58), designed to defend the Church and all established institutions "against the triple alliance of infidelity, liberalism and papistry."[16] This is more high and dry than High Church, more Tory than Anglican. Indeed, it might seem to be the quarterly counterpart to the newspaper *John Bull* (1820–92), which was "in the Church interest" politically but whose tone was too scurrilous ever to allow it to be described as a religious journal. The *Church of England Quarterly Review*, however, was not scurrilous; its editor was a clergyman; it defended the established order because it included the Established Church.

The next journal, the *Ecclesiastical Gazette* (1838–1900), not only had no party; it had no opinions at all. It was "not intended to be a vehicle for theological discussions or opinions, but a record of facts, and a general medium of intelligence" which would be "acceptable to all parties."[17] Distributed free to all clergymen, it was intended by its publisher, John W. Parker, primarily to be a vehicle for advertisements, which in fact supported it. Much of its advertising dealt with clerical "situations wanted" in the form of presentations to benefices to be bought or sold. When that business was restricted by law, the *Ecclesiastical Gazette*, which had been profitable, soon came to an end.

The *Church and State Gazette* (1842–56) might seem to be a weekly counterpart to the *Ecclesiastical Gazette*, but it was a newspaper whose purpose was to defend the union of church and state. Conservative in politics, it criticized extremists of both the High and Low parties. But at the end of 1856 it was purchased by a faction of extreme High Churchmen, who transformed it into the *Union* (1857–62),[18] later the *Union Review* (1863–75), the organ of the "corporate reunion" movement.

Another neutral periodical had an origin and a sequel that were unique. E. W. Cox, a barrister, had founded the *Law Times*, which in turn spawned many other legal periodicals. In order to attract advertising from publishers, the *Law Times* generated the *Critic*, a periodical of general reviewing characterized, like the legal journals, by factual reporting rather than opinion. The *Critic* claimed a large clerical readership, for whom Cox and John Crockford, his business manager and publisher, projected a special journal devoted entirely to ecclesiastical literature and news. This was the *Church Journal*, begun in May, 1853, which soon changed to the fortnightly *Clerical Journal* (1853–69), to serve the clerical profession as the *Law Times* served the legal or the *Lancet* the medical: "the *Clerical Journal* is of no party. It is purely a *Church Journal*; the organ of the *Clerical Profession*; the Chronicler of *Facts*."[19] This ideal was perhaps too pure for the Victorian clergy, among whom impartiality was no virtue. The journal survived but did not establish itself in that undisciplined profession.

The experience of conducting the *Clerical Journal* made its publisher aware of the need for a biographical directory of the clergy more ample than the *Clergy List*. Letting one thing lead to another, a policy that made the Cox periodicals into a publishing empire that eventually included the *Field* and the *Queen*,[20] Crockford began in 1855 the publication of a *Clerical Directory* as a supplement to the *Journal* in parts included in each issue (with entries in the order in which they were received from clergymen). The project grew to vast proportions, with a paid editor and "an outlay of *more than Five Hundred Pounds for Postage Stamps alone*."[21] The whole was issued as a volume in 1858. Serial publication may not have been planned, but new editions were published (as *Crockford's Clerical Directory*) in 1860, 1865, and 1868. Periodicity was established with biannual publication from 1870 to 1876 and annual issues thereafter. The (anonymous clerical) editor from 1869 also began the famous "Prefaces," originally as a general reply to readers and exhortation to clerical respondents, but evolving into an annual review of the state of the Church. *Crockford's* did not achieve quasi-official status until it was taken over by Oxford University Press in 1921, but it had already supplanted its rival.

The long-dormant parliamentary body of the clergy, the Convocation of the Province of Canterbury, began to resume its activities in 1851, and the Reverend C. Warren attempted to record its proceedings in *Synodalia* (1852–53), later the *Journal of Convocation* (1854–58). Two parliamentary shorthand reporters then commenced the *Chronicle of Convocation* (1859–) in the style of *Hansard's Parliamentary Debates*, verbatim reports (corrected by the speakers) published six weeks after the debates, with official documents.[22] This became, like *Hansard's*, the official record and an invaluable historical source. The convocation of the Province of York had its own *Journal* from its beginning in 1861, and the unofficial Church Congresses, which admitted laymen, also had their *Authorised Report* of their annual meetings, which began in 1861.

SOCIETIES

The oldest Church society was the Society for Promoting Christian Knowledge (SPCK), founded in 1699. Its earliest efforts were directed towards charity schools, a movement that lost momentum during the eighteenth century; but its most important work was done as a publisher of religious literature. It was slow to enter the field of periodicals, not even publishing an *Annual Report* until 1811. In 1832, however, a General Literature Committee was formed to publish works not specifically religious, in response to the availability of cheap literature deemed unsuitable. Specifically in response to the success of the "useful knowledge" *Penny Magazine*, the Committee published the *Saturday Magazine* (1832-1844), a penny weekly issued on Saturday to avoid profaning the Sabbath but obviously (though never admittedly) intended for reading on Sunday. It was an instant success, claiming a circulation of 70,000,[23] and lasting as long as the vogue of useful penny magazines continued. Thereafter the SPCK published a number of other popular periodicals, but none achieved the success of the *Saturday Magazine*, although a halfpenny monthly miscellany, *Dawn of Day* (1878-1928), had a good run.

The Society for the Propagation of the Gospel (SPG), founded in 1701 and originally specializing in missions in the Americas, had published annual reports from 1704 but was nearly dormant by the end of the eighteenth century. Its revival was accompanied by periodical publication, quarterly papers under various titles being distributed to members from 1839, with a Welsh edition as well.[24] A regular periodical, the *Monthly Record of Church Missions* (1852-55), was published with J. W. Colenso (later a colonial bishop, controversial for his biblical criticism) as its first editor. Its format of one article per number was perhaps unsuitable, and it was transformed into a true illustrated magazine, *Mission Field* (1856-1941), the most successful of the SPG periodicals. The Society published children's magazines from 1852, and its ladies' association published the *Grain of Mustard Seed* (1881-98; then *Women in the Mission Field*, 1899-1903).

The Church's extensive efforts for the elementary education of the lower classes had been organized from 1811 by the National Society for Promoting the Education of the Poor in the Principles of the

Established Church. The National Society started an official journal in 1847, the *Monthly Paper of the National Society* (1847–75).[25] As more matter became available for publication, this journal was converted to a weekly, the *School Guardian* (1876–1937). More specialized periodicals were later issued for and eventually by the Society's schoolteachers.

The threat of legislation against the rights of the Church (at first the abolition of church rates, later disestablishment) prompted the formation of the Church Institution in 1859. From 1862 to 1864 it issued the *Church Institution Circular* weekly during sessions of Parliament. Later it offered a monthly, the *National Church* (1872–1919).

Two other Church organizations were responses to initiatives beginning among nonconformists. The temperance movement, largely nonconformist, had an Anglican counterpart, the Church of England Temperance Society, which published several periodicals. The most important was the *Church of England Temperance Magazine* (1862–72, then *C. of E. Temperance Chronicle*, 1873–88, then *Temperance Chronicle*, 1888–1914), which became one of the four major temperance journals, high-class rather than popular.[26] The success of the nonconformist Salvation Army stimulated an evangelical clergyman, Wilson Carlile, to form a rival body affiliated with the Established Church, the Church Army. His counterpart to Booth's *War Cry* was an equally aggressive *Battleaxe* (1883–86), which became the *Church Army Gazette* (1886–).

THE CHURCH IN WALES

In Wales, the Church of England was established but not national. It was largely English in speech as well as origin, slow to translate itself into the Welsh language still spoken by many of the people, and hence it became a minority in Welsh-speaking areas. Nonetheless there was an Anglican Church in Wales and eventually in Welsh, and it developed a number of periodicals, mostly short-lived.

Apparently the first Church periodical in Welsh was *Y Gwyleidydd* (1822–37), a magazine that was general but unable to avoid religious controversy. The most successful magazine was a weekly, *Yr Haul* (1836–), founded and edited for thirty years by David Owen, a vigorous controversialist.

Religion was then the all-consuming interest of the Welsh people. Even politics appealed to them mostly because of the various implications of the relations between Church and State. *Yr Haul* was unashamedly controversial because controversy was the very breath of religion at the time.[27]

Owen was succeeded by William Spurrell and Ellis Roberts, who maintained the orthodox and conservative position of the journal. Other Church magazines generally found that there was room for only one of the kind. The only one of any duration was the less acrimonious *Yr Eglwysydd* (1847-62), produced by clergymen led by Archdeacon Clough. *Y Cyfaill Eglwysig* (1862-) served the needs of Welsh Church Sunday Schools. A number of newspapers were attempted; the only survivor, after some mergers, was *Y Llan a'r Dywysogaeth* (1881-).

SCOTLAND

The Episcopal Church of Scotland was a very small minority in that Presbyterian land; disestablished since 1689, it only began to revive in the nineteenth century. Its periodicals were few and generally short-lived, the most notable being the *Scottish Magazine* (1849-54). Eventually, however, it produced a successful monthly, the *Scottish Standard Bearer* (1890-).

IRELAND

The Anglican Church of Ireland was formally united to the Church of England in 1801 but was separated and disestablished in 1869. It was always the church of a privileged minority, the "ascendancy," which lost its privileges in the course of the nineteenth century. Rejected by most of the Irish nation, this church regarded itself as perpetually embattled, besieged by the Roman Catholic majority: "We regard the great evil of Ireland to be the domination of Popery."[28] Defense of privilege and anti-Catholicism were therefore the main themes of its press.

The Anglicans of Ireland were served by the English Church press, but a feeling that a specifically Irish publication was needed for the defense of the Church led to the founding of the *Christian Examiner*

(1825-69), a monthly that unabashedly devoted much of its space to anti-Catholic polemic. It was in financial trouble from 1835, but it nonetheless survived until disestablishment.[29] Another general monthly with a heavy burden of anti-Catholic controversy was the *Irish Ecclesiastical Journal* (1842-52). On the other hand, the *Irish Ecclesiastical Gazette* (1856-99; then *Church of Ireland Gazette*, 1900-) was founded solely as a journal of church news, distributed free to all Irish clergymen and largely supported by advertisements. Although it eventually published leading articles and letters, it remained "the most moderate and sound of the Irish Church journals."[30] It served the disestablished Church of Ireland after 1869, along with the *Irish Church Advocate*, the successor of the *Achill Missionary Herald.*

PARISH AND LOCAL PERIODICALS

The Church of England appears to have been slower than the nonconformists to develop a local press. The record is unclear, partly because local periodicals of this type were rarely copyrighted and are therefore unrecorded and partly because the word *parochial* often was used in the titles of journals dealing with the politics of the parish as a civil unit, the parish pump rather than the parish church. The parish church magazine (though there may have been earlier exemplars) dates from the initiative in 1859 of J. Erskine Clarke, vicar of St. Michael's, Derby, also known for successful children's magazines such as *Chatterbox* (1866-). Clarke commenced the *Parish Magazine* (1859-) as twenty pages of inside matter available at wholesale to parishes, which could then enclose them in four pages of cover with local news or advertisements. The idea built slowly: after two years some sixty parishes had subscribed, about 15,000 copies, not enough for self-sufficiency; but it eventually caught on and became commonplace.[31] The *Parish Magazine* was a unique combination of central initiative and localization.

A number of ruridecanal magazines appeared in the latter decades of the century, reflecting the development of clerical meetings at this subdiocesan level. Diocesan journals are a still later development, except for annual calendars or clergy lists; the earliest of these was published for Lichfield in 1855, and all dioceses had them by 1880.[32]

THE SIMONY PRESS

A type of periodical peculiar to the Established Church grew out of its legal and business aspects. The advowson—the right to nominate the clergyman of a parish—was a species of real property, capable of being bought and sold or even (in effect) rented by the sale of the "next presentation." Where these transactions were entered into by or for clergymen with a view to speedy possession of the benefice, they approached simony, which was both sinful and a breach of the law. Nonetheless, a small profession of clerical agents or brokers existed throughout the century to make these arrangements as well as to effectuate exchanges of livings and the placement of curates. Such offers were advertised occasionally in the regular press, such as *John Bull* or the *Times*, and frequently in religious newspapers: the *Record* and the *Guardian* for the convenience of their respective parties, but especially the *Ecclesiastical Gazette*, which lived on its advertising revenues. Some clerical agents found it convenient to print their own lists, often on a monthly basis. This frequency qualifies them as periodicals but perhaps not as publications, since they were "for private circulation only," sent on request and confidentially to prospective clients. They were usually not copyrighted; only occasional copies survive, and bibliographic listings are rare.[33] The first known examples date from 1844; their heyday was the 1870s, when a select committee and a royal commission revealed (and deplored) the business of clerical agents.[34] The Leviathan of clergy-mongering was W. Emergy Stark, who regularly put out five monthly lists, each for a specific clientele, with titles such as *Church Preferment Gazette* and a total annual printing of 10,960 copies in 1884.[35] His periodicals ran from the 1860s to the 1890s; perhaps the reforming Benefices Act of 1898 put them out of business.[36]

6

EVANGELICALS

The evangelical revival, beginning in the eighteenth century, provided the motive force behind the general revival of religion in the nineteenth century. The evangelical impulse manifested itself in three denominational forms. There were those evangelicals who remained loyal to the Church of England, becoming a party rather than a denomination. There were new denominations, founded largely under the impulse of John Wesley and bearing the name of Methodist. There were also groups of the older Dissent, Congregationalist or Baptist, who were stimulated to renewed life by a similar impulse. All these elements were active—for example, in issuing periodicals—in their denominational forms. But there was also a common fellowship, indeed a culture, of evangelicals. They could work together to promote morality in the nation and "vital religion" in the family, to oppose "popery," and especially to enhance the spiritual and practical well-being of classes regarded as dependent or inferior: children, women, servants, and laborers. They preached; they organized; most characteristically, they published tracts. Among other things, they issued periodicals.

The first periodical of nondenominational evangelicalism was, appropriately, the *Evangelical Magazine* (1793–1904), the earliest of the second generation of religious magazines but curiously old-fashioned in format: "The Work will uniformly be conducted upon the principles of the late Gospel Magazine, devoid of personality and acrimonious reflections on any sect of professing Christians"[1] (in other words, not so narrowly Calvinist as to offend Wesleyans). It followed the *Gospel Magazine* (1766–84) in its "accounts of triumphant deaths and remarkable providences,"[2] but it innovated in illustration by giving portraits of eminent ministers. The "editors" (really contributors, whose names were stated) were twenty-four ministers, some of them clergymen of the Church of England; but the Congregationalist element became dominant. The first editor was John Eyre, secretary of the nonconformist London Missionary Society; he was succeeded in both posts by George Burder in 1802. From that year the *Christian Observer* tended to draw away the Anglican evangelicals, making the *Evangelical Magazine* essentially nonconformist; but it soon faced competition first from the general nonconformist (but largely Congregationalist) *Eclectic Review* and later from explicitly Congregationalist denominational journals.[3] The *Evangelical Magazine* nonetheless prospered and continued on its noncontroversial theological and pietistic course for over a century.

Another magazine of the old style, reusing an old title, was the *Spiritual Magazine* (1825–52), serving all "whether Episcopal, Independent, or Baptist,"[4] but under nonconformist control. In 1837 it merged with a similar monthly, *Zion's Casket*, adding that title to its own and reducing the price to 2d., "the cheapest of all our contemporaries."[5] The effort to meet the competition may have given the journal an additional fifteen years of life.

The religious press was largely responsive to or imitative of innovations in the secular press, and this tendency was evident in its response to the success of the *Penny Magazine*, published from 1832 to 1845 by the Society for the Diffusion of Useful Knowledge (SDUK) for the expanding literate portion of the lower classes. The SDUK was secular and radical, and a need was immediately felt to counteract its presumed infidelity by a similar but religious publication. The result was the *Christian's Penny Magazine* (1832–38), an illustrated "weekly miscellany, conducted upon the principles of the Protestant Reformation, and suited to every denomination of Christians," according to its masthead. Noting that Britain had become "a nation of readers," the *Christian's Penny Magazine* acknowledged its reactive character: "there is a mass of reading supplied in the cheapest form, of a character which is antichristian and destructive. Shall we make no corresponding efforts to vindicate the honour of our Divine Christianity?"[6] The articles were more often religious than "useful," a fact that may account for the magazine's relative lack of success. A similar venture was the monthly *Zion's Trumpet* (1833–68), subtitled "the Penny Spiritual Magazine." The original publisher was Edward Palmer, publisher of the *Spiritual Magazine*; he broke with *Zion's Trumpet* in 1834, when the printer, John Nichols, became the publisher. The profits were given to the Aged Pilgrims' Friend Society, and the use of ministers and local agents to promote the journal may account for its longevity, the greatest of any penny magazine.[7] Strictly Calvinist, it too was more religious than "useful."

Evangelicals were first in the field with another type of periodical, the *Christian Lady's Magazine* (1834–49), edited by Charlotte Elizabeth, the nom de plume of the prolific writer Charlotte Elizabeth Tonna, née Browne. "She felt as a woman who, by the good providence of God, was chosen to prepare for the Christian females of the land, a certain portion of literary entertainment, which it was her duty to render as solidly instructive as she could."[8] Too conservative to be feminist, she acknowledged that there were topics "the discussion of which we consider better adapted to periodicals of a more masculine stamp"[9] (church reform and "conflicting interpretations of Unfulfilled Prophecy" were cited as examples). But she faced up to the question of whether it was

> lawful and expedient for us publicly to "intermeddle with all wisdom" in spiritual matters. That we are not excluded from this happy prerogative is clear from many passages in holy writ; that a boundary is assigned, beyond which it were unbecoming presumption in us to press, is quite as evident.[10]

The *Christian Lady's Magazine* was far from bland, freely dealing with controversial subjects such as factory and housing reform and Charlotte Elizabeth's favorite hobbyhorse, anti-Catholicism (she was simultaneously editor of the *Protestant Magazine* for five years). She admitted (and wrote) fiction (but not "love-tales"[11]), but her most effective technique was the didactic essay in the form of a dialogue in which "uncle" instructs "niece." She developed a personal relationship with her readers, down to the moving announcement of her own impending death from cancer in 1846. None of her would-be successors could maintain this relationship, and the magazine died a few years later.

Another specialized periodical was the *Servant's Magazine* (1838–69), published for women domestics by the London Female Mission. Noting that servants had become fond of reading, it sought "to direct this taste into a useful channel"[12] by giving not "mere amusement, but practical utility."[13] "Utility" included moral instruction in various forms, but sections such as "The Servants' Hall" (conversations on domestic subjects) and "My Mother's Note-Book" (short "how-to-do-its") gave practical information of the sort that Mrs. Beeton would later popularize. Although it was directed to an acknowledged subordinate class, the *Servant's Magazine* was only mildly patronizing.

The next type of specialized religious periodical to emerge was the family magazine, responding to the growing habit of family reading and the need for suitable reading during the unoccupied hours of a British Sunday. Competition with the respectable secular press often meant that the evangelicalism of these journals would be diffuse or attenuated. The pioneer in this field was the Religious Tract Society with the *Leisure Hour* (1852–1905) and the more explicitly religious *Sunday at Home* (1854–1940), both very successful. Certain publishers came to specialize in this field, notably the house of Cassell,[14] whose first major venture, not explicitly religious, was *Cassell's Illustrated Family Paper* (1853–67), continued monthly as *Cassell's Magazine* (1867–74). John Cassell was more religious and more venturesome with the *Quiver* (1861–1956), "designed to advance the cause of Religion in the Homes of the People," a penny weekly that included, besides the usual religious articles and a sermon, a serialized tale by a well-known author. Cassell could celebrate an "extensive circulation" and boast that such rich fare "marks an era in the history of cheap Religious Literature."[15] The era had really begun a year earlier with *Good Words* (1860–1906), the first major production of Alexander Strahan, who built up a stable of religious or quasi-religious periodicals in Edinburgh and later in London. The most explicitly religious was the *Sunday Magazine* (1864–1906), edited in Scotland and therefore exclusively serious but high-quality Sunday reading, with a variety of signed authors and illustrators. Strahan's publishing empire, which included the *Contemporary Review*, collapsed between 1872 and 1881 because of poor management,[16] but the journals survived because of their merit and interest.

A very different specialty was represented by the *Foreign Evangelical Review* (1852–53), designed "to furnish British readers with a selection from the many valuable papers that from time to time appear in the Denominational Quarterlies of the United States"[17] and also Continental journals. This format was soon enlarged by the addition of original articles and transformed into the better-known *British and Foreign Evangelical Review* (1853–88), which eventually completed its course as the *Theological Monthly* (1889–91). The review was appropriately published in Edinburgh, for Calvinist Scotland served to mediate European religious scholarship to an insular England. The review was nonetheless very conservative and orthodox, providing heavy theological fare to a largely ministerial audience.[18]

A second wave of evangelical revival, beginning in Ulster in 1859 under stimulus from America, produced a weekly, the *Revival* (1859–70), the product of an enterprising young publisher, Richard Cope Morgan. Originally intended to publicize the Ulster revivals and to encourage their spread in England, the *Revival* made most of its early sales in bulk to sponsors who distributed copies gratis, much like tracts. As the revival impetus died down, Morgan wisely transformed the *Revival* into a general "news magazine for the evangelical subculture."[19] In 1870 it received a more enduring name as the *Christian* (1870–1969). Its coverage of the Moody and Sankey evangelistic campaigns of 1873–75 and 1882–83 established the *Christian* as an enduring organ of nondenominational evangelicalism.

A rival journal catered to another characteristic interest of the evangelical subculture, an interest in Scriptural prophecy, especially apocalyptic. This journal was *Signs of the Times* (1867–75), "a serial of prophetic exposition, Jewish intelligence, and revival news," edited by the Reverend Michael Baxter, who avowed himself a "Clergyman of the Church of England" but was thoroughly interdenominational in his coverage. In 1876 Baxter transformed his prophetic monthly into a more general weekly entitled the *Christian Herald* (1876–), containing little news other than revivals but featuring sermons (including some by Spurgeon), religious biography, essays, and tales. This journal too met the needs of its subculture and enjoyed a substantial circulation. One may note that, although Baxter left the prophetic specialty for general evangelicalism, numerous prophetic journals continued to be published.

WEEKLY NEWSPAPERS

This discussion has so far dealt only with magazines. Newspapers presented a special problem for evangelicals. A desire for news smacked of worldliness, and much of what passed for news—crime, the theater, or partisan politics—was unfit to be read by good Christians and especially their womenfolk. But modern practical men need the news, and the medium was already so powerful that a desire was felt to place a Christian representative within it. A religious daily paper, requiring a large staff, was never practical, but a weekly seemed possible by the end of the eighteenth century. It was characteristic of the early religious newspapers that they felt obliged to apologize for their existence:

> The Press is certainly the most powerful engine which can be applied to the public mind; and of all its productions, NEWSPAPERS appear the most effective, because circulated to the greatest extent, and read by thousands with avidity, who scarcely ever read any other publication. That these are too generally employed in the cause of Scepticism, Vice, and Faction, cannot be denied; and to wrest this weapon from the hands of the enemy, and use it in the cause of Religion, Virtue, and Social Union, is the general object of this Plan.[20]

Even this statement was not enough without an assurance of morality in subject and phrase: "it will be so guarded in its expressions, as to leave no hesitation in the minds of good men as to the safety of introducing this newspaper into any branch of their families."[21] Evangelicals, who were Victorians before Victoria, were explicit about what their newspapers would *not* report. Nonetheless, they denied any specific religious character for these journals, claiming to be general newspapers; but they used sufficient evangelical code words for their intended audience to recognize them.

The first effort was the *Weekly Register* (1798-99?), "designed for serious families," which is known only from a prospectus, a stray issue, and a notice in a magazine.[22] The stray issue proves that it lasted at least thirteen months, but it probably was premature, as no other attempt was made for nearly two decades. On January 1, 1817, there appeared the *Philanthropic Gazette* (1817-23), "a weekly journal of intelligence, foreign and domestic, adapted for families, schools, societies, etc." The editor both asserted and denied his religious character:

> The Bible is his religious creed; and his politics the British Constitution of 1688. Believing in the doctrine of a superintending Providence, he will endeavour to guide his readers to that "invisible hand," which directs the moral government of the world. . . . And yet . . . this work is not intended as the vehicle of religious news.[23]

The *Philanthropic Gazette* outlasted and absorbed a rival of Methodist origin, the *Christian Reporter* (1820-22). But it too failed, and the first lasting religious newspapers were founded under denominational auspices, the nonconformist *World* in 1827 and the Anglican *Record* in 1828.

A second opportunity for nonsectarian evangelical newspapers came in the 1850s, when the repeal of the "taxes on knowledge" opened the way for a cheap press. Prompt to take advantage of this development was the *Christian Cabinet* (1855-64), which boasted itself "The Pioneer of the Religious Penny Press" and "A Weekly Newspaper for the Churches." Emphasizing that it was "perfectly unsectarian,"[24] the paper gave space to the great Baptist preacher Spurgeon for a copyrighted column; it also had a temperance column. A similar venture was the *London Christian Times* (1863–64), later the *Illustrated Christian Times* (1865–66), finally the *Christian Times* (1866–71), also "a religious journal" of "evangelical principles"[25] but no denomination. But the only religious journal of evangelical principles to survive this era was the specifically nonconformist *Christian World*.

NO-POPERY

The least attractive feature of British evangelical Protestantism was its fierce anti-Catholicism. "No-Popery" had been a constant element in English national sentiment, given new prominence in the nineteenth century with the Roman (and Anglo-) Catholic revival. Anti-Catholicism developed an extensive network of organizations, speakers, and writers, nondenominationally evangelical in religion. *Protestant* in a title invariably denoted anti-Catholicism.

Catholic Emancipation in 1829 stimulated a first wave of anti-Catholic reaction, which obtained a permanent organization in 1836 with the Protestant Association, founded under Tory auspices. Its primary publication was the *Protestant Magazine* (1839–65), free to subscribers of ten shillings annually (an upper- and middle-class audience) and designed to promote coordination among branch associations in pressing for the restoration of "our protestant constitution."[26] To reach the lower classes in the manner of the penny press, the Protestant Association issued the *Penny Protestant Operative* (1840–48), seeking to tap another vein of anti-Catholicism by encouraging the formation of Protestant Operative Societies.[27] Each issue had a sensationalized story of martyrdom under Queen Mary, complete with a woodcut illustration of popish cruelty.

Another ancient vein of anti-Catholicism was found in Ireland's Protestant minority and their British upholders, who sponsored missions to convert Irish Catholics as if they had been heathen. The *Achill Missionary Magazine* was a specifically Anglican example of this activity. Less denominational was the *Irish Missionary Magazine* (1844–45), continued briefly in 1846 as the *Protestant Advocate.*

These two streams of No-Popery merged after 1845 in a second wave of anti-Catholic reaction provoked by an increased government grant to the Irish Catholic seminary of Maynooth College.[28] Several organizations grew out of this movement, which was reinforced by a parallel reaction against the growth of tractarian Anglo-Catholicism, which, to evangelicals, was indistinguishable from the Roman variety. The first organization was the Protestant Reformation Society, which published the *British Protestant* (1845–64), later *Protestant Churchman* (1865–1907), as well as other periodicals and innumerable tracts. The confused election of 1847, in which Maynooth was mixed up with Protection, saw many temporary periodicals, among which was a *Protestant Elector.* Of more lasting importance was the formation in 1847 of the Evangelical Alliance, intended to rally evangelicals of all denominations against all forms of Catholicism. Its principal organ was *Evangelical Christendom* (1847–), monthly until 1899. But the Evangelical Alliance developed into something more positive than its initial anti-Catholicism, eventually becoming a worldwide ecumenical association of evangelical bodies.

Continuing the anti-Catholic wave of the 1840s were two enduring groups organized in the next decade. The Scottish Reformation Society tapped the strong anti-Catholicism of that Calvinist country, a uniting force despite the recent split in the Established Kirk. Its monthly organ, the *Bulwark* (1851–), claimed an early circulation of 30,000 and distribution throughout the British Isles. Directed against both "Popery and Puseyism,"[29] it lasted well beyond its initial impetus and was the strongest anti-Catholic voice at the end of the century. In England there was founded in 1851 the Protestant Alliance, intended to replace the weakening Protestant Association without its Tory bias. Its organ was a monthly letter simply entitled *Protestant Alliance* (1853–1930; then *Reformer*, 1930–), expanded into a magazine in 1898.[30]

Late-nineteenth-century anti-Catholicism was directed more against Anglo-Catholic ritualism than against Romanism itself. The special organ of this anti-Catholicism was the *Protestant Times* (1881–88), later the *Protestant Observer* (1888-1917), whose editor was Walter Walsh, author of the notorious *Secret History of the Oxford Movement* (1897).[31]

RELIGIOUS TRACT SOCIETY

Evangelicals of all persuasions were great organizers of societies. One of the earliest societies was also the most important in terms of publication. This was the Religious Tract Society (RTS), founded in 1799 for that most evangelical of purposes, the printing and distribution of tracts or pamphlets, the favorite means of religious expression apart from the sermon. The tract was the principal rival of the periodical as the medium of evangelism; but the periodical was destined to prevail. It was soon found that even tracts could be periodicalized: Hannah More's Cheap Repository Tracts, the undisputed hit of that genre, was issued monthly from 1795. "With a story, an address, and a ballad issued every month, they were periodicals in all but name."[32] Eventually, the Religious Tract Society also became an issuer of periodicals, despite its name.

It was perhaps inevitable that one of the Society's first efforts should be a *Tract Magazine* (1824-46), halfway between periodicalized tracts and a "Christian miscellany," and that it should, like other societies, publish a house organ for subscribers, the *Christian Spectator* (1838-56; then *Religious Tract Society Reporter*, 1857-75), resumed quarterly as the *Religious Tract Society Record of Work at Home and Abroad* (1877-1900, continuing under other titles).[33] It was not inevitable, and was indeed remarkable, that a tract society should discern and fill a need for periodicals as such in other areas, some of them pioneering. It published one of the first and longest-lasting children's magazines, the *Child's Companion* (1824-). Originally subtitled "Sunday Scholar's Reward" and distributed at Sunday schools, this preachy journal may have been more of an infliction than a reward, but it often supplied the only available reading and had some "genuine features as a periodical—verses about animals, notes on natural history and anecdotes from English history."[34] This journal and Carus Wilson's *Children's Friend* were prototypes of an important if dreary genre. The RTS similarly responded to the vogue of penny "useful knowledge" magazines and the felt need "of stemming the torrent of moral poison with which the Penny Press is inundating the land"[35] with the *Weekly Visitor* (1833-35; then the monthly *Visitor*, 1836–51),[36] religious in tone but not in subject matter.

By the 1850s the Religious Tract Society had become a regular publisher of periodicals, showing remarkable adaptability. The *Leisure Hour* (1852–1905), "a family journal of instruction and recreation," was its response to the vogue of family reading, symbolized by its frontispiece depicting paterfamilias reading to the household; it was religious in tone but varied in its subject matter. More daring was the Society's entry into Sunday reading, the *Sunday at Home* (1854-1940), directed to the working classes "as a profitable employment of those intervals of the Lord's day which are not devoted to Divine Worship and the reading of the Holy Scriptures."[37] The suitability on Sunday of any reading not explicitly religious was a touchy subject among evangelicals, and the Society's apology displays both realism and embarrassment, speaking of

> those four millions of our working-men, of whom it has been computed that only six out of every hundred attend any place of public worship. . . . to provide a journal which on the Lord's day may, to some extent, supersede the secular and the infidel publications which are now so largely received by them–is the object of this magazine. . . . it is necessary to accommodate ourselves, in some respects, to the classes with whom we have to deal. If we adopt the more sermonic form, or confine our attention to religious subjects exclusively, our labour will be thrown away, for we shall inevitably fail to gain admission to the very class we seek to benefit. . . . although these topics are not exclusively of a biblical or a theological character, their treatment shall be thoroughly and unmistakeably religious.[38]

In contrast to the refreshing sense of the *Sunday at Home* was a periodical directed at the class that had been the traditional recipient of the Society's tracts, the laborer. The *Cottager* (1861–65) showed some recognition that England was no longer an ordered rural society by changing its name to the *Cottager and Artisan* (1865–1919),[39] but it remained as preachy as the traditional tracts in its short tales and homilies, though varied with illustrations and items of useful knowledge such as gardening.

The RTS appeared in its most attractive light as a publisher of periodicals for young people in the last quarter of the century. The stimulus was the popularity of the penny dreadfuls, which at last gave boys something they really wanted to read; the antidote had to be an exciting, readable journal with no evident sign of religion about it—not even an acknowledgement that it was published by the RTS. "All this enlargement, liberty, romance and science were to appear at their best" in the *Boy's Own Paper* (*BOP*, 1879-1967), a hugely successful and thoroughly enjoyable weekly newspaper that "aimed to portray real boys."[40] Though edited at first by a clergyman, Dr. J. Macaulay, it betrayed no sign of religious purpose; in its serialized novels, often by name writers, there was "blood and thunder" enough, though within the bounds of decency. Under its next editor, G. A. Hutchinson, a natural communicator with boys, the cause it served was the late Victorian cult of manliness; it may have contributed more to imperialism than to Christianity. The *BOP* is almost the only Victorian religious periodical that can be read with pleasure a century later.

The success of the *BOP* stimulated a parallel journal, the *Girl's Own Paper* (1880–1927; continuing under other titles). It also concealed its religious affiliation[41] and avoided overt moralizing. Necessarily less bold than the *BOP* (the RTS might countenance manliness but not feminism), the *Girl's Own Paper* nonetheless was open to wider spheres for women, catering both to the majority of girls who expected to become wives and mothers and the growing minority who sought education and careers. The two journals were a remarkable achievement for the Religious Tract Society, which still maintained its traditional role in both tracts and periodicals.

OTHER ORGANIZATIONS

The Ragged School Union, founded in 1844 by the great Anglican evangelical Lord Ashley (later Earl of Shaftesbury), was a nondenominational mission of improvised schools for the poorest of the poor in slums, street waifs who could be taken off the streets and given very rudimentary schooling. In 1849 it commenced a house organ for contributors, the monthly *Ragged School Union Magazine* (1849-75; then *Ragged School Union Quarterly Record*, 1876–87; then *In His Name*, 1888–1907; finally *Shaftesbury Magazine*, 1908–), which claimed that "nearly *60,000* copies of the Magazine have been circulated among all classes of Christians, including a large portion of the nobility and gentry."[42] The Union also published a children's magazine.[43] The Education Act of 1870, which made elementary education available to all children, made the ragged schools superfluous, but nobody wants to waste a good organization; the Union and its house organ survived by taking on other functions and names.

A great nineteenth-century movement was the establishment of Sunday schools, originally teaching reading as well as the Bible. Most of these schools were attached to specific churches, both established and nonconformist, and they had their denominational organs for subscribers, students, and teachers. The *Sunday School Times* (1860-1925) was a nonsectarian weekly "suitable both for the Sabbath-school and the home circle."[44] A nonconformist group, the Sunday School Union, was the most important publisher of periodicals for teachers and students, notably the weekly *Sunday School Chronicle* (1874-1928).[45] There were many such periodicals, some dating back to the 1820s.

One of the most celebrated nonsectarian evangelical efforts, still in being, was the Juvenile Mission of Dr. T. J. Barnardo, which began as revivalism and ended as a charity for destitute children. Initially the subject of controversy, Barnardo found it useful to establish a periodical for his own and other home missions, *Night and Day* (1877- ; entitled *National Waif's Magazine*, 1899-1906). "Social questions having relation to Christian faith and practice will frequently be discussed, but purely doctrinal and dogmatic questions will be avoided,"[46] he said in an unusual acknowledgement that revivalism had passed over into social welfare. He also published a weekly juvenile magazine under a variety of titles.[47]

Mention should be made of the Pure Literature Society, founded in 1854, which did not publish periodicals but helped to distribute some 140,000 copies of evangelical journals each year.[48]

An important self-help evangelical movement was the Young Men's Christian Association (YMCA), founded by (Sir) George Williams in 1844. The national association issued reports, lectures, and papers from 1845 to 1862, a *Quarterly Messenger* (1863-73), and a number of magazines thereafter; local YMCAs, especially in Birmingham and Manchester, were equally vigorous in publishing journals. The later Young Women's Christian Association centrally issued a monthly letter from 1872 and two magazines from the 1880s.

7

Nonconformity

Facing the established Church of England (which, with all its divisions, remained one church) were the various denominations of Nonconformity or Dissent. The bodies which had seceded at the Restoration—the "Three Denominations" of Congregationalists (or Independents), Baptists, and Presbyterians (replaced in the eighteenth century by the Unitarians)—constituted the Old Dissent, together with the Quakers (Friends), who shared similar Puritan origins. These were reinforced from the eighteenth century by the products of the evangelical revival, principally Methodists, who constituted the New Dissent, along with some new denominations formed in the nineteenth century. There were also some movements common to Nonconformity in general, which, by mid-century, numbered at least as many active members as the Established Church.

The Three Denominations had long been accustomed to work together in the Protestant Dissenting Deputies, who pressed their claims on the government. In the 1790s, when numerous groups sought representation in the periodical press (the *Evangelical Magazine* was founded in 1793), it seemed appropriate for the Old Dissent to have its own magazine. But the 1790s were also the years of the Tory reaction to the French Revolution, when dissent of any kind was regarded as potentially revolutionary. The result was that the *Protestant Dissenter's Magazine* (1794–99), a monthly of what was by now the standard form, took an apologetic and cautious line, disclaiming any representative character and any "intention to interfere in any political contests; much less to introduce anything that might tend to inflame the minds of readers against any measure of government."[1] Therefore "all controversy on *the present affairs of state* will be excluded,"[2] and the magazine would confine itself to the religious instruction of the members of its denominations. This position was safe enough, perhaps too safe, too tame to invite either persecution or enthusiasm. Whether because of this tameness or the competition of the *Evangelical Magazine*, the journal did not last.

The next attempt at a nonconformist periodical was more successful and indeed transcended the usual limitations of religious journalism. This was the *Eclectic Review* (1805-68), a monthly "Review of Books on a New Plan,"[3] so named because it would include in its reviewing the best and most noteworthy books, whatever their source. It was indeed a review in the sense about to be established by the great quarterlies such as the *Edinburgh* (though it was cheaper and not quarterly), the articles all being in the form of reviews of books, scientific, literary, political, or theological. There was nothing specifically religious about it, except that it was controlled by Nonconformists, pledged its profits to the Bible Society, and proclaimed a coy "approbation" of "the Doctrinal Articles of the Church of England, which we conceive to be congenial with those of the Kirk of Scotland, of the principal Churches of Europe and America, and of a vast majority of those Secessions which have arisen wherever Britons have dwelt."[4] Two of its early editors, Daniel Parken (1806-12), a cofounder, and Josiah Conder (1813-36), a Congregationalist layman who purchased the review, established its literary character. Its writers (except for the Utilitarian James Mill) were more eminent in Nonconformity than in general letters, but they were the "intellectual aristocrats of Nonconformity," and "occasional articles published in the *Eclectic Review* during its best years reached the standard of the *Edinburgh* or the *Quarterly*."[5]

The studied moderation of the *Eclectic Review* was modified somewhat when Conder sold it to an eminent Baptist minister, Thomas Price, whose editorship (1837-50, 1850-55 with coeditors) produced controversies. Price followed Edward Miall of the *Nonconformist*—indeed he anticipated Miall—in adopting a voluntaryist or disestablishmentarian position on church-state issues. This lost the review the support of moderates such as Robert Vaughan, who in 1845 founded the *British Quarterly Review*.[6] Price also managed to alienate the rising star of Congregationalist journalism, the aggressive John Campbell of the *Christian Witness* and the *British Banner*. In 1850 the ailing Price sold the *Eclectic* to one William Linwood. Campbell found heresy both in Linwood's past association with Unitarians and in a remark in the *Eclectic* about Emerson's "happiness";[7] it was inconceivable to a Calvinist that a Unitarian could be saved. The *British Banner* (Campbell's own organ) commenced a fierce attack headed *"Infidelity! The 'Eclectic Review' and its Editor! Alarming Manifesto on the Subject of Religion and Human Happiness!"*[8] The sensitive (and possibly unorthodox) Linwood took fright and withdrew from the *Eclectic*, giving it back to Price.

Worse was to come. Price, still ailing, required coeditors and finally sold the review to one of them, J. E. Ryland, in 1855. Ryland was soon attacked by Campbell in the *British Banner* for a favorable short notice of a poem, *The Rivulet*, by one T. T. Lynch, a Congregationalist minister who had denounced Campbell in 1850. This trivial poetic effusion (more a leak than a rivulet) became the center of a major controversy in which Campbell bid for dominance over Congregationalist journalism and in turn faced a counterattack that almost split the Congregational Union.[9] The controversy was too long and intricate to be discussed here; it ended with the status quo ante bellum as far as the *Eclectic Review* was concerned, although there is a period of uncertain editorship between 1856 and 1860. In that year the review was taken over by the prolific author Edwin Paxton Hood, who restored its literary distinction; but the days of this form of religious journalism were passing, and the *Eclectic Review* ended its career in 1868.

A secession of moderate Congregationalists from the *Eclectic Review* produced its only rival as a high-quality Nonconformist periodical, the *British Quarterly Review* (1845–86). Price's commitment to disestablishmentarianism in 1844 provoked Robert Vaughan, president of the Lancashire Independent College, to organize a less extreme organ of Nonconformity, differing also in that it was a quarterly review and competed at the highest level of journalism. He faced opposition from the *Nonconformist*, which attacked his prospectus, and from some trustees of his college, over whom he won a victory for academic freedom when the board voted to "disavow all right to control the literary engagements of the professors of this college."[10] The review had both lengthy articles and short reviews of books, giving ample coverage to religious subjects but devoting most of the space to literature, science, and especially politics. Vaughan edited the review successfully for twenty-one years, though he had to renew its guarantee fund in 1857. Retiring at the age of seventy-one, he was succeeded in 1866 by Henry Allon, with whom was associated another Congregationalist minister, H. R. Reynolds, through 1874, after which Allon edited the review alone. The core of the writing staff were a number of Nonconformist ministers, but Vaughan had secured other writers, more eminent but less clearly Nonconformist, including G. H. Lewes, Coventry Patmore, and Herbert Spencer, while Allon added others, including the historian E. A. Freeman, who expected to be paid the *Edinburgh*'s rates (one pound per page) instead of the usual seven guineas a sheet.[11] At its best the *British Quarterly Review* could sometimes rival the great reviews; like them, it was pirated in America, where the nonconformist denominations were mainstream Protestantism. Allon's greatest success was to draw an article from Gladstone, on which occasion in 1879 the review abandoned its practice of anonymity. But by the time the review's fortunes (like those of other reviews) were declining; circulation, once as high as twenty-five hundred, fell near to five hundred in the 1880s. Its termination in April, 1886, coincides with the split in the Liberal party with which Nonconformists were allied, but it is more likely to be due to the change in taste from heavy reviews to more lively magazines; as the veteran Nonconformist journalist Edward Baines put it, "the public taste seems to revolt from long series of publications on one model."[12] The *British Quarterly* had been "the voice of Dissent without dissidence during Nonconformity's most influential era."[13] A brief attempt was made to replace that voice by merging the defunct review with the moribund *Congregationalist* as the *Congregational Review* (1887-91).

Nonconformity acquired a political identity in struggles for equal rights, particularly opposition to church rates, a local levy for the upkeep of the established church. The imprisonment of one of his congregants for nonpayment radicalized a Congregationalist minister, Edward Miall, who transformed this struggle into a movement for the disestablishment of the Church of England. With the motto (taken from Burke) "the dissidence of dissent and the protestantism of the protestant religion," Miall founded and edited a weekly paper, the *Nonconformist* (1841-80). This was politicized Nonconformity, not only denouncing the established Church but adopting the full radical political program.

Readers of this excellent periodical will look in vain for an article of mystical aspiration or religious meditation. Under colour of making war against clericalism, embodied in the worship of the Establishment, it spoke of nothing but free trade, the franchise, and the individual's political rights, and thus, instead of making Radicalism Christian it ended by secularizing Christianity.[14]

The strident and single-minded politicization of the Nonconformist cause offended many moderates, but Miall became a major political force, winning election to Parliament in 1852. The *Nonconformist* enjoyed several decades of success (circulation around 3,000), and Miall's son Charles succeeded him on his retirement. When the circulation fell, the *Nonconformist* was merged with the *English Independent* as the *Nonconformist and Independent* (1880–89; then *Independent and Nonconformist*, 1890–1900; other titles to 1915), taking on a more specifically Congregationalist character.

The *Nonconformist* was Miall's personal organ. In 1844 he inspired the formation of a national organization, the British Anti-State Church Association, later the Society for the Liberation of Religion from State Control or simply the Liberation Society. This great pressure group at first used the *Nonconformist* for its communications, but in 1855 it established its own official organ, the *Liberator* (1855–), a monthly circulated primarily among the Society's subscribers. Other periodicals were started to advance particular Nonconformist political causes. In the election of 1847, an ad hoc semiweekly, the *Nonconformist Elector*, was issued during July and August to guide nonconformist voters into bloc voting;[15] the confused results did not encourage a repetition of this experiment. Later, public education and temperance became political issues that often seemed to be distinctively Nonconformist; the latter produced a vast number of periodicals.

Nondenominational Nonconformity produced its first newspaper in 1827, the *World* (1827–32), owned and edited by Stephen Bourne. Its first function seems to have been to report on the May meetings at Exeter Hall of evangelical and denominational societies; it turned to general news after the meetings ended.[16] The *World* failed after five years and was replaced by the newly founded *Patriot*, edited by Congregationalists. Indeed the Congregationalists supplied the newspaper needs of Nonconformity in general for many years. John Campbell's *British Banner* (1848–58) and *British Standard* (1857–67), being his own organs, were not strictly denominational; but they must be discussed as part of the journalistic history of Congregationalism with which his personality is so intimately involved.

A specifically nonconformist newspaper was set up by two evangelical gentlemen, Sir Culling Eardley and John Henderson, as the *Christian Times* (1848–58; then *Beacon*, 1858–59). Committed to the voluntary principle ("We have no disposition to sacrifice our Nonconformity to our Catholicity"),[17] it sought to raise the standard of family newspapers: "the religious periodical press has not kept pace with the progress of mind in this country."[18] The *Christian Times* gave value (sixteen pages) for money (six-pence); but the price showed that it aimed at too narrow a segment of the nonconformist readership.

The first nonconformist newspaper to take full advantage of the repeal of the stamp tax was the *Christian World* (1857–), founded by a Baptist minister, Jonathan Whittemore. Describing itself as "a cheap family newspaper, conducted on pure principles,"[19] it combined the cheapness of a penny weekly (hitherto directed at the working classes) with the provision of family and Sunday reading sought by the middle classes. Whittemore attained a creditable circulation of 22,000; but the real making of the *Christian World* was the accession to the editorial chair of a professional journalist, James Clarke, who joined the staff about 1859 and succeeded Whittemore on his death in 1860. Clarke, the first professional editor of a major religious journal, brought the touch of the professional to the *Christian World.* He took immediate advantage of the repeal of the paper duties in 1861 by doubling the size of the journal.[20] He included fiction and attracted well-known nonconformist ministers as writers, particularly of travel narratives. The circulation passed 100,000 in 1867 and eventually reached 120,000, the largest of any religious newspaper. The *Christian World* became a major institution of Nonconformity. Clarke built on its standing to spin off subsidiary publications: a monthly supplement, the *Literary World* (1868–1919); the *Christian World Pulpit* (1871–), reprinted sermons; another monthly supplement, the *Christian World Family Circle Edition* (1878–84; then *Family Circle*, 1885–97; then *Fiction and Fact*, 1898); and others. He became a publishing entrepreneur, leaving his journals to two of his sons.

A distinguishing feature of the *Christian World* was its regular involvement in politics, unusual at that time for religious journals. From the first, it was liberal or progressive, supporting the North in the American Civil War and giving lifelong support to Gladstone. Its insistence that "the sphere of religion includes politics, and every other worthy human concern" caused it to be nicknamed the Worldly Christian by some.[21] This position, combined with its encouragement of liberal theology, caused it to be denounced by the great Baptist preacher Spurgeon in the Down Grade controversy that embittered his last years. Only a Victorian would have considered the *Christian World* exciting enough to be denounced; a modern reader finds it relatively bland. The editor who took it into the twentieth century, Arthur Porritt (1899–1936), renewed its editorial strength.

The other great nonconformist newspaper at the end of the century was the *British Weekly* (1886–), brought out by the evangelical publishers Hodder and Stoughton. The new paper was entirely the creation of its editor, William Robertson Nicoll, a Scottish minister who had been ordered to go south and give up preaching for the sake of his health. He had already dealt with Hodder and Stoughton as editor of the *Expositor*, and they accepted his suggestion of a "high class weekly journal for the advocacy of social and religious progress."[22] At the price of a penny, it had to reach a large audience: "We must have 20,000 subscribers, and there is not that number of intelligent people in the country—so we must condescend to weak minds."[23] The condescension consisted of serialized tales (J. M. Barrie was a contributor) and some sensational reporting, such as a series on "Tempted London" in 1887. The greatest sensation was caused at the very outset with the serial publication of a religious census of London, a useful piece of what would now be called investigative journalism. The *British Weekly* was paying its way by 1888. It was also providing some solid reading matter, "among the best of the weeklies for intelligent men."[24] Robertson Nicoll was a serious intellectual figure, and he "hoped to reach the vast number of educated Nonconformists in Scotland and England who take no Christian paper, and despise the Nonconformist papers for their want of culture."[25] In addition to the *Expositor*, the *British Weekly*, and some spin-offs, he founded the *Bookman*, an important monthly not specifically religious, in 1891.[26]

Notwithstanding its religious character, including a religious column on the front page, the main thrust of the *British Weekly* was political, advocating "what is known as Advanced Liberalism. We are believers in progress because we are believers in the advancing reign of CHRIST."[27] The *British Weekly* was "intended to provide an organ for the Christian democracy of the country."[28] Like the *Christian World*, it claimed a readership over 100,000; unlike the *Christian World*, the political element came to overshadow the religious one. Always attached to the Liberal party, as was Nonconformity generally, Robertson Nicoll specifically attached himself to the nonconformist Liberal Lloyd George. He became so influential during World War I that he was called "the man who made Lloyd George." Lloyd George rewarded his supporters, and Nicoll was made a knight and a Companion of Honour before his death in 1923.[29] He had made the religious editor a power in the land, but more so politically than religiously.

Evangelical nonconformists were as addicted to the formation of societies as were evangelicals generally. The missionary enterprise particularly called for such organizations. In addition to denominational societies, there was formed a common nonconformist body, the London Missionary Society (LMS), in 1795, largely under Congregationalist leadership. From the beginning it published its annual reports and an occasional publication called *Missionary Transactions*, but its chief medium of communication was a section of the *Evangelical Magazine* (which shared much the same leadership). In 1813 this section was formally organized as the "Missionary Chronicle," and the *Transactions* were regularly published. Belatedly, these two publications were made into a proper periodical as the *Missionary Magazine and Chronicle* (1837-66; then *Chronicle of the London Missionary Society*, 1867-), with a circulation of 20,000.[30] The LMS also published a children's magazine, the *Juvenile Missionary Magazine* (1844-87; then the *Juvenile*, 1888-94; then *News from Afar*, 1895-).

Another movement in which nonconformists took a special interest was the Sunday school movement. Jonathan Whittemore, the founder of the *Christian World*, also founded the *Sunday School Times* (1860-1925), which remained under the control of his successors. The coordinating agency for nonconformist Sunday schools was the Sunday School Union, which established as its weekly organ the *Sunday School Chronicle* (1874-1928), intended to assist teachers of Sunday schools; the Union also published several other periodicals. (Curiously, the other great nonconformist educational body, the British and Foreign School Society, had hardly any periodicals.)

Toward the end of the century, the nonconformist denominations (who now preferred to be called Free Churches) sought a general structure of interdenominational cooperation, forming the National

Council of the Evangelical Free Churches in 1896. The Methodist Hugh Price Hughes, who inspired the Free Church movement, also inspired it to issue periodicals:

> No modern movement realises itself, becomes clearly articulate to mankind and can put forth its strength in harmonious activity, until it possesses an organ in periodical literature. Under the conditions of existing civilisation, every Movement must have a Newspaper or a Magazine.[31]

The first organ was the monthly *Free Churchman* (1897–). In 1899 the National Council started a second monthly, the *Free Church Chronicle* (1899–1934); it also issued annual *Proceedings* and a *Year Book.*

8

THE OLD DISSENT

CONGREGATIONALISTS

The Congregationalists (or Independents, as they were also called) were the largest group of pre-Wesleyan dissenters. Solidly middle-class, they were able to support a learned ministry, trained in those dissenting academies that provided the best education in England prior to the reform of the universities. Heirs of the Puritans, they were strict Calvinists; but they were awakened by the evangelical revival. Proud of their Independency, they were hesitant about organizing as a denomination. Separated only by infant baptism from the Baptists, they cooperated readily. With their better education, the Congregationalists took the lead in common Nonconformist periodicals, so that it is often hard to distinguish them from denominational publications. Perhaps this is why the first purely Congregationalist periodical did not appear until 1818.

This was the *London Christian Instructor* (1818–24; then *Congregational Magazine*, 1825–45; then *Biblical Review*, 1846–50), a monthly of the conventional type. On its reorganization as the *Congregational Magazine* in 1825, new departments were added, including an "American Miscellany" reporting on American Protestantism and showing notable sympathy for the separation of church and state.[1] The undoing of the *Congregational Magazine* may be attributed to the rivalry of John Campbell's more popular journals after 1844 and the retirement of the long-time editor, John Blackburn. The magazine was renamed the *Biblical Review* and entrusted to a committee of theological professors; inevitably "it met the common fate of Congregationalist periodicals."[2]

During the struggle for the Reform Act of 1832, there appeared a newspaper, the *Patriot* (1832-66; then *English Independent*, 1867-79), in the Whig interest politically, but religious in character. Claiming to speak for Nonconformity in general, with Baptist supporters, the *Patriot* was dominated by Congregationalists, with Josiah Conder of the *Eclectic Review* as its editor until 1855. It was the only newspaper organ of the Old Dissent for many years, confined to the middle class by the high price (at first 7d.) required by the stamp tax and also by the moderation of its politics. The circulation declined in the decade after 1855, and the *Patriot* was merged with the *British Standard* to form the *English Independent* (an explicitly Congregationalist title) in 1867, lasting until 1879, when it was merged with the *Nonconformist.*[3]

The denomination achieved a national organization in 1832 as the Congregational Union, which adopted the *Congregational Magazine* as its organ. Seeking a cheaper magazine, it accepted the offer of John Campbell of the Moorfields Tabernacle to manage the *Christian Witness* (1844-71). The Scots-born Campbell was already known as a contributor to the *Patriot* and the *Eclectic* and as the leader of the successful campaign to reduce the monopoly price of the Authorized Bible. Campbell "was truly a 'Son of Thunder,' and storms naturally gathered around him."[4] He proved to be the greatest religious editor of the mid-century and perhaps of the century. He knew how to appeal to the religious tastes of the lower middle class and the class immediately below it, as near to a mass audience as Victorian religion could reach. Within a year the *Christian Witness* had a steady circulation over 30,000, producing a profit that was the chief support of the denomination's Aged Ministers Fund. The ebullient Campbell had stated that he began the magazine as a year's experiment, adding characteristically that "the Public, not the Editor, are now on their probation."[5] The public passed the test.

Campbell sought an even wider audience, "the Millions! . . . cheap Bibles, and cheap Periodicals, for the Millions of England!"[6] Denouncing quarterly reviews as elitist (he disliked the *British Quarterly Review* founded in 1845), he proposed a penny monthly companion to the *Christian Witness*, the *Christian's Penny Magazine* (1846-81), also edited by himself. This did not quite reach the millions, but it did achieve a circulation over 100,000 within a year, "to which, in the history of Religious Periodical Literature, there is no parallel."[7] For once Campbell did not overstate the case. Campbell achieved his journalistic success by the vigor and liveliness of his style,[8] without compromising the seriousness of his journals. Though he personalized his magazines, he respected their status as organs of the Congregational Union and generally did not engage them in his more idiosyncratic controversies, reserving these for his own unofficial periodicals. He was both an ornament and an embarrassment to his denomination, which was forced by the quarrels of his other journals to deprive the *Christian Witness* and the *Christian's Penny Magazine* of their status as organs of the Congregational Union in 1857.[9] But Campbell's retirement from their editorship in 1864 was marked by fulsome testimonials.

While still editing his magazines for the Union, Campbell was invited by the managing committee of the *Patriot* to start a newspaper of his own. This was the *British Banner* (1848–58), for which Campbell accepted no payment except a substitute for his pulpit (his voice was failing). In this role Campbell was free of restraints, and it was in the *British Banner* that he engaged in his most bitter controversies, particularly the *Rivulet* affair, which almost wrecked the Congregational Union and led to its dissociation from its magazines.[10] The *British Banner*, like the *Patriot*, claimed to speak for Nonconformity in general, but it was clearly the organ of Campbell, journalistically a denomination in himself. "He revelled in being a denominational Press baron. . . . He transformed differences of opinion into dramatic clashes of personality."[11] But he was wise enough to give the public what it wanted, which was news spiced with polemics, despite his original intention to provide "a medium between a mere secular Journal and a congeries of didactic dissertations."[12] He sought a circulation of 100,000,[13] unprecedented for a religious newspaper in the days of the stamp tax. Anticipating the abolition of the tax and planning to report on the Crimean War, Campbell increased the frequency in 1855 to thrice weekly, unequalled except by the *Record* under Haldane (an appreciative opponent). Campbell reduced this frequency in 1856 to twice weekly. When he moved to the *British Standard* in 1857, the *Banner* became again a weekly, but even so it could not compete.

In 1856–57, while still under attack in the Congregational Union, Campbell fell out with the Committee of the *Patriot*, whose offices he shared. The Committee, nominally proprietors of the *British*

Banner, proposed to displace the publisher (business manager), Daniel Pratt, with whom Campbell had worked harmoniously. Campbell decided that he "must be entirely independent of all Proprietary Bodies, Committees, and Contractors,"[14] and resigned from the *Banner*, amicably, to set up his own weekly newspaper, the *British Standard* (1857-66), with Pratt as publisher. Most of the readers of the *Banner* transferred their allegiance to the *Standard*; they followed the editor, not the journal. Campbell was fully independent now. He enlivened the *British Standard* with a uniquely personal column of "Answers to Correspondents," turning the editorial chair into a throne. Only failing health forced him to retire at the end of 1866, after which the *British Standard* was merged with the *Patriot* to form the *English Independent* in 1867.

Many Congregationalists tended to disparage denominational literature, and it was to counteract this tendency that the trustees of the *Christian Witness*, on its failure in 1871, decided to start another, rather austerely intellectual, monthly, the *Congregationalist* (1872-86). The first editor was R. W. Dale of Birmingham, the most eminent Congregational minister of the latter part of the century, who had begun as an admiring teenager in Campbell's Tabernacle but had become a liberal in theology and politics. Dale was succeeded in 1879 by James Guinness Rogers, another distinguished minister; but neither could stem the tide that was setting against old-fashioned denominational magazines. On the failure of the *Congregationalist*, which coincided with that of the *British Quarterly Review*, Rogers attempted a *Congregational Review* (1887-91); but reviews were also going out of fashion.[15]

The Congregational Union of Scotland, perhaps the largest non-Presbyterian Protestant denomination in that country, published the *Scottish Congregational Magazine* (1835-80; then *Scottish Congregationalist*, 1881-).

BAPTISTS

The Baptists differed from the Congregationalists only on the point of adult baptism; they were somewhat lower in their social standing; sharing the same congregational polity, they were slower to unite nationally. They differed among themselves. General Baptists held that Christ died for all men, Particular Baptists that He died for the elect; in the nineteenth century, Strict and Particular Baptists insisted on closed communion and maintained a rigid Calvinism.

The General Baptists, a small and declining body, were the first in the field of periodicals. In 1798 their New Connexion appointed Daniel Taylor to conduct the *General Baptist Magazine* (1798–1800) of the conventional sort. After its failure, Taylor's brother Adam was urged to undertake the *General Baptist Repository* (1802–59; then *General Baptist Magazine*, 1860–91; then *Baptist Union Magazine*, 1892–95; then *Church and Household*, 1896–1901), at first a modest semiannual, to make their scattered churches acquainted with each other.

Thomas Smith of Tiverton started a semiofficial Particular Baptist organ, the *Baptist Magazine* (1809–1904), the profits to be devoted to widows of ministers. He was so successful that his monthly was said to have drawn away the Baptist readers of the *Evangelical Magazine.*[16] The magazine began a second series in 1861 with a trio of editors, among them the young C. H. Spurgeon. The *Baptist Magazine*, in private hands since 1838, survived the century. The official Baptist General Union, on the other hand, "failed to achieve influence through publishing."[17] There were many private-venture Baptist periodicals, often published in the provinces, where Baptists were stronger. One of these was of major regional importance: *Seren Gomer* (1818–1931), the first Welsh-language newspaper.

A Leeds printer, John Heaton, who had started a successful penny monthly, the *Church* (1844–91), ventured to begin a weekly newspaper, the *Freeman* (1855–99; then *Baptist Times and Freeman*, 1899–), to provide a newspaper for all groups of Baptists. A need for such an organ must have been generally felt; it was successful enough (over 2,000 copies) that Heaton had to move it to London in 1856. After some decline in sales, a halving of the price to twopence in 1871 trebled the circulation.[18] Politically Liberal, as were most Baptists, the *Freeman* is the periodical to be read in order to ascertain Baptist opinion in the late nineteenth century.

While the Baptists did not achieve much in denominational organization, they were first among Dissenters in missionary organization, founding the Baptist Missionary Society (BMS) in 1792. From 1800 they published the reports of their missionaries as *Periodical Accounts* (1800–37). From 1819 they published a monthly organ, the *Missionary Herald* (1819–21; then *Missionary Herald of the Baptist Missionary Society*, 1821–1911; continuing under other titles), containing missionary reports, organizational news, and reports on other missionary societies. The BMS also published a *Juvenile Missionary Herald* (1845-1908; then *Wonderlands*, 1909-).

Special mention ought to be made of the great Baptist preacher C. H. Spurgeon, whose Metropolitan Tabernacle and its associated institutions were almost a denomination in themselves. Spurgeon allowed some of his sermons to be printed in various periodicals, but he founded his own sermon magazine, the *New Park Street Pulpit* (1856-62; then the better-known *Metropolitan Tabernacle Pulpit*, 1863-), which reached a circulation of 25,000. Spurgeon preached three sermons each Sunday; these were taken down by shorthand reporters, revised by Spurgeon, and published before the week was out. Under the title *The Sword and the Trowel* (1865-), taken from Nehemiah 4:17, 18, Spurgeon published a monthly magazine to which he contributed articles to "be a supplement to our weekly sermon and . . . enable us to say many things which would be out of place in a discourse."[19] The profits of both journals went to support Spurgeon's Pastor's College. *The Sword and the Trowel* was the vehicle in 1887 for Spurgeon's denunciation of his own denomination, from which he withdrew, saying that its faith was on the "down grade."[20]

UNITARIANS

Most of the originally Presbyterian chapels had drifted during the eighteenth century into Unitarianism, which thus became the third denomination of the Old Dissent. Not very numerous, the Unitarians were the most intellectually advanced and literarily active of Dissenters, producing many periodicals and attracting proportionately the greatest scholarly attention.[21]

The first Unitarian periodical was the most distinguished religious journal of its day, Joseph Priestley's *Theological Repository* (1769-71, 1784-88). This eminent philosopher and scientist produced a learned, liberal, and argumentative periodical, idiosyncratically and irregularly published. No other professed Unitarian periodical of the eighteenth century survived, though Unitarians found several literary outlets in journals not professedly religious.

A wayward minister and inept editor supplied the antecedents of another distinguished magazine. William Vidler, passing through a stage of Universalism, produced the *Universalist's Miscellany* (1797-1801), which, when he became a Unitarian, became the *Universal*

Theological Magazine (1802–05). On its failure, it was purchased by another minister, Robert Aspland, who gave it a new birth as the *Monthly Repository* (1806–37). Aspland's model was Priestley's *Theological Repository*, "open to *free and impartial theological inquiry and discussion*,"[22] but more literary and with the conventional departments of a religious magazine. Unitarian theology was too free and impartial to draw many readers, and it took nine years for the journal to pay its way; but it was well established when Aspland sold it in 1826 to the official British and Foreign Unitarian Association. It was a typical denominational magazine (to the extent that the Unitarians were a typical denomination) when the editorship was assumed in 1828 by William Johnson Fox, then minister of the South Place Chapel. Under Fox the scope and authorship of the magazine were widened in an effort to compete with the great quarterlies, and for the remainder of its career it became a major literary periodical. Writers of national importance, such as Harriet and James Martineau, John Stuart Mill, and Robert Browning, were among its contributors. But this larger dimension was obtained at the price of its value to the denomination. Fox, wishing to be freed from the denominational tie (from which he was personally drawing away), bought the magazine himself in 1831. From 1832 it was the organ of Fox and his friends, and its religious character diminished;[23] by 1834 it could hardly be called a religious journal at all. From 1836, when Fox sold it to R. H. Horne, it ceased to be a Unitarian periodical.

Aspland had meanwhile commenced a monthly in 1815 to parallel the *Monthly Repository* for humbler readers "whom more bulky, laboured and expensive works are not likely to reach."[24] This was the *Christian Reformer* (1815–63), largely written by Aspland himself with assistance from some *Monthly Repository* contributors. Pioneering as a serious religious magazine for the lower classes and not at all condescending to them, the *Christian Reformer* was less literary and more practically moral and religious than its eminent counterpart. When the *Monthly Repository* ceased to be religious, Aspland expanded the *Christian Reformer* in 1834 to serve as a denominational organ. Dying in 1844, he was succeeded by his son Robert Brook Aspland.

The lapse of the *Monthly Repository* also spurred the creation of a more serious monthly journal, the *Christian Teacher* (1835–44), the organ of a new breed of Unitarians who added an emphasis on religious sentiment to Priestley's rationalistic individualism. This new emphasis, which differentiated the *Christian Teacher* from the *Christian Reformer*, became evident when J. H. Thom of Liverpool succeeded J. R. Beard as editor in 1838. He brought in friends such as James Martineau, J. J. Tayler, and Charles Wicksteed, also Unitarian ministers. Thom was impatient of the limitations of a denominational monthly (the *Christian Teacher* became quarterly in 1840). In an 1843 manifesto, he acknowledged that the journal was addressed to Unitarians because they were "the only nucleus of any interest or influence we could ever hope to possess," but he desiderated "a Periodical, the servant of no sect, loving the spirit of the gospel but afraid of no truth."[25] This ideal was too much for most Unitarians, who preferred a more denominational interest in their periodicals; but it stimulated Thom's colleagues to transform the *Christian Teacher* into the first of the great series of Unitarian quarterly reviews, the highest form of journalism.

The new "Quarterly Journal of Theology and Literature" was named the *Prospective Review* (1845-55) to suggest "the Duty of using Past and Present as a Trust for the Future,"[26] emblematic of its catholic liberalism of thought. The editors were Thom and his friends, all ministers in the northern counties, meeting regularly as "cabinet councils"[27] to organize the work. Among the contributors were Francis Newman and younger men such as W. L. Roscoe, R. H. Hutton (both briefly coeditors), and Walter Bagehot. The quality of the articles was high, but their authors were unpaid, for the review was financially unsound due to its low circulation—approximately the 500 carried over from the *Christian Teacher.* A private circular was sent out in 1850 asking for financial support; but the real source of the difficulty was one that could not be stated, namely that the *Prospective Review*, despite its professed impartiality, was regarded as denominational by the general public, while that same impartiality lost it the support of its denomination. It was "caught between the Unitarians who did not think it represented them, and the general public who thought that it did."[28] Martineau, the most eminent of the editors, had been seeking a more general audience by writing for the *Westminster Review*, which he even sought to purchase. Martineau instead transformed the *Prospective* into a new review with a new title, edited by younger men under his and Tayler's supervision.

The result was the *National Review* (1855-64), which became the most distinguished Unitarian review and something more, fully the equal of the three great quarterlies. The editors were two young men beginning great literary careers, Martineau's disciple, R. H. Hutton, and a non-Unitarian, Walter Bagehot. Martineau had a free choice of subjects; Tayler, the editors, W. R. Greg, and W. C. Roscoe contributed regularly. A prospectus promised to have "a more constant reference to general principle" and "to combine with a habit of free enquiry, the faithful adherence to realized and definite truth."[29] Faithful adherence to these principles (which implied but did not specify Unitarianism) brought general recognition of the high tone of the review. Starting with a guarantee fund drawn from nineteen contributors (Lady Byron was one), the review was financially independent by 1861 with a circulation over 1,000. But the American Civil War cut off important American sales, and in 1862 Hutton, who had converted to Mauricean Anglicanism, felt that he had to withdraw from a periodical nominally Unitarian. Ironically, he was replaced by a Broad Church Anglican, C. H. Pearson, who added to the non-Unitarian contributors (such as J. F. Stephens and E. A. Freeman) the names of Mark Pattison, M. E. Grant Duff, and Goldwin Smith as well as other liberal Anglicans. The prominence of "liberal parsons"[30] over sturdy dissenters exacerbated the tensions between Martineau's school and conventional Unitarians, represented by the *Christian Reformer* and the weekly *Inquirer*, which had criticized the *Prospective* as well as the *National Review*. Yet Pearson was restrained by the non-Unitarian Bagehot from removing Unitarian theology altogether and resigned in 1863, leaving Bagehot as sole editor. Other outlets were opening up for the disparate though brilliant staff of the *National Review*: Hutton had the *Spectator* and Bagehot the *Economist*, and the liberal Anglicans were to have the *Contemporary Review*; Tayler was looking to found a new, strictly Unitarian review. When the *National* ceased to appear as a quarterly in April, 1864, only Martineau was left without a periodical organ, spending the rest of his long life writing great unread books. Bagehot attempted to revive the *National* in November, 1864, but he found no audience; the issue contains "an unconscious epitaph in what is perhaps the greatest essay published in this quarterly,"[31] Matthew Arnold's "The Function of Criticism at the Present Time," lamenting the absence of "free disinterested play of mind" in periodical literature.

The strictly Unitarian element among the supporters of the *National Review* was transferred to the *Theological Review* (1864–79), which was projected by Tayler to replace the *Christian Reformer*, which failed in 1863. A bimonthly so as not to interfere with the *National* (which it soon replaced), the *Theological* was more confined to religious subjects but open to both sides of Unitarianism under the editorship of Charles Beard and the supervision of a committee of other ministers led by Tayler. The progressive element predominated, producing some conflicts; but, on becoming a quarterly in 1866, the *Theological Review* opened its pages to non-Unitarians liberal in religion, including several foreign contributors. It was learned as well as liberal, "too learned and too liberal to attract a large body of subscribers."[32]

Another minister, R. A. Armstrong, sought to "grasp the torch" of "the succession of Reviews devoted to the free discussion of theology"[33] with the *Modern Review* (1880-84), a quarterly devoted to dealing with the problems raised for theology by science. Even more than its predecessors, this able liberal periodical suffered from lack of funds after the initial support ran out, and its avoidance of political subjects denied it a general audience. Its failure in 1884 marked the end of the series of great Unitarian reviews. An attempt to revive Unitarian magazines, the best of which had also ended, was made in 1886 with the *Christian Reformer* (1886-87), supported by all sides of Unitarianism; but this did not find an adequate circulation and soon failed.[34]

For their number, the Unitarians were unusually active in the publication of newspapers. The first (and the eventual survivor) was the *Inquirer* (1842-), originally a general liberal newspaper with a religious character. The original editor, William Hincks, a London minister, had to survive two proprietors who quickly gave up on the journal; but a cheaper printer and an appeal for subscriptions brought the circulation at first to 600 and eventually to nearly 1,000 copies. By 1843 the *Inquirer* had become a more conventional religious newspaper. Hincks retired as editor in 1847, and the journal was sold to the printer, Richard Kinder, in 1851. From 1851 to 1853 the *Inquirer* was edited by R. H. Hutton and staffed by Walter Bagehot and other young men, who were later to be contributors to the *National Review*. In these years there was a youthful playfulness in the writing, unusual among religious newspapers; the most outrageous was Bagehot, with a series of letters sardonically praising Louis Napoleon's coup d'état in France.[35] Hutton retired because of illness in 1853, being succeeded by his friend J. L. Sanford until 1855. From 1856 through 1887 the *Inquirer* was edited by another

London minister, Thomas Lethbridge Marshall, who "strove, not always successfully, to mediate between what was known as the 'Old' and the 'New' schools of Unitarianism";[36] in fact, the *Inquirer* was pretty consistently on the "Old" side, critical of the *National Review* and Martineau. Marshall was succeeded by his assistant, the Reverend W. G. Tarrant, who moved closer to the "New" position and improved the circulation in the face of competition, aided by reductions in the price, eventually one penny.

The first Unitarian response to the repeal of the newspaper taxes was the *Unitarian Herald* (1861–89), a penny weekly founded in Manchester by four ministers, J. R. Beard (associated with the *Christian Teacher* and the *Theological Review*), William Gaskell (associated with Elizabeth Gaskell, the novelist), Brooke Herford, and John Wright; Gaskell and Herford served throughout the journal's lifetime. The *Herald*'s first number asserted "a closer alliance among ourselves" and "a more vigorous and affirmative tone to the world outside" as winning for Unitarians recognition "among the positive religious agencies of the time."[37] Eight thousand copies were printed, but such a circulation could not be maintained, especially after a third newspaper was added to the overcrowded field. In 1889 the *Unitarian Herald* was merged into that newspaper, the *Christian Life* (1876–1929). This was founded by Robert Spears, secretary of the British and Foreign Unitarian Association and editor of a popular monthly, the *Christian Freeman* (1859–1909). The *Christian Life* "was the organ of an aggressive Unitarianism of the Scriptural and conservative type"[38] favored by Spears.

QUAKERS

The Quakers (Society of Friends) were also a product of the Puritan era, but their separation from the world distinguished them from other Dissenters. During the eighteenth century they had cultivated quietism, but evangelical influences reached them in the nineteenth century. Largely middle class and often wealthy, they were active in philanthropic work and in peace and antislavery societies. Their numbers were small (16,000 in 1840); uniquely in this age of revival, they were steadily declining until 1860, largely because members who married outside the sect were disowned. Yet this small but distinguished body produced an extensive periodical literature.

From 1813 the Quakers had published a unique periodical, the *Annual Monitor*, consisting entirely of obituaries of Friends who had died during the year. Although the biographies often consist largely of edifying deathbeds, they are a superb record of a denomination, usable by religious and social historians.[39] The Friends are undoubtedly the best documented denomination, member for member.

In 1843, two monthly Quaker magazines simultaneously burst upon the scene. One had had a predecessor: the *Irish Friend* (1837-42), published by the small community in Belfast. This magazine ended when the editor emigrated to America, and his relatives turned over the subscription list to William and Robert Smeal of Glasgow, who commenced the *British Friend* (1843-1913).[40] Unknown to them, some English Quakers had started the *Friend* (1843-). The two journals coexisted in a most Friendly fashion, neither competing nor conceding. The *Friend* was the more evangelical, which in the Quaker context meant more liberal regarding the customary distinguishing usages.[41] Both eventually became Liberal in politics. The *British Friend* became liberal in theology from 1891.[42] In 1892 the *Friend* became a weekly, eventually absorbing its Friendly rival.

The most ambitious Quaker periodical was the *Friend's Quarterly Examiner* (1867-1946), not a review but a magazine, founded by W. C. Westlake. Intended as a semiannual under the title of *Friend's Examiner*, it was promptly "quartered" with the second number. It was open to all, with most contributions being signed (editorial and denominational responsibility was disavowed). Contributors were unpaid or "voluntary";[43] many periodicals failed to pay their authors, but here the practice was elevated to a principle. Early contributors included a Seebohm and a Rowntree, signs that the magazine had penetrated the progressive elite of Quakerism.

9

The New Dissent

WESLEYAN METHODISTS

Most of the new Nonconformist denominations of the nineteenth century were the fruits of the Methodist revival, whose chief figure was John Wesley; but only a portion of those who called themselves Methodists belonged to Wesley's own Connexion. Wesley's genius as an evangelist lay in organization: having formed what was a denomination in all but name, he built up the ancillary institutions that it needed, including a publishing house or Book Room, a formula that was copied by all the secessions from his Connexion. He saw the need for a periodical organ, modeled on the magazines that had been created in the 1760s but free from (and designed to counter) the narrow Calvinism that disfigured the *Spiritual* and *Gospel Magazines*. Wesley's own freewill position had been stigmatized as Arminian, after the Dutch theologian Jacob Arminius; Wesley adopted this pejorative name (as he had earlier adopted *Methodist*) after reading Arminius, and the first number of his magazine contained his Life of Arminius, based on original sources. Wesley determined to publish a magazine in August, 1777, issued a Prospectus in November, and, in January, 1778, commenced the *Arminian Magazine* (1778–97; then *Methodist Magazine*, 1798–1821; then *Wesleyan Methodist Magazine*, 1822–1914; continuing, now as *Methodist Magazine*), which was destined to become the oldest surviving religious periodical in the world.

Wesley's *Arminian Magazine* was a monthly miscellany characteristic of himself: a defense of the doctrine of salvation open to all; a biography of a holy man; accounts and letters of the experiences of the pious; and poetry—"But we faithfully promise not to insert any Doggerel"[1] —mostly hymns, largely by his brother Charles. As with everything Wesleyan, John Wesley maintained a tight control, dismissing his first assistant, Thomas Olivers, for bad proofreading and for inserting pieces without his approval.[2] This control, both of the denomination and its organ, was bequeathed on his death in 1791 to the "Conference" of one hundred preachers, who imposed a strict ministerial rule. The magazine (hawked by preachers at the chapels and an important source of funds) was edited, along with all denominational publications, by a "connexional editor," at first George Story. In 1798, Wesley's enthusiasm for Arminius having died with him, the Conference sensibly changed the title to the *Methodist Magazine.* From 1804 to his death in 1821, the learned and conservative Joseph Benson was the editor, raising the circulation to twenty thousand. He was succeeded from 1821 to 1824 by Jabez Bunting, who had already begun his rise to a near-dictatorial rule of the Connexion. Bunting began a new series in 1822 under the title *Wesleyan-Methodist Magazine*, characteristically emphasizing the authentic succession of ministerial authority from Wesley himself.[3] When Bunting returned to the office of Secretary in 1824, he was succeeded as editor to 1842 by the able Thomas Jackson, but Bunting maintained a close supervision. Hence the magazine was most noted for its conservatism, literary, religious, and political. Even after Bunting passed from the scene and Methodists moved closer to liberalism in politics, the *Wesleyan Methodist Magazine* was stolidly conservative in theology; in the *Essays and Reviews* controversy, it not only defended orthodoxy but defended it for orthodox reasons, and with some show of learning (except in classical languages). Changing its title twice in the twentieth century and with a more popular format, it remains, as the *Methodist Magazine*, "the oldest religious Magazine in the World," as its masthead boasts.

From 1816 the Wesleyan Methodists published monthly *Missionary Notices.* After 1818 this was incorporated in the *Methodist Magazine*, but a number of copies continued to be printed for separate distribution.[4] In 1839 the publication was revived as *Wesleyan Missionary Notices* (1839–1904).

The first Methodist attempts at newspapers were outside the usual official control. A printer, James Nichols, projected the *Christian Reporter* (1820–22) with Bunting's assistance, but they quarreled over the trial of Queen Caroline, and the unsupported paper soon collapsed.[5] A decade later there appeared the *Christian Advocate* (1830–39), "intended for circulation amongst the Wesleyan Methodists" but stating that it was published by "private men,"[6] no preacher among them, and with no official authority. This independence, however respectful, may have alarmed Bunting and determined him to have an official newspaper to support his position. This became clear during the schism of 1834–35, when both sides issued temporary fortnightlies, the *Watchman's Lantern* (1834–35) by the anti-Buntingites and the *Illuminator* (1835–36) by Buntingites in Liverpool.

Simultaneously with the latter, Humphrey Sanwith, a lay Buntingite, started the weekly *Watchman* (1835–84), "especially pledged to uphold . . . the principles and economy of Wesleyan Methodism, as settled by its venerable Founder, and by the Conference since his decease," though denying that it was an "official organ"[7] of the Conference. Its bias was made clear in the first issue by an attack on the anti-Buntingites as anti-Wesleyan.[8] It continued in its conservative course, appealing largely to ministers and the better-educated laity, at a relatively high price (7d. at first, 5d. to 1860, 3d. thereafter). It was "a journal very conscious of its dignity."[9] In 1863 (after Bunting's death) the *Watchman* came under common management with the *Methodist Recorder* (1861–) as a corporation half-lay and half-ministerial.

The *Methodist Recorder* had been founded as a penny weekly in 1861 by a committee of six ministers to provide a cheaper alternative to the *Watchman*. It succeeded too well: the *Watchman*'s circulation declined from 3,200 in 1855 (very good for a stamped paper) to 2,000 in 1865 and 1,000 in 1870. In 1884 the *Watchman* was entirely driven out of business by its cheaper partner. The company that produced the *Methodist Recorder* was legally independent of the Conference and avoided partisanship in Methodist politics. The paper was first edited by the Reverend William Morley Punshon (1861–81), but it was established as a major religious newspaper by the Reverend Nehemiah Curnock (1886–1906), who gave up his pastorate to become a full-time editor and was "a pioneer in the art of press photography and reproduction."[10] The *Methodist Recorder* was destined to outlast all its rivals.

One such rival was the product of the last crisis of Bunting's reign as the "Methodist Pope." This was the *Wesleyan Times* (1849–67), put out by anti-Buntingites who sought not secession but legitimate opposition within Wesleyan Methodism. "As Wesleyans, we need a second Newspaper. One already exists. . . . It is Conservative, *alias* Tory. It dreads democracy." The *Wesleyan Times* would instead be "a Newspaper that shall be as a faithful exponent of the liberalism of the body."[11] The *Wesleyan Times* served both reformers within the Connexion and those who seceded to form new bodies. The latter, however, found organs of their own.

By mid-century, the Wesleyan Methodists felt that they were able to produce a quarterly review. The first proposal had been made in 1839 by a young theological student, James Harrison Rigg, who was to become the review's editor forty-four years later. In 1853, without benefit of the usual prospectus or manifesto, the *London Quarterly Review* (1853-1931) was commenced, a stodgy review of the standard type. Its subjects were mostly religious, but literature and science were also reviewed. From 1858 to 1862 the review was retitled the *London Review* before reverting to its original title, much to the confusion of librarians and bibliographers.[12] The review avoided Methodist factionalism, but it took a more advanced social position than the early leadership had favored.[13] Toward the end of the century original articles were added to the reviews. In 1932, in connection with the merger of the denominations, the *London Quarterly Review* merged with the Primitive Methodist *Holborn Review* under the combined title; in an abortive attempt at further ecumenism, this merged with the Anglican *Church Quarterly Review* in 1968.

Although the Methodists had shown that they could creditably sustain a review and a magazine, the newspaper seems to have been their preferred medium. A group of laymen, having no official standing and not limited to any particular sect of Methodism but devoted to the Liberal party, commenced the *Methodist* (1874-84), "a weekly newspaper and review."[14] It offered some general but mostly religious news and comment; the new departure was a children's section. In 1884, on learning that the popular preacher Hugh Price Hughes was about to start his own newspaper, the proprietors of the *Methodist* resolved to shut down their paper. "Its place will be more than supplied by a journal whose promoters have every reason to anticipate for it a larger measure of success, a wider range of influence, and a much longer career."[15]

This promise was fulfilled in the *Methodist Times* (1885-1937), "a journal written by young Methodists for young Methodists,"[16] dominated by the personality of Hughes, presenting younger and better-educated Methodists, and aspiring to be the voice of what came to be known as the Nonconformist Conscience. Hughes combined evangelical pietism with Liberal politics and social activism: "it is our supreme duty not merely to save our own souls, but to establish the Kingdom of God upon earth. . . . Above all, we must do our utmost to promote the social welfare of the people."[17] His vigorous if often harsh pen was employed in the campaign for Social (that is, sexual) Purity among those in public life, and he is credited with a major role in bringing about the fall of Parnell in 1891 over his affair with Kitty O'Shea. This was the high-water mark of the *Methodist Times*, which lost some Nonconformist support when Hughes took a stridently imperialistic position during the Boer War. Perhaps this excessive involvement in politics, this wielding of the Nonconformist Conscience as a political weapon, corroded that Conscience itself: "the struggle for political power coarsened their moral sensibility."[18] However that may be, the *Methodist Times* was a power in the land, at least until Hughes' death in 1902.

Among many other Wesleyan Methodist periodicals, one should mention the *Methodist Temperance Magazine* (1868–1906; continuing under other titles), an important organ in a cause that had originated among Methodists. The Methodists of Ireland, having achieved reunion, published in 1883 the Belfast-based *Irish Christian Advocate* (1883–85; then *Christian Advocate*, 1885–1923; again *Irish Christian Advocate*, 1923–), a weekly family journal.

METHODIST NEW CONNEXION

While the Wesleyan Methodist Connexion was the original and largest Methodist denomination, others were formed from it by expulsions and secessions growing out of opposition to the clericalism of the ruling ministerial Conference and its repression of lay and local initiatives. The first secession was that of the Kilhamites, followers of Alexander Kilham, who was expelled in 1797 for his efforts to obtain a greater voice for laymen in connexional affairs. They organized as the Methodist New Connexion, with laymen and preachers having an equal voice, but imitating many details of the original body, including the Book Room and its magazines—features that were to be standard in later secessions. The *Methodist New Connexion Magazine* (1798–1907) was the principal denominational organ throughout the nineteenth century, originally published in Manchester but later moving with the Book Room to London.

PRIMITIVE METHODISTS

As official Wesleyan Methodism became clericalized, it turned its back on many of the spontaneous and sensational practices that had characterized early Methodism. From 1807, the rejection of camp meetings led to secessions, led by Hugh Bourne and William Clowes, known as Ranters or Camp-Meeting Methodists, but officially organized in 1812 as the Primitive Methodist Connexion. They drew their strength from artisans, miners, and countryfolk, becoming the only major nonconformist denomination whose roots and continuing support were in the working classes. Notwithstanding this background, the Primitive Methodists were the most sophisticated producers of periodicals among the Wesleyan secession connexions.

Bourne, who supervised the Book Room, began a magazine in 1819 under the name *A Methodist Magazine.* Ill health interrupted his editorship, and the magazine was itself interrupted after eight months, Bourne publishing three substitute numbers during 1820.[19] In 1821 the magazine was regularly established as the *Primitive Methodist Magazine* (1821–98; then *Aldersgate Primitive Methodist Magazine*, 1898–1932), with all the departments of a denominational magazine, but simpler and sometimes more sensational in reporting "providences."[20] This continued as the Connexion's official organ until it merged with the main Methodist body in 1932. The Connexion also issued, as early as 1824, the *Primitive Methodist Children's Magazine* (1824–51; other titles to 1932), one of the first denominational children's magazines and an immediate success.[21]

Primitive Methodists took the lead in publishing the *Revivalist* (1853–64), not strictly a denominational journal but rather the voice of Methodist revivalism, especially stressing Wesley's doctrine of entire sanctification. The journal itinerated from Hull to Louth to London during its career.

Also ostensibly nondenominational but conducted by Primitive Methodists was a venture that started not as a periodical but as a series of three volumes of essays in 1858–89 entitled the *Christian Ambassador.* In 1863, under C. C. M'Kechnie, the *Christian Ambassador* commenced as a quarterly periodical (1863–78; then *Primitive Methodist Quarterly Review*, 1879–1909; then *Holborn Review*,

1910–32). Quarterly reviewing was a somewhat daring venture for a denomination whose members had little education, but M'Kechnie's stated goals suggest that he did not feel that the *Christian Ambassador* was different in kind: "to defend the cause of Evangelical Godliness against hostile assault, to aid in the diffusion of religious truth, to stimulate thoughts on subjects of everlasting importance, to kindle holy emotions, to constrain to practical conformity to the image of Christ."[22] In the twentieth century, as the *Holborn Review*, the periodical attained real distinction as a major religious review before merging in 1932 with the *London Quarterly Review*.

In 1868 the Primitive Methodists founded a penny weekly, the *Primitive Methodist* (1868–1905; other titles to 1932), "a journal of denominational and general news," according to its masthead. The news was more denominational than general, and the general news was strictly religious; but it met a need. There was a special section for temperance news. It faced and eventually absorbed a Manchester competitor, the *Primitive Methodist World* (1883–1908).

BIBLE CHRISTIANS

Similar to the Primitive Methodists in that their founder was expelled by the Wesleyans for irregular outdoor preaching, but with a rural base originating in the Southwest, were the Bible Christians, organized in 1818. Their organ, originally published in the obscure village of Shebbear, Devon, was the *Bible Christian Magazine* (1822–1907), "being a continuation of the Arminian Magazine," as its masthead boasted in a claim to the true Wesleyan succession. It was imitative also in being published by the Book Room and sold "by all the itinerant preachers."[23]

LATER SECESSIONS

During Bunting's reign as Methodist Pope, attempts to reduce the despotic control of the Conference of leading ministers were repeatedly made; when they failed, they produced secessions. One such affair in 1834 produced the Wesleyan Methodist Association, which published from its Book Room a monthly organ, the *Wesleyan Methodist Association Magazine* (1838–57).[24] A serious wave of secessions beginning with the expulsion of three dissidents in 1849 produced several new bodies, Wesleyan Reformers and Protestant Methodists.

In 1857 many of these joined with the Wesleyan Methodist Association to form the United Methodist Free Churches, and the magazine was retitled the *United Methodist Free Churches Magazine* (1858–91; then *Methodist Monthly*, 1892–1907). Wesleyan Reformers who did not amalgamate formed the Wesleyan Reform Union, with a congregational polity, which published the *Wesleyan Reform Union Magazine* (1861–65; then *Christian Words*, 1866–).

COUNTESS OF HUNTINGDON'S CONNEXION

This is a curious small body, formed in the late eighteenth century to provide a denominational haven for congregations served by the chaplains of that patroness of all things evangelical, Selina, Countess of Huntingdon. Anglican in liturgy, congregational in polity, Calvinist in theology, and above all evangelical, the Connexion maintained chapels of its own but also provided services and links for other evangelical bodies. It found an organ in the quarterly *Evangelical Register* (1824–43; then *Countess of Huntingdon's New Magazine*, 1850–51; then *Harbinger*, 1852–66). In the tradition of helpfulness to other evangelical bodies, the Connexion offered the services of its magazine to the new Free Church of England, publishing it jointly for both groups under various titles from 1867.

WALES

In Wales, Nonconformity as a whole came to be the national religion. The largest single nonconformist body, and the only denomination specifically Welsh, was the Calvinistic Methodists (officially the Presbyterian Church of Wales). This was the product of independent evangelical revivals by Welsh-speaking contemporaries of Wesley; only in 1811 did Thomas Charles organize the movement as a separate denomination. Its first organ was *Y Drysorfa* (1831–). Later in the century *Y Goleuad* (1869–1918) was an important voice.[25]

Welsh-speaking Wesleyan Methodists were also present, expressing themselves through *Y Gwyliedydd* (1877–1909).

MORAVIANS

The Moravians (United Brethren) were a German (originally Czech) pietist group, devoted to missions, who passed through England on their way to America, founding a church in London at which Wesley experienced his own conversion. The English branch of this far-flung body remained small, serving as a base for missions elsewhere; appropriately, its first major publications were *Periodical Accounts* (from 1790) of missions, later the *Missionary Reporter* (1861–65; 1870–78; other titles, 1879–). A slight expansion of the denomination produced an annual almanac from 1869 and a proper magazine, the *Messenger* (1873–90; then *Moravian Messenger*, 1890–).

SALVATION ARMY

This distinctive outgrowth of Methodism was the creation of William Booth, a New Connexion minister who withdrew in 1861 to become an independent traveling evangelist. Given the East London Mission (later Christian Mission) in 1865, he found success in reaching unchurchable slum-dwellers through sensational outdoor services. Missions were opened outside London, and a national organization was developed in the 1870s under Booth's autocratic control. Military metaphors came increasingly into use; the name "Salvation Army" was adopted in 1879, and "General" soon replaced "general superintendent."

The progress of Booth's mission was recorded in periodicals: the *East London Evangelist* (1868–69), originally local; the *Christian Mission Magazine* (1869–78); the *Salvationist* (1879). Beginning December 27, 1879, Booth issued a half-penny weekly in the new military style, the *War Cry* (1879–). "Why a weekly *War Cry*? Because the Salvation Army means more war . . . to old readers of *The Salvationist*, this explanation will suffice."[26] Military metaphors ran riot, including reports of battles and expeditions. Yet there was an engaging freshness: "The remarkable incidents contained in it, couched, as they often are, in language which to some may appear eccentric and extravagant, are the very means by which we attract the attention of those who would be otherwise indisposed to read the solemn, instructive, and warning truths of the Gospel."[27] The *War Cry*, edited and published by Booth (aided by his son Bramwell) at the Salvation Printing Office, rose from a circulation of 20,000 to 110,000 in one year. The Salvation Army and its *War Cry* stimulated the Anglican response of the Church Army and its *Battleaxe*.

PLYMOUTH BRETHREN

The most extreme evangelical sect was the Plymouth Brethren, founded by John Nelson Darby, a former Church of Ireland clergyman who reacted against ecclesiasticism by founding a denomination composed of a saved remnant who sought the Holy Spirit in a worship devoid of ministers and liturgy. In 1830 he made his English base in Plymouth. Following Darby's principle that "separation from evil is God's principle of unity," the Brethren split into several groups of Exclusive and Open Brethren, distinguished by the degree to which they refused communion to each other. Their first periodical, to which Darby contributed extensively, was the *Christian Witness* (1834-41).[28] *Present Testimony* (1849-73) claimed to be "the Original Christian Witness Revived."[29] The longest-lasting periodical was the *Bible Treasury* (1856-1920), later *Bible Monthly* (1921-). The missionary efforts of the Plymouth Brethren, few and scattered but influential in the origins of American fundamentalism, were represented in England by the *Missionary Echo* (1872-84), later *Echoes of Service* (1885-).

CHRISTADELPHIANS

This American millenarian sect was one of the few of its kind to effect a lodgment in Britain, complete with a periodical. Founded in 1848 and based on interpretation of Scriptural prophecies, its system of beliefs was so rich and complex that the first several issues of its periodicals had to be devoted to mere statements of doctrine. The periodical was the monthly *Ambassador of the Coming Age* (1864-68; then *Christadelphian*, 1869-), published in Birmingham by Robert Roberts. A second periodical was unsuccessfully attempted in 1865.[30]

10

Presbyterians

Presbyterian is the term used in Britain and countries of British settlement for that branch of Protestantism known on the Continent as Reformed or, more loosely, Calvinist. Specifically, Presbyterianism was the national religion of Scotland, popular as well as official. However, the established Church (Kirk) of Scotland was not necessarily the church of all Scotsmen. The religious history of Scotland from the final establishment of the Kirk in 1689 to the Disruption of 1843 was a history of successive secessions from the Establishment, usually on points of discipline concerning the relation of the church to the state, and of secessions from the secessions. From 1820 there was a countertendency of reunions of these secession bodies (but with secessions from the reunions), which ultimately led to the reunion of (nearly) all in 1929. (Only in Scotland could there be a United Secession Church.) Those who seek to draw up a scorecard of religious periodicals must first draw up for Scotland a scorecard of denominations, seceding and merging.

There were, however, a number of nondenominational periodicals that expressed the common Presbyterianism and indeed the common evangelicalism of Scotland. Except for the *Evangelical Repository* (1854–88), a theological quarterly, these have been treated in the chapter on Evangelicals. The *Bulwark* was the organ of the Scottish Reformation Society, the strongest anti-Catholic organization. There was the *British and Foreign Evangelical Review*, bringing to Britain the thought of America and Germany, more attended to in Scotland than in England. There were the family publications issued by

Alexander Strahan in London but edited in Scotland: Norman Macleod's *Good Words*, broadly inclusive, and the more Scottishly Sabbatic *Sunday Magazine*. The religious literature of Scotland, though it had a peculiar character, was not isolated from that of England or Ireland.

CHURCH OF SCOTLAND

The established Kirk, dominated by latitudinarian Moderates during the eighteenth century but with a growing Evangelical element, was slow in issuing periodicals. The first of any importance was the *Edinburgh Christian Instructor* (1810–40), strictly religious but including, besides its denominational intelligence, original articles and extensive reviews and lists of new books. After the death in 1830 of its founder, Dr. Andrew Thompson, it was edited to 1835 by Marcus Dods, who engaged in controversy with the Irvingite *Morning Watch*, the organ of a charismatic schism in the Presbyterian chapel in London.[1] The magazine represented the Evangelical wing of the Kirk but upheld the Establishment against the growing Voluntary movement.[2] Also devoted to the Establishment were the *Presbyterian Review* (1831–48)[3] and the *Church of Scotland Magazine* (1834–38).[4] None of these journals, nor the *Presbyterian Magazine* (1832–36), had any official sponsorship. The only official publication was one that was characteristic of many Scottish denominations, the *Home and Foreign Missionary Record* (1838?, 1839–62; then *Church of Scotland Home and Foreign Missionary Record*, 1862-1900),[5] with its parallel children's magazine.

The conflict between the Moderate and Evangelical parties in the Kirk came to center around the issue of patronage, the right of the landlord since 1712 to impose his choice of minister on the parish. To abolish this contradiction of Presbyterian self-government, the Society for Improving the System of Church Patronage in Scotland was founded in 1824, from 1829 issuing the *Church Patronage Reporter* (1829–32; then *Anti-Patronage Reporter*, 1833–34). The issue became acute when the General Assembly of the Kirk took up the cause from 1834 but could secure no redress from Parliament. The nonintrusionist movement finally found its periodical voice in 1840 with a twice-weekly newspaper, the *Witness* (1840–64). The editor was the popular self-taught geologist Hugh Miller, who had achieved celebrity in religious circles with his *Letter to Lord Brougham* (1839) on this issue. He was equally self-taught as an editor and even more successful. "Miller was in his element. 'His business,' says Dr. Guthrie, 'was to fight. Fighting was Miller's delight.' . . . There was in him, says Professor Masson, 'a tremendous ferocity. It amounted to a disposition to kill.'"[6] These qualities, often uncomfortable to Miller's associates, were just the thing for a popular newspaper editor. The circulation, beginning at 800, rose by the end of 1841 to 1,700, not only the largest of any religious newspaper but more than any secular paper except the *Scotsman.*[7] After the Disruption of 1843, the *Witness* served as the newspaper of the new Free Church, but it was Miller's own organ rather than that of any institution.

After the Disruption, the established Church had only the *Missionary Record* as its official organ, though *Macphail's Edinburgh Ecclesiastical Journal* (1846–63) was an unofficial voice, as was the *Edinburg Christian Magazine* (1850–59). In 1878, the General Assembly, not without misgivings as to the effect on the *Missionary Record*, authorized a monthly parish magazine, which appeared as *Life and Work* (1879–), the first Scottish religious penny magazine. The circulation rose within a year to 76,000, largely sold through the ministers or issued with local supplements in parishes.[8] Supplements were issued for Gaelic speakers, women, and young men. At the beginning of 1901 the *Missionary Record* was incorporated into *Life and Work.*

FREE CHURCH OF SCOTLAND

The greatest event in nineteenth-century Scottish religious life was the Disruption of 1843, when the nonintrusionist element in the General Assembly, frustrated by the use of the courts to force patrons' nominees on unwilling parishes and by Parliament's refusal to grant relief, withdrew to form the Free Church of Scotland (Free Kirk). They took with them a third of the ministers, rather more of the people, and all but one of the missionaries, foresaking churches, manses, and endowments. By extraordinary efforts they raised the funds needed to erect a parallel national church. They found it easy to replicate the official organ, since the editor of the *Missionary Record* passed over to them. The *Home and Foreign Missionary Record for the Free Church of Scotland* (1843–50; then *Home and Foreign Record*, 1850–56; then *Free Church of Scotland Weekly Record*, 1861–62; then *Free Church of Scotland Monthly*, 1862–1900) was able to speak in its first number of "our last publication,"[9] claiming continuity with the original journal. The *Record* soon had a circulation over 7,500 and made a profit.[10] There were also available to the Free Kirk the services of Hugh Miller's *Witness*, though the independent Miller fell out of favor with "the clerical magnates"[11] of the denomination by 1846, when he beat down an attempt to force a subeditor on him. The *Witness*, though it effectively served the Free Kirk, was thereafter Hugh Miller's organ. "Probably no single man has so powerfully moved the common mind of Scotland, or dealt with it on more familiar or decisive terms."[12] But the price that had to be paid for Miller's personal journalistic triumph was that the *Witness* could outlive his death in 1856 by only a few years.

The Free Kirk also created new periodicals; except for the acts and proceedings of the General Assembly, these were unofficial but not always independent. The *Free Church Magazine* (1844-53) received neither recognition nor adequate financing;[13] later the *Presbyterian* (1868-73) met a similar fate. But another venture attained considerable success and even distinction, deliberately competing with the *Edinburgh* (too secular) and *Quarterly* (too conservative) *Reviews*. This was the *North British Review* (1844-71), a quarterly that professed not to be the organ of any denomination (but everybody knew it served the Free Church) nor to be "a Theological Journal" ("But topics of every kind will be treated by individuals accustomed to view them in their highest relations; and Papers of a more strictly religious character will be frequently introduced").[14] In fact, the *North British Review* sought the best of both worlds, religious and literary, and it provides the classic case of religious "periodicals with ambitions of becoming organs of national standing. To these the term 'religious review' was a burden, a skin to be sloughed off, or more precisely, to be outgrown."[15] The problem did not seriously trouble the first editors, who were well connected to the early leadership of the Free Kirk; they felt free to bring in distinguished writers, even of other denominations, but the proportion of theological articles was much higher than in the great quarterlies. But circulation, which had begun at a promising 4,000, settled below 2,000, and financial difficulties led the publisher, W. P. Kennedy, to bring in a younger editor, A. C. Fraser, a noted philosopher. Fraser sought to attract both circulation and eminent authors in England, bringing the *North British* into the leadership of public opinion.[16] The list of authors is impressive, still continuing Scotsmen (not all of the Free

Church) and adding Englishmen largely of Broad Church views. But the religious liberalism thus introduced was uncongenial to the Free Church leadership. The crisis came in 1856, when a liberal review of Chalmers's works challenged the verbal infallibility of Scripture. William Cunningham, principal of New College, Edinburgh, denounced the article, and Kennedy forced Fraser's resignation as editor in 1857. There was an immediate loss of both stature and circulation, from which the *North British* recovered only after Kennedy ceased to be publisher in 1860. W. C. Blaikie, editor from 1860 to 1863, achieved much but concluded that "it would have been better for me to have left it alone."[17] David Douglas, editor and publisher to 1869, restored its literary character at the price of making it the organ of an Edinburgh coterie.[18] In 1869 the review was sold to English liberal Roman Catholics, led by Lord Acton, who sought to replace the *Home and Foreign Review* with one that would be political and historical rather than religious.[19]

In 1886 the Free Church colleges founded the quarterly *Theological Review* (1886-90; then *Critical Review*, 1890-1904).

EARLIER SECESSIONS AND THEIR OFFSHOOTS

The first secession from the Church of Scotland came at the time of its establishment. The Cameronians, a militant group of Covenanters, refused to join a church or recognize a state that did not accept as perpetually binding the Covenants of 1638 and 1643. They organized as the Reformed Presbytery in 1743. Their periodical organs were the *Covenanter*[20] (1830-34?; then *Scottish Presbyterian*, 1835-54; then *Reformed Presbyterian Magazine*, 1855-76). In 1876 most of them joined the Free Church.

The first secession of the eighteenth century, and the first over the issue of patronage, produced the Associate Presbytery in 1733. This split in 1747 into two sections, known as Burghers and Anti-Burghers, according to their acceptance or refusal of the civil oath; and around the turn of the century both groups divided into Auld Lichts (Old Lights) and New Lichts. Despite their fissiparous tendencies, these groups produced the first Scottish religious magazine, the *Christian Magazine* (1797-1820; then *Christian Monitor*, 1821-25; then *Edinburgh Theological Magazine*, 1826-32; then *United Secession Magazine*, 1833-47). This was intended as the Scottish counterpart of the *Evangelical Magazine.*[21] At first it was the joint product of both parties of Secessionists, with the editorship rotating among a number of ministers; but after 1802 it passed into the hands of the Anti-Burghers.[22] In 1820 elements of both groups merged to form the United Secession Church; in 1827 other elements merged to form the Original Secession Church. The *Christian Magazine* went with the former, adding a department of "religious intelligence" characteristic of denominational magazines and commencing a series of changes of title that eventually produced the *United Secession Magazine.* In 1846 the United Secession Church produced its own *Missionary Record* with the usual complementary *Juvenile Missionary Magazine.* But in 1847 the denomination merged with the Relief Church to form the United Presbyterian Church, and the periodicals were merged as well, the missionary magazines simply adding *of the United Presbyterian Church.* The combination of the *United Secession Magazine* and the *Relief Magazine* was eventually named the *United Presbyterian Magazine*[23] (1847-1900; then *Union Magazine*, 1901-04). Meanwhile the Original Secession Church had waited until 1847 to produce its organ, the *Original Secession Magazine* (1847-50, 1852-?); but in 1852 much of this body merged with the Free Kirk.

A second secession in 1761 produced the Relief Church (to give relief to those who wished to withdraw from the Establishment). Their organ was the *Christian Journal* (1833-45; then *Relief Magazine*, 1845-46) until the merger that produced the United Presbyterian Church.

These churches were voluntary or nonestablished, and many of their members adopted a voluntaryist position opposed to any establishment of religion. This took the form of the Voluntary Church Association, which produced the *Voluntary Church Magazine* (1833-41). This disestablishmentarian position[24] went further than the anti-patronage movement that eventually produced the Free Kirk.

Secessionists supported the Scottish Missionary Society, which published the *Scottish Missionary Register* (1820-46) and the *Scottish Missionary Chronicle* (1832-39).

IRISH PRESBYTERIANS

Scotsmen had migrated to Ireland, particularly to Ulster, since the seventeenth century, and Presbyterians were the most numerous Protestant element in that province. After divisions parallel to those in Scotland, they reunited as the Presbyterian Church in Ireland in

1840. Their first periodical, a monthly, was the *Orthodox Presbyterian* (1829–40). A private venture, the *Monthly Missionary Herald* (1837–43), was taken over by the Mission Board of the Church and became its *Missionary Herald* (1843–1946).[25] The *Monthly Messenger* (1851–56, 1857–85), edited by the Reverend Thomas Millar of Lurgan until 1856, was originally designed for his own flock, but it attracted a nondenominational evangelical audience, preparing the way for the Revival of 1859; it was "altogether free from sectarian bias,"[26] meaning that it was open to other Protestants. The Dublin-based *Evangelical Witness* (1862–73), a monthly, made way for the *Witness* newspaper in 1874. The Irish Mission of the Church (to Roman Catholics) published *Plain Words* (1862–76); forced to discontinue this title because of a copyright conflict, it was succeeded by the *Presbyterian Churchman* (1877–94), more of a denominational organ, which was replaced by the *Irish Presbyterian* (1895–). The function of the mission to Catholics was taken up by the *Key of Truth* (1880–82; then *Christian Irishman*, 1883–). There were numerous other periodicals, especially missionary and juvenile.

As was the case with the Roman Catholics of Ireland, religious magazines were of less importance in the maintenance of sectarian consciousness than newspapers, whose identification as Protestant was as much political as religious. Until 1842 the needs of Ulster Presbyterians were met by general local newspapers in Londonderry, Newry, and Belfast. A specifically Presbyterian journal appeared as the *Banner of Ulster* (1842–69), published twice weekly in Belfast and powerful in its day. It was replaced definitively by the weekly Belfast *Witness* (1874–1941), a general newspaper that not only served as the Church's organ but was an advocate of Temperance and (after 1886) "strongly Unionist in Politics."[27]

PRESBYTERIAN CHURCH OF ENGLAND

Most of the original Presbyterian chapels in England had turned to Unitarianism, but there was a remnant that remained faithful to trinitarian Dissent. Their numbers were increased in the course of the nineteenth century by Scotsmen migrating to England. The two elements slowly merged to form the Presbyterian Church of England, beginning in 1836. Their principal journal was the *Weekly Review* (1862–81), somewhat unusual in being a "Journal of Opinion"[28] rather than a newspaper, serious and intelligent. There was also a monthly organ, originally the *English Presbyterian Messenger* (1845-67; continuing under a number of titles).

IRVINGITES

Edward Irving, minister of the Scottish Church in Regent Square, London, in the 1820s, believed in the imminent second coming of Christ. To propagate his millenarian doctrines, which included the expectation of charismatic gifts, Irving published, with the aid of the banker Henry Drummond, the quarterly *Morning Watch* (1829-33), "an able little paper which carried his teaching into hundreds of Evangelical homes."[29] In 1831 prophesying and speaking in tongues broke out in Irving's church. He was removed from the ministry, but his followers formed a new chapel, which eventually became a new denomination, the Catholic Apostolic Church, with an elaborate hierarchy and rich liturgy far removed from the original Presbyterianism. Before this development was well under way, the *Morning Watch* had ceased publication; and the genius of the Catholic Apostolic Church was directed toward ritual rather than periodicals.

11

Roman Catholics

The Roman Catholic press started slowly and tentatively. English Catholicism had been shaped by two centuries of persecution: the chief concern of Catholics had been to remain unnoticed. Even when an active Catholic press had developed, some old Catholics were not sure that it was a good thing: "If a newspaper was desirable at all . . . it should be distinguished for its tact, and reticence, and conciliatory language. The remnant of the English Catholics was convinced that its safety was bound up in the universal belief in its harmlessness."[1]

The earliest Catholic periodicals were produced by London booksellers specializing in Catholic literature, acting also as stationers, printers, and publishers. One of them, James Peter Coghlan, was in the 1750s the official printer of the *Ordo Recitandi*, a directory of worship and church calendar. A rival, James Marmaduke, translated the *Ordo* into English and brought out the *Laity's Directory* as an annual from 1759. Coghlan followed suit in 1768, and after Marmaduke's death in 1788 Coghlan's *Laity's Directory* had the field to itself for fifty years. The present *Catholic Directory*, a conventional denominational directory, began in 1838.[2]

In the early nineteenth century, the most active publisher of periodicals was William Eusebius Andrews, a printer from Norwich, who set up his press in London in 1813 and immediately started a monthly magazine, the *Orthodox Journal.* He had the patronage of Bishop Milner, a controversial Ultramontane not popular with the Catholic lay leadership; the *Orthodox Journal*'s role in the quarrels between Milner and the Catholic Association made it "the most important English Catholic periodical of the time."[3] Milner broke with Andrews in 1819, and the *Orthodox Journal* lasted only one more year. It was replaced by a weekly newspaper, the *Catholic Advocate* (1820–21). Andrews resumed the *Orthodox Journal* in 1823–24. Then he again attempted a weekly newspaper, the *Truth-Teller*; but a newspaper, with its stamp duty, was too rich for the blood of the small and divided Catholic community, and the *Truth-Teller* was converted in 1825 into a "weekly pamphlet." This lasted until 1829, when Andrew tried a third series of the *Orthodox Journal* for a year. In 1832 Andrews started a weekly miscellany, delightfully named the *Weekly Orthodox Journal of Entertaining Christian Knowledge* but generally known as *Andrews' Penny Orthodox Journal*, continuing to 1834. Resumed in 1835 as the *London and Dublin Orthodox Journal of Useful Knowledge*, this found a wider circulation and lasted until 1846, surviving its publisher and editor, who died in 1837.[4]

Andrews's rival was the firm of Keating and Brown, which had in 1801 published a short-lived monthly, the *Catholic Magazine and Reflector.* Patrick Keating published and his son George edited the *Publicist*, a monthly, in the last half of 1815, to oppose Andrews's *Orthodox Journal.* Henceforth the firms were rivals in both business and church politics. In 1816 the Keatings started another monthly, the *Catholicon* (1816–18), revived as the *Catholic Spectator* (1823–26). In 1828 George Keating attempted a weekly newspaper, the *Catholic Journal*, to oppose Andrews's *Truth-Teller.* The *Catholic Journal* lasted a year until the editor resigned.[5] In 1839 the Keating firm, now in its third generation, published the *Penny Catholic Magazine*, a weekly possibly intended to rival the *London and Dublin Orthodox Journal.* It lasted only one year.[6]

There was another old Catholic bookstore in London, the house of Booker, which between 1837 and 1840 came under the control of a relative, Charles Dolman, with high ambitions for Catholic literature. In 1838 the firm became the second publisher of the *Dublin Review*, founded two years earlier; Dolman kept it until 1844.[7] Also in 1838, Dolman picked up a monthly, the *Catholic Magazine*, founded as the *Edinburgh Catholic Magazine* in 1832–33 and resumed in London in 1837; it lasted until 1844.[8] Dolman started a new monthly in 1845 as *Dolman's Magazine.* He terminated this in 1849 and abandoned periodicals, but he allowed his cousin Thomas Booker to publish a journal as its successor and continued its editor, Rev. Edward Price.

This was the *Weekly Register*, which lasted until Price resigned in January, 1850.[9] Booker then started a monthly, the *Catholic Register and Magazine*; this died in the same year, but its title was revived in 1855 in order to be merged in the *Weekly Register*.

The initiative in Catholic periodicals (there were sixty-seven in the first half-century) passed from bookseller-publishers to literary gentlemen. Charles Butler, of an eminent "old Catholic" family, commenced the *Catholic Gentleman's Magazine* in 1818. Although it was "well got up,"[10] it lost money and lasted only a year. In 1822 Ambrose Cudden started a monthly *Catholic Miscellany*. In 1826 he sold it to a publisher but continued to edit it. When the publisher failed in 1828, the *Catholic Miscellany* was purchased by the Reverend T. M. McDonnell of Birmingham, who revived it under his own editorship until 1830.[11]

McDonnell provides a link to a more important periodical, the *Catholic Magazine*, a monthly founded in 1831 as the organ of the English Cisalpines, survivors of an English Catholic Enlightenment about to be swept away by the Ultramontane revival. The *Catholic Magazine* was controlled by a number of clergy in the Midland District, with McDonnell as "acting editor"; the historian John Lingard was a contributor. Perhaps the best of the early English Catholic journals, the *Catholic Magazine* engaged with distinction in several controversies; but eventually its conductors discovered that the Enlightenment had ended.[12] They withdrew at the end of 1835, and the magazine soon expired after appearing irregularly in 1836 as the *Catholicon*.

In 1836 the leader of the rising Ultramontanes, Nicholas Wiseman, then rector of the English College in Rome, founded the first and most enduring of Catholic quarterlies, the *Dublin Review* (1836–1969). The idea was suggested to Wiseman by Michael J. Quin, an Irish lawyer in London, who became the first editor and who brought in Daniel O'Connell as patron and coproprietor.[13] The title may have been a compliment to O'Connell, or it may have suggested a Catholic counterpoise to the *Edinburgh Review*;[14] but the *Dublin Review* was always published in London. It had none of the old Catholic reticence. An article by Wiseman gave the Anglican Newman his "first real hit from Romanism"[15] by citing Augustine's words *securus judicat orbis terrarum*; it was perhaps the *Dublin*'s greatest moment.

Wiseman, in Rome until 1840 and a bishop thereafter, required a resident editor in London. Quin resigned after only two numbers. A permanent editor was eventually found in H. R. Bagshawe, a barrister, who served from 1837 to 1863, doing the donkeywork but never in real command. Wiseman had ultimate control and took an active if sporadic part. Charles W. Russell, professor at the Irish seminary of Maynooth, was effectively an associate editor.[16] Bagshawe resigned on being appointed a County Court judge in 1861. In the confusion, the *Dublin* missed deadlines and even issues at a time when a clear voice of orthodoxy was needed to oppose the liberal Catholicism of the rival *Rambler*, later the *Home and Foreign Review*.[17]

To rescue the *Dublin*, Wiseman transferred it to his protégé and eventual successor, Henry Edward Manning.[18] Manning appointed as editor in 1863 the ablest lay Ultramontane, William George Ward. This appointment was the salvation of the *Dublin*, which commenced a vigorous controversial career. Ward's interests were confined to theology and philosophy, on which he wrote most of the articles: "You will find me," he told a subeditor, "narrow and strong–*very* narrow and *very* strong."[19] His narrowness left much freedom in literature, politics, and secular history to his subeditors. Ward retired in 1878, and about that time Manning presented the *Dublin* to his own protégé and successor, Herbert Vaughan. Vaughan gave the editorship to Cuthbert Hedley, a Benedictine monk, who moderated the tone and broadened the scope of the review. Hedley, who was made a bishop in 1881, resigned as editor in 1884. Vaughan nominally became editor, but the work was done by an assistant, W. E. Driffield.[20] When Vaughan was promoted to archbishop of Westminster in 1892, he appointed Canon James Moyes as editor; the ownership of the *Dublin* was later bequeathed to the archdiocese.

The first weekly newspaper to survive was the *Tablet*, founded in 1840 by a convert, Frederick Lucas, a barrister. His financial support failed in 1841, and he was replaced by the printer, a Protestant named Cox.[21] Lucas had won much support but also many enemies by his too-vigorous advocacy of Catholic claims[22] and his support for Irish concerns. Cox entered into a cabal with some conservative Catholics, including Quin, formerly of the *Dublin Review*, and this cabal led to a rupture in February, 1842. Lucas restarted the journal under his own control, calling it the *True Tablet*, while Cox inserted Quin as editor of the nominally continuous *Tablet*. The two *Tablets* fought each other (once even physically) for several months; but Lucas kept the subscriber list and won support from the Irish.[23] By

July, Lucas emerged as the victor, resuming in 1843 the original name of the *Tablet.* He became more radical. A visit to Ireland during the Famine converted him to Irish nationalism, to the displeasure of his English supporters.[24] Becoming more Irish than the Irish, Lucas moved his journal to Dublin late in 1849 and entered politics as an Irish Independent Member of Parliament in 1852. The Irish phase of the *Tablet* lasted until Lucas died in 1855.

The next year the *Tablet* was purchased by an English barrister, John Wallis, who brought it back to London, altering its politics to his own Toryism. He edited the *Tablet* vigorously for twelve years; but his Toryism, palatable to Cardinal Wiseman, displeased Wiseman's successor, Manning. In 1868 Wallis sold out to Manning's protégé Herbert Vaughan, who wanted a high Ultramontane organ during the first Vatican Council. Vaughan edited the *Tablet* until he became a bishop in 1872, promoting his subeditor, G. E. Ranken, to editor. He was succeeded in 1884 by Vaughan's relative and future biographer, J. G. Snead-Cox, who remained editor until 1920 and consolidated the position of the *Tablet* (from 1892 the property of the archdiocese of Westminster) as a solid, temperate, and politically Conservative journal.[25]

The 1840s brought a wave of converts from the Oxford Movement, and inevitably some of these educated men, especially married ex-parsons unable to pursue their clerical vocations in the Roman Church, found an outlet in periodicals. One such was John Moore Capes, who founded a weekly, the *Rambler*, at the beginning of 1848. After some experimentation, the *Rambler* settled down as a monthly magazine from September, 1848. The *Rambler* established itself as the organ of the lay converts and was initially favored by Cardinal Wiseman.[26] In 1854, a younger convert, Richard Simpson, joined the staff, becoming subeditor in 1856. Simpson, with a taste for scholarship and an irreverent wit, produced several provocative articles that marked the *Rambler* as distinctly liberal—meaning, among Catholics, supporting freedom of intellectual speculation and scholarship within the Church—and brought it into conflict with the hierarchy. Simpson could not refrain from writing theology despite his lay status.[27] An unflattering reference to the anti-intellectualism of "the little remnant of Catholic England" prompted an attack on the *Rambler* by Wiseman himself in the *Dublin Review* in 1856.[28] By 1857 the *Rambler* was not simply the convert organ but the organ of a liberal Catholic movement; indeed it was the movement.

At this point Capes, ill and short of money, resigned the editorship to Simpson and soon sold the *Rambler* to a partnership of his brother Frederick, Simpson, and the young Sir John (later Lord) Acton. The leading member of this team proved to be Acton. Not a convert, Acton was distinguished by his cosmopolitan background and his education in German historical scholarship. He drew the *Rambler* into the international liberal Catholic movement.[29] Unfortunately, this development was at a time when the rival movement of Ultramontanism was prevailing and finding English spokesmen such as Manning and Ward under the patronage of Wiseman. Controversies were sparked during 1858 by provocative articles or even phrases. Two articles on education (which the bishops regarded as their exclusive domain) in early 1859 produced episcopal action.[30] Wiseman and two bishops demanded that Simpson (deemed the enfant terrible of the magazine) resign as editor.

To save the *Rambler*, the owners persuaded the most eminent convert, Newman, to take the editorship. To ease his burden, the *Rambler* was made into a bimonthly, marking a stage in its evolution to the status of a review.[31] Newman objected not to the principles but to the "tone" of Simpson's *Rambler*, and he retained its openness to venturesome ideas. This policy was not what the hierarchy expected, and, upon a hint from his bishop, Newman resigned after two issues, but not before he had published an article "On Consulting the Faithful in Matters of Doctrine," which was related to Rome.[32] Acton then assumed the editorship, with a convert, Thomas F. Wetherell, as subeditor.[33] The *Rambler* reverted to its old ways, though with a more scholarly style. The issue between liberal Catholics and Ultramontanes was, in fact, more than a matter of tone. In 1861 the bishops tried to bring the *Rambler* to heel through the publisher, James Burns; but this plot was foiled by a deft switch to a Protestant publisher.[34] But formal censure by the bishops, or by Rome itself, seemed likely. Acton and Simpson decided in 1862 to transform the magazine into a quarterly review with a new name. The *Home and Foreign Review* (1862-64) thus became the rival of the newly revived *Dublin Review*.

The *Rambler* had been lively; the *Home and Foreign Review* was distinguished. It was the only Catholic periodical—almost the only religious periodical—to rival in merit the three great reviews. Though it continued the principles of the *Rambler*, the *Home and Foreign* sought to appeal to a wider audience. Neither its readers nor its contributors were exclusively Roman Catholic or English.[35] It was distinguished for its "scientific character,"[36] a level and breadth of erudition unmatched by any periodical. A unique feature of the *Home and Foreign* was the numerous brief reviews of British and foreign books, reviews written by scholarly experts. Nonetheless, the *Home and Foreign Review* lasted only two years. It stood for a principle, freedom of scholarship, which was an issue in the conflict of Ultramontanism and liberal Catholicism. A papal brief of December, 1863, initimated a condemnation of that principle. Acton could neither abandon his principles nor challenge the authority that condemned them. He determined to "sacrifice the existence of the Review to the defense of its principles."[37] The *Home and Foreign* ended its career in April, 1864. Matthew Arnold pronounced its epitaph in words that may apply to all religious journalism:

> Our organs of criticism are organs of men and parties having practical ends to serve, and with them those practical ends are the first thing and the play of mind the second; so much play of mind as is compatible with the prosecution of those practical ends is all that is wanted. . . . Directly this play of mind wants to have more scope, it is checked, it is made to feel the chain. We saw this the other day in the extinction, so much to be regretted, of the *Home and Foreign Review.* Perhaps in no organ of criticism in this country was there so much knowledge, so much play of mind; but these could not save it. The *Dublin Review* subordinates play of mind to the practical business of English and Irish Catholicism, and lives.[38]

Silenced as expressly Catholic journalists, Acton, Simpson, and Wetherell made two journalistic ventures in secular guise. In 1867–68 they attempted a weekly newspaper, the *Chronicle*, with Wetherell as editor; but the *Chronicle* primarily served the cause of Gladstonian liberalism.[39] In 1869 they took over the *North British Review*, hitherto the organ of the Scottish Free Kirk, and sought to make it a nondenominational successor of the *Home and Foreign Review.* In 1871, however, Wetherell's health broke down, and Acton and Simpson were disheartened by the final victory of Ultramontanism at the Vatican Council of 1870. The *North British Review* was allowed to expire.[40]

One year after the *Rambler*, a weekly newspaper, the *Catholic Standard*, was begun in 1849. Its founder was a Frenchman, E. Robillard, who was in financial trouble in 1852.[41] In 1854, the *Catholic Standard* came into the hands of the convert Henry Wilberforce, son of the liberator of the slaves and brother of "Soapy Sam," bishop of Oxford. It was this good man's fate to be overshadowed by more distinguished connections, and his journal shared this fate. In 1855 the *Catholic Standard* was merged with Booker's defunct *Weekly Register*, and the combined journal was known by the latter name.[42] This maneuver may have been intended to establish an English rival to Lucas's *Tablet*;[43] but Lucas's death made this pointless. Nonetheless, the *Weekly Register* continued its rivalry with the *Tablet*, Wallis being Conservative and Wilberforce Liberal; their rivalry was a feebler counterpart to that of the *Dublin Review* and the *Rambler*. Wilberforce eventually wearied of the burden of bringing out a weekly.[44] In 1864 he sold out to another convert, Robert Walker.[45] Little is known of the *Weekly Register* for the next decade and a half except for a malicious attack by its Rome correspondent on Newman in 1867. In 1881 the *Weekly Register* was acquired by Cardinal Manning "to save it from extinction."[46] Manning gave it to Wilfrid Meynell, who edited it with his wife, the poet Alice Meynell, for nineteen years. Meynell had a more important venture of his own, the monthly *Merry England*, founded in 1883. *Merry England* had a distinguished list of literary contributors, including Meynell's own discovery, Francis Thompson, in the dozen years of its existence.[47] The *Weekly Register* passed in 1899 to a recent convert, Robert Dell, who embroiled it in the Modernist controversy, and in 1900 the periodical passed to the more moderate Frank Rooke Ley. It was transformed in 1902 into the *Monthly Register*, which died the same year. Its failure removed the only Catholic periodical of theologically liberal inclinations.[48]

The 1850s saw the beginnings of Catholic popular journals, including some for the growing Irish population in Britain. Most notable was the *Lamp*, "devoted to the Religious, Moral, Physical and Domestic Improvement of the Industrious Classes,"[49] founded in 1850. The *Lamp* went through a rapid series of changes until 1862, when it was bought by Mrs. Fanny Margaret Taylor (later Mother Magdalen Taylor). She sold it in 1871 to the convert Mrs. Lockhart, under whom Meynell had his first editorial experience. There were several other managements until the *Lamp* was extinguished in 1905.[50]

The first major popular newspaper after the repeal of the stamp tax was the *Universe*, a penny weekly started in 1860 under the inspiration of Cardinal Wiseman and the management of a lay fraternity, the Society of St. Vincent de Paul. The managers were led by George J. Wigley, London correspondent of the militant French Ultramontane journal *l'Univers*, after which it was modeled. At first the *Universe* eschewed politics; when it was found that politics had to be included in order to raise the circulation, the original staff resigned. The printer, a London Irishman, Denis Lane, became proprietor. He admitted politics, secured a considerable rise in circulation, and ran the *Universe* with a very firm hand until his death in 1906, when it was the leading Catholic paper.[51]

The next important Catholic periodical was the *Month*, founded in 1864 by Mrs. Taylor, of the *Lamp*, to reach a higher-class audience. She had the fortune to obtain *The Dream of Gerontius* from Newman, but her principal support came from the Society of Jesus. When she found the *Month* unprofitable, she sold it in 1865 to the Jesuits, who thenceforth produced it at the Farm Street community in London. The Jesuits transformed the *Month* into a serious monthly review of some scholarly and controversial distinction. Their most notable editor was the convert Henry Coleridge, a great-nephew of the poet. The editors were closely supervised by Jesuit provincials from Peter Gallwey, who had helped to start the *Month*, to John Gerard, editor before and after his term as provincial.[52] Farm Street was known as the "scriptorium,"[53] with priests assigned there primarily to write for Jesuit publications. One priest was the future Modernist George Tyrrell, whose writings caused some trouble around the turn of the century. On the other hand, this Jesuit periodical refused poems by Gerard Manley Hopkins, S. J.; the *Month* confined itself to prose since 1865. It accepted contributions from laymen, including the naturalist St. George Mivart. Under Gerard's management, the *Month* survived the doctrinal difficulties of some of its authors.[54]

Two other weekly newspapers must be noticed. One began in 1867 as *Catholic Opinion*, founded by Mrs. Lockhart and edited by her son, Father William Lockhart. It was purchased in 1873 by that great acquirer of periodicals, Herbert Vaughan, to be an educational supplement to the *Tablet.* He sold it in 1876 to Father James Nugent, the "Apostle of Liverpool," who merged it with a struggling local paper, the *Northern Press*, founded in 1860 and renamed *Catholic Times* in 1870; the merger was called the *Catholic Times.* It was edited by an Irishman, John Denvir, who made it the Home Rule organ in England.[55]

Another newspaper was established in 1884 under the inspiration of Cardinal Manning as the organ of "Catholic Industrial Democracy." This was the *Catholic Herald*, published by Charles Diamond for the next fifty years. Diamond's social politics was unpopular with much of the Catholic public. Only after 1934 did the *Catholic Herald* become a mass-circulation paper, competing with the *Universe* (the largest) and the *Tablet.*[56]

By the mid-1880s, the Catholic press was fully elaborated. Diocesan magazines began to appear then, and local and regional newspapers, particularly in the North, appeared in the 1890s. A number of religious fraternities and temperance organizations issued periodicals. The leading Catholic schools and colleges began to publish. One of their journals was more than a house organ and aimed for a serious national audience: the *Downside Review*, founded in 1880 by the Benedictines of that abbey and school.[57]

IRELAND

The Catholic religious press of Ireland was much less significant than its English counterpart, even though Irish Catholics were far more numerous. This circumstance was not due to reticence—Catholic Irishmen were extraordinarily vigorous journalists—but to the near impossibility of distinguishing their religious from their political press. In Ireland, *Catholic* is as much a political as a religious term. A historian of the Irish press pleads for the largest definition of the Catholic press:

> Nor by the Catholic Press do we mean solely the religious Press, for the Catholic point of view is manifest in a large number of journals and magazines which are not exclusively religious in character. By the term "Catholic Press". . . I mean simply periodicals under the control of Catholics, and not officially non-sectarian.[58]

This definition is too broad for our use, but it helps to explain the apparent paucity of periodicals that may be cited as specifically religious.

For most of the century, Catholic spokesmen, ecclesiastical as well as lay, found a religious newspaper press unnecessary, expressing themselves through general secular, lay-owned papers. Daniel O'Connell had the *Pilot* (1828–49); Archbishop Murray of Dublin utilized the *Dublin Evening Post* during the 1840s; Archbishop MacHale of Tuam made the *Connaught Patriot* his organ.[59] The most important newspaper was the Dublin *Freeman's Journal*, owned from 1850 by the Protestant Gray family; Sir John Gray reached an understanding with Cardinal Cullen in the 1860s, and thereafter the *Freeman's Journal* served as the organ of the hierarchy. On the one occasion when it deviated from the official line (over Parnell in 1891), frantic efforts were made to replace it;[60] the *Freeman's Journal* soon came to heel. Only two papers may claim to be regarded as specifically religious. The *Catholic Telegraph*, which replaced the *Weekly Telegraph* in 1856, printed a considerable amount of Catholic news from all over the world as well as other religious articles; it survived until 1867.[61] The *Irish Catholic*, also a lay weekly, was founded in 1888; although it was not approved by the hierarchy, it bore a more distinctively religious cast, printing important sermons in full.[62]

A self-conscious attempt to create a Catholic religious press was made by the publisher James Duffy in 1847–48 with the monthly *Irish Catholic Magazine.* An article in the first issue demanded "A Catholic Literature for Ireland." But the late 1840s were a bad time for any new venture in Ireland.[63]

The next effort was more distinguished. The Catholic University of Ireland, founded in 1854 with Newman as rector, wanted an organ to display the work of its professors.[64] Newman envisioned something like a learned journal, a "dry professorial production,"[65] not religious but literary and scientific. The result was the *Atlantis*, begun in 1858 as a semiannual, in two departments, literary and scientific. Newman was the nominal editor, but the scientific department was managed by William K. Sullivan, professor of chemistry, who was the working editor; late in 1858 the literary department was taken over by the Egyptologist Peter le Page Renouf. A general learned journal was an unusual thing, and its few readers were puzzled by its hybrid character. They were, however, treated to some excellent scholarship: the science was as dry as Newman wished, and the literary side, which included contributions by Newman and some English Catholic friends, published pioneering translations by Eugene O'Curry, precursor of the Gaelic revival. But the financial base of the *Atlantis* was insecure, and in 1860 it was announced that it would be published at "irregular intervals" as articles (and money) could be obtained.[66] Single issues were published in 1860, 1862, 1863, and 1870. Catholic

Ireland did not yet have the resources to sustain a purely academic periodical.

The idea of a Catholic University magazine did not die, however. In 1887 a group of professors at University College (successor of the Catholic University) founded a monthly, the *Lyceum.* Not as formidable as the *Atlantis*, the *Lyceum* nonetheless promoted "a higher Catholic literature,"[67] discussing literary, scientific, and social issues from a Catholic but nonpartisan point of view.[68] In 1894 the *Lyceum* was replaced by the *New Ireland Review*, with contributors who made it an organ of the Irish literary renaissance: W. B. Yeats, J. M. Synge, George Moore, and the Gaelicists Douglas Hyde and Eoin MacNeill (not all Catholics). In 1909 University College joined the National University of Ireland, and in 1911 the *New Ireland Review* came to an end.[69]

Two periodicals of general Catholic interest were the products of religious orders. The *Irish Monthly*,[70] founded and edited by the Jesuit Father Matthew Russell from 1873 to his death in 1912, was essentially a nonsectarian literary magazine of quality, giving a start to many writers, including Yeats. The Dominicans of St. Saviour's Priory founded the *Irish Rosary* in 1897 as a popular illustrated magazine; it later became a more serious periodical.[71]

The most important Catholic religious periodical was produced for the diocesan clergy with the sanction of authority. This was the monthly *Irish Ecclesiastical Record*, founded in 1864 by Archbishop (later Cardinal) Cullen of Dublin. As part of Cullen's strict control of all ecclesiastical matters, the *Record* was managed by his nephew Patrick F. Moran and his secretary, George Conroy.[72] The *Irish Ecclesiastical Record* was directed to a clerical audience; its articles had a largely ecclesiastical character but included contributions by laymen and about general subjects, notably Irish history.[73]

The Irish sustained the burden of the missionary efforts of British Catholicism, and this effort produced periodicals, notably the *Annals of the Propagation of the Faith* from 1837. There were also two Irish Catholic Directories from the 1830s.[74]

SCOTLAND

A *Catholic Directory for Scotland*, published at various places since 1829, is the oldest Scottish Catholic publication. The rest were local papers, serving the Irish immigration. The most important was the *Glasgow Observer* (1885-).

12

OTHERS

SWEDENBORGIANS

The theology of Emmanuel Swedenborg (1688–1762) was a rational mysticism newly revealing the spiritual sense of the divine Word. Swedenborg's English disciples organized the New Church (or Church of the New Jerusalem) in the 1780s. This small group was active in intellectual and missionary work. Their organ was the quarterly *Intellectual Repository for the New Church* (1812–29; then monthly as *Intellectual Repository and New Jerusalem Magazine*, 1830–81; then *New-Church Magazine*, 1881–), whose early volumes included serial publication of translations of Swedenborg's works.[1]

MORMONS

The Mormons (Church of Jesus Christ of Latter-Day Saints) are a product of American revivalism claiming supplementary revelations, notably the *Book of Mormon.* They sent their first missionaries to England in 1837, seeking converts to emigrate to their settlement; in 1840 another mission began with considerable success. One missionary, Parley P. Pratt, landed in Liverpool on April 6, 1840, and commenced a periodical on May 1—a testimony to the recognition in both countries that each denomination needed a periodical. This was the *Latter-Day Saints Millennial Star* (1840–1945; now *Millennial Star*), first monthly, then fortnightly, then weekly. To explain the complex Mormon belief system, the *Millennial Star* printed copious extracts from the *Book of Mormon* and other revelations and from their American periodical, the *Messenger and Advocate*; the frequent publication of reports and journals makes the *Millennial Star* a source for Mormon history. For a dozen years the Mormons enjoyed much success, sending thousands of emigrants to Utah. The revelation in 1852 of the lawfulness of polygamy was proclaimed in England by the *Millennial Star*, boldly but belatedly, on January 1, 1853. The decline of Mormonism in England has been dated from this event;[2] but the denomination and its organ survived.

THE JEWISH PRESS

At least half the periodicals with "Jewish," "Hebrew," or "Israel" in their titles are not Jewish at all but rather the work of conversionist missionaries or of the British Israel movement. Nonetheless, there was a genuine and substantial Anglo-Jewish press.

The Jewish community in England dated only from Cromwellian times; a well-organized communal life had been developed before the nineteenth century. A constant trickle of immigration from continental Europe and of emigration to present and former British colonies resulted in a greater international flavor to British Jewry than was characteristic of most denominations. Their periodicals sought their models from continental Jewish rather than British religious publications, and the editors were often immigrant scholars. This was perhaps not true of the first Jewish periodical, the *Hebrew Intelligencer*, a monthly that appeared in 1823. Its end, after the third issue, was characteristic of a problem that faced the Jewish press: a communal worthy, offended by some remarks, applied pressure on the printer, who had to refuse to print further issues.[3] It was eleven years before the next periodical appeared, a learned monthly, the *Hebrew Review*, edited by the Swedish-born Rabbi M. J. Raphall. This scholarlike journal lasted until 1836.

The founding of the Jewish newspaper press was a direct response to the situation created by the Damascus ritual-murder accusation of 1840: "It was not until the foul attacks on us and our religion, with which some newspapers teemed at the time of the Damascus affair, that British Jews began to feel how necessary it was that they, likewise, should possess a periodical of their own."[4] The result was at first two newspapers, started almost simultaneously by two independent groups. Jacob Franklin, a public-spirited statistician and accountant, led a group that founded the *Voice of Jacob* in September, 1841, a fortnightly that for a while was the more successful newspaper and lasted until 1847. Two months later, on November 12, 1841, there appeared the *Jewish Chronicle*, a weekly that was destined to become the oldest and perhaps the greatest Jewish newspaper in the world.

The *Jewish Chronicle* was founded by a printer and bookseller, Isaac Vallentine, employing as editors a rabbi, David Meldola, and the master of the Jews' Free School, Moses Angel. They represented the Hebrew and English sides respectively of a journal that carried a Hebrew cotitle, *Sefer Zikkaron*, on its masthead and included "text books" (such as a Hebrew-English dictionary) as well as religious instruction, Jewish news, and original articles. The venture started well, until Vallentine made the mistake of publishing the editors' names. The vestry of Meldola's synagogue required him to withdraw; and the *Jewish Chronicle* ceased publication after March 20, 1842, surrendering to the *Voice of Jacob*, edited for a year by Angel.

In October, 1844, Vallentine recommenced the *Jewish Chronicle* as a fortnightly. The dominant figure came to be a businessman, Joseph Mitchell, who both provided the funds and served as editor. With a wider appeal, cheaper and more vigorous, the revived *Jewish Chronicle* soon got the better of the *Voice of Jacob* and had the field to itself. A weekly again from 1847, the *Jewish Chronicle* obtained the services of a German-born scholar, M. H. Bresslau, as coeditor; and Bresslau brought a touch of German scholarship and an interest in continental Judaism to the journal. (It always had an interest in English-speaking Jewry abroad, especially in the British possessions, for which it was long the organ.) The Mitchell-Bresslau partnership[5] ended on Mitchell's death in 1854; Bresslau bought the paper but soon found the task too great.

Meanwhile, another continental scholar who had settled in England, Dr. Abraham Benisch, had started a rival newspaper, the *Hebrew Observer*, in 1853. The Jewish community could not support two newspapers; the two journals merged in December, 1854. By early 1855, the combined paper passed completely under Benisch's control. To render the journal self-supporting and independent of subsidies, Benisch practiced a rigid frugality, combining the functions of proprietor, editor, publisher, printer, and principal writer, aided only by his wife. The result was success, helped by the abolition of the stamp tax in 1855 and an increase in advertisements. The paper took on a definite form, with the first and last page devoted to advertisements (including family announcements, later a very important item) and with two pages of literary matter, a page of editorial articles, another of general news, and one or two of correspondence. By 1861 Benisch could afford to employ a printer and publisher and confine himself to editorial work.

In 1868 there appeared a rival to the *Jewish Chronicle* in the form of a penny newspaper, the *Jewish Record.* This lasted only four years, but the *Jewish Chronicle* was forced to respond to the competition. Benisch's response was to publish a penny edition of the *Jewish Chronicle* parallel to its regular threepenny edition. This meant that he competed with himself; unsurprisingly, by 1869 he was in financial straits. At this juncture, three prominent London Jews bought the paper in order to save it, installing as editor a patent agent with literary flair, Michael Henry. Henry dropped the penny edition but reduced the price of the paper to twopence. The "new series" was simpler in style but larger in number of pages, a format retained for seventy years. English-born and typically Victorian, Henry built up a large group of contributors who made the *Jewish Chronicle* the literary expression of English Jewry. This Englishing of the paper continued even after Henry's untimely death in 1875, when, under a peculiar arrangement, Benisch resumed the ownership until his own death in 1878.

By his will, Benisch gave the *Jewish Chronicle* to the Anglo-Jewish Association, stipulating that the management was to be assigned to Asher Myers, his printer and publisher since 1869. The Association sold the paper to Israel Davis and S. M. Samuel, who associated Myers with them in the ownership and made him editor. Not himself a literary man, Myers drew literary men to his paper, which obtained the services of all the notable Jewish writers, including some, such as Lucien Wolf and Israel Zangwill, known outside Jewry. The *Jewish Chronicle* sponsored Jewish literary projects and favored the study of Jewish history. It also reported on Jewish news from other countries, especially after the beginning of persecution in Russia in 1881. In 1891 it published a monthly supplement, entitled *In Darkest Russia*, for a year. Myers was not, however, sympathetic to Zionism, though he gave space to Herzl.

Myers was entitled to describe the *Jewish Chronicle* as "The Organ of the Anglo-Jewish Community,"[6] though it faced rivals continuously from 1873. Myers' editorship was ended only with his death in

1902. He was succeeded by the surviving owner, Israel Davis, a barrister who had played an active role during Myers' editorship. In 1907 the paper was restructured as a limited company, managed by L. J. Greenberg. It remains the oldest surviving Jewish periodical in the world.

From 1873 there was a rival newspaper, the *Jewish World*, founded by an eccentric journalist of independent means, G. L. Lyon. This lively and controversial paper, which styled itself "The Leading Organ of the Anglo-Jewish Community,"[7] was not a serious threat to the *Jewish Chronicle*; the circulation was under 500 when Lyon sold it in 1897. The new owner, S. L. Heymann, installed as editor S. L. Bensusan, who quadrupled the circulation by expanding the paper and making it more attractive, but at ruinous cost. In 1900 the *Jewish World* was taken over by a syndicate that made another effort to rival the *Jewish Chronicle.* With Lucien Wolf as editor, they were almost successful; but eventually they were beaten, bought out, and merged. Other rival newspapers appeared, but never for long; the most important was the *Jewish Standard*, subtitled *The English Organ of Orthodoxy*, which had a distinguished but unsuccessful career from 1888 to 1891.[8]

The Jewish press was not confined to newspapers. A high-class quarterly review was commenced in 1888 by the scholar Israel Abrahams and by Claude Montefiore, leader of Liberal Judaism. They started "tentatively" a journal of Jewish literature, religion, and history, without precedent in England, "a medium in which scholars may register the results of their research, and theologians the results of their thoughts."[9] The *Jewish Quarterly Review* professed "absolute impartiality" among the various schools; it admitted articles by Christian biblical scholars such as Driver, Cheyne, and Sayce as well as Jewish writers of the caliber of Cyrus Adler, Heinrich Graetz, Wolf, and Zangwill. Scholarly to a greater degree than other quarterly reviews, the *Jewish Quarterly Review* both created and satisfied the want for such rich fare. It lasted twenty years and then was transferred to America under the aegis of Dropsie College.

Nothing in the nineteenth-century Jewish press corresponded to the monthly magazines so favored by Christian bodies. A Jewish children's magazine was first started in 1897 with *Young Israel*, founded by L. J. Greenberg; not entirely juvenile in its appeal, it was suspended in 1901 but later resumed as a supplement to the *Jewish Chronicle.* Greenberg was also one of the founders of the *Jewish*

Year Book, which first appeared in 1896. In these respects the Jewish press was slow to develop.

Mention should be made of Anglo-Jewish publications in languages other than English. A Yiddish paper was attempted in 1867, perhaps prematurely, since the major immigration from eastern Europe did not come until the 1880s; another attempt in 1878 also failed quickly. Numerous, generally short-lived Yiddish publications appeared in the 1880s and 1890s. Not all of these would qualify as strictly religious periodicals; they were more correctly ethnic publications; but the distinction between the ethnic and the religious element is not as significant among Jews. Some papers were political in character: the *Poilisher Yiddel*, which appeared briefly in 1881, was the first Yiddish socialist paper in the world. Others were humorous. The first Yiddish periodical to establish a secure position in England was the *Yiddish Express*, which was founded in Leeds as a weekly in 1895, attained the greatest circulation of any "jargon" paper, and moved to London as a daily in 1899. More periodicals followed in the twentieth century.[10]

Literary journals entirely in Hebrew were attempted at various times from 1878, but none lasted more than a few issues until the weekly *haYehudi*, a one-man production by Isaac Suwalski, kept going from 1898 to 1913.

THEOSOPHISTS

Theosophy is an esoteric and occult creed claiming a secret knowledge derived from the ancient wisdom of India. Truly international, the Theosophical Society was founded in America by Madame H. P. Blavatsky and others; migrating with them to India in 1879, its first organ, the *Theosophist*, was published in that year in Bombay. On her further migration to England, Madame Blavatsky published *Lucifer* (1887-97; then *Theosophical Review*, 1897-1907). On her death in 1891, she was succeeded as editor by the remarkable Annie Besant, ex-atheist, ex-Fabian, and future Indian nationalist. The official organ of the Theosophical Society in England was *Vahan* (1891-1920).

SPIRITUALISTS

A similar interest in the occult, coupled with a deep desire for the survival of the soul despite the loss of doctrinal faith, produced spiritualist movements during the last half of the nineteenth century, transcending formal denominations. Of the many spiritualist journals, the "most important"[11] was *Borderland* (1893–97), covering without much discrimination "telepathy, clairvoyance, crystal-gazing, hypnotism, automatic writing," edited by a crusading journalist of nonconformist origins, W. T. Stead, who sought "to democratize the study of the spook."[12] Less eminent but longer-lived was the *Medium* (1870–95).

The more scientific side of spiritualism was represented by the Society for Psychical Research, founded in 1882 by respectable intellectual figures including F. W. H. Myers and Oliver Lodge. The Society issued *Proceedings* from 1883 and a monthly *Journal* from 1884.

POSITIVISTS

It was not necessary to go to India or the "other side" to find surrogates for Christianity. Auguste Comte (1798–1857) had developed a rationalistic philosophy that traced the mental progress of mankind in three stages, theological, metaphysical, and positive; he then compensated for this nontheistic creed by proposing an elaborate Religion of Humanity. Positivism won several eminent adherents in England, including John Stuart Mill (with qualifications) and Frederic Harrison. Some of Comte's English disciples organized a Positivist Church. Inevitably, the church required a periodical organ, which was belatedly supplied by the *Positivist Review* (1893–1923; then *Humanity*, 1924–25). The first editor (to 1900) was E. S. Beesley; Harrison was the most frequent contributor;[13] the articles mostly dealt with social and political issues, but some were philosophical or ethical.

THE LABOUR CHURCH

A large portion of the working class was disaffected towards organized Christianity because of its class bias but nonetheless retained vague religious sentiments. An attempt to found a church in which workers would feel comfortable was made by a Unitarian minister, John Trevor. The Labour Church that he started in 1891 (becoming the Labour Church Union in 1893) was devoid of doctrine and vague in its religious character, serving as a small-scale wing (mostly in Lancashire and Yorkshire) of a labour movement in the process of becoming a Labour Party.[14] Trevor, with the backing of an eminent Unitarian minister, Philip H. Wicksteed, supplied the entire organization of this new church and produced its organ, the *Labour Prophet* (1892-98). This penny monthly had to be replaced by a smaller quarterly, the *Labour Church Record* (1899-1901). This did not long survive the withdrawal of Trevor, ill and poor, who had "to discontinue my work for the Labour Churches, and to give myself wholly to the work of making a living. . . . Finding it necessary to work in the open, I have taken up chicken raising on a large scale."[15] The movement lingered for a while after the failure of its organ and then died.[16]

The vague combination of religious feeling and social brotherhood that produced the Labour Church also spawned various Brotherhood Churches and Ethical Societies. The South Place Ethical Society in London, with a more "highbrow" membership, published the *South Place Magazine* (1895-1909; other titles thereafter).

13

FREETHOUGHT

A study of periodicals dealing with religion must include periodicals opposed to religion, especially in the nineteenth century, when atheism, agnosticism, and secularism developed as organized movements of unbelief. Contemporary Christians labeled these tendencies "infidelity," but the best generic term is "freethought."[1] English freethought, though it had Enlightenment precursors, emerged in the welter of radical democratic movements stimulated by the French Revolution and released into activity after the peace of 1815. The flurry of pamphlets and periodicals that soon appeared attacked both political institutions and organized religion, so that it is often impossible to categorize a periodical specifically as radical or as antireligious. Some periodicals particularly attacked the Church of England (and its wealth); others attacked organized Christianity in general. Their positive standpoints varied from Paineite deism to eccentric heresy to atheism. These journals were intended to stir up the middle and lower classes, and they aroused fears of revolution in the dominant classes and the Church.

The upholders of the established order in church and state had one powerful weapon: the law. Law is always on the side of the possessors; it was especially so in an age when Parliament represented property rather than population. In common law, blasphemy was a crime; anti-Christian pamphlets and journals were frequently prosecuted, usually with success until 1842. The favorite medium of the radical and antireligious press was the newspaper because of its frequency and cheapness; and for newspapers statute law had created special terrors. Since 1712, partly with a view to stifling criticism, there had been a stamp tax on newspapers; in 1815 this had been raised to fourpence, in effect pricing legal newspapers out of the reach of the lower classes. Radical newspapers, which refused to pay the tax, were an illegal underground press, with publishers, printers, and distributors liable to fine and imprisonment. To facilitate prosecution, one of the "Six Acts" of 1819 (60 George III c. 9) defined a newspaper as "any paper which contained public news, intelligence, or occurrences, any comments thereon or on matters of Church and State; and which was printed for sale and published periodically within 26 days; and which was no larger than two sheets and sold for less than 6d. exclusive of the duty."[2] The law did not make clear "whether a paper was a newspaper if it infringed one of the clauses . . . or only if it infringed all of them."[3] Under the broadest definition, many religious magazines published more often than monthly, even though they did not regard themselves as purveying news, were liable to the crippling tax; but none were prosecuted.[4] The duty did inhibit the growth of a religious newspaper press, but its intent and use was to shut down the radical and antireligious press, which responded with a campaign of defiance in the period 1816–22 and again in the "War of the Unstamped" from 1830 to 1835, eventually securing the reduction of the tax to a penny.[5]

Most of the radical journals of the first newspaper war, 1816–22, subsumed their anti-Church or antireligious positions within a generalized radicalism that attacked most political and social institutions, so that it is difficult to separate out a distinct antireligious press. The hero of the movement was Richard Carlile,[6] a disciple of Thomas Paine in radicalism and deism, who printed and published a number of periodicals, notably the *Republican* (1819–26), and who spent over nine years in prison (from which he continued to edit his journals). Carlile is also the link to the illegal periodicals of the 1830s. He conducted discussions in 1829–31 at the London Rotunda, the center of radical and freethought activity, which also provided a forum for the eccentric Reverend Robert Taylor, who sought to demonstrate the mythological basis of Christianity and whose lectures were published by Carlile as periodicals under titles such as the *Devil's Pulpit* (1831-32). Carlile's own weekly miscellany, the *Gauntlet* (1833–34), was basically political but became "increasingly preoccupied with the need for church reform,"[7] by which radicals meant confiscation of church property.

The agitation for parliamentary reform that began in 1830 sparked a revival of the unstamped radical press, and renewal of prosecutions by the Stamp Office caused much of the agitation to be directed against the tax itself in the "War of the Unstamped." Many of the unstamped periodicals were primarily political or included attacks on the Established Church in their attacks on the establishment in general; but in the course of this struggle distinctly anti-Church and even anti-Christian periodicals emerged. Thomas Parkin's *Christian Corrector* (1831–32) was a weekly "miscellany in which Parkin denounces organized religion, supports the appropriation of church property, and repeatedly employs Christian doctrine to sanction revolution."[8] *A Slap at the Church* (January–May, 1832), a weekly miscellany edited by John Cleave and William Carpenter, unusual in being illustrated (some illustrations by George Cruikshank), attacked tithes and argued that Church property belonged to the state. It was succeeded by the *Church Examiner* (May–December 1832), which counseled refusal to pay church rates; "as a result of a Stamp Office prosecution . . . it was forced to convert into a 2d. monthly"[9] in November. Supernatural Christianity was attacked in such journals as Samuel Cornish's *Rationalist* (1833) and one of the several publications of Henry Hetherington, the *Bible of Reason* (1836). The reduction of the stamp tax to a penny in 1836 and the rise of a legitimate penny press made most of these periodicals unnecessary; few survived the victory of their principle of free expression; but Hetherington continued active in publishing, and his conviction for blasphemy in 1840 provides a link to the next decade. Meanwhile a link between freethought and social radicalism had been forged by the *New Moral World* (1834–45), founded by Robert Owen as the organ of his utopian cooperative socialism but after 1838 tending to emphasize "rational religion."

In the 1840s freethought became an organized movement. This was largely the work of George Jacob Holyoake, whose long and prolific career reached into the twentieth century and combined freethought with social and political radicalism. The conviction of an atheist, Charles Southwell, after publishing four numbers of the *Oracle of Reason* (1842–43), brought Holyoake into the rationalist struggle. He carried on the *Oracle* and publicly protested against the persecution of blasphemy to the extent that he himself was convicted of it, though his conviction was practically the last.[10] Holyoake formed the Anti-Persecution Union, whose organ was the *Movement*

(1843-45). He was also involved in forming the Rationalist Society and contributed to its organ, the *Herald of Progress* (1845-46). Holyoake replaced this with the *Reasoner* (1846-61; then *Counsellor*, 1861) under his own editorship, with varying formats and frequencies. The *Reasoner* described itself as "a Weekly Journal of Materialism, Communism, and Republicanism–regarding Theology as a speculation and Religion as a practical error–and substituting in the place of Religion Systematic Morality."[11] Holyoake was agnostic in theology, utilitarian in morality, and positively secularistic, emphasizing the improvement of conditions in this world; he was not an atheist, having no negative creed to proclaim. Ill health forced Holyoake to end the *Reasoner* in 1861 and issue the *Counsellor* as a "meanwhile journal."[12] In 1862 he joined with the rising star of atheism, Charles Bradlaugh, in the latter's *National Reformer*, but soon left when his share of the journal was cut in half; there was a basic antipathy between their positive secularist and negative atheist views. Until 1872 Holyoake intermittently revived the *Reasoner* under various titles.[13] In 1876 he reemerged with the *Secularist*, which was soon renamed the *Secular Review* (1876-77, 1877-88; then *Agnostic Journal*, 1889-1907). In 1877 the now elderly Holyoake transferred this to Charles Albert Watts, a second-generation rationalist printer and editor, but he continued to write for it. Holyoake's last freethought journal was a monthly, the *Present Day* (1883-86), "to restore secularism to its original broad base; to show that the foolish day had passed when men could be shocked into truth by sensation, or kicked into it by outrages."[14] Holyoake's longevity and productivity were matched only by the relative reasonableness of his writing.

Whereas Holyoake's motto for the *Reasoner* had been a mild *Nescio Deus* (I do not know God), an explicit and militant atheism characterized the other Protean figure of freethought, Charles Bradlaugh. Already a well-known atheist and radical lecturer under the name of Iconoclast (a pseudonym he often used for his articles), Bradlaugh entered journalism late in the history of a magazine founded as the *London Investigator* (1854-57; then *Investigator*, 1858-59). This had started as a secularist journal with some support by Holyoake, but the editor, Robert Cooper, found Holyoake's agnosticism insufficiently militant; there was also a financial quarrel with the Holyoake brothers. Ill health forced Cooper to transfer the editorship to "Anthony Collins" (William H. Johnson), who renamed the journal the *Investigator* and completed the breach with Holyoake and mere secularism, proclaiming that "the *Investigator* is the only British Journal which advocates Atheism."[15] In November, 1858, Bradlaugh assumed the editorship, announcing that his policy would be "aggressive" and that "there is no middle ground between Theism and Atheism."[16] Financial problems ended the *Investigator*'s career in August, 1859.

Using the device of a limited company to safeguard himself against loss, Bradlaugh started in the next year a weekly, the *National Reformer* (1860–93). At times Bradlaugh was only coeditor controlling half the paper, sharing it with Joseph Barker for the first year, uneasily with Holyoake for part of the second, and with John Watts from 1863 to 1866. Thereafter, Bradlaugh made the *National Reformer* "the most famous atheist publication."[17] Bradlaugh attained national fame himself, first when he was prosecuted (with Annie Besant, his coeditor at the time) for publishing a pamphlet on birth control and again when he was elected to Parliament in 1880 but repeatedly denied his seat because of his atheism until 1886. The years of this struggle saw the high-water mark of the atheist cause. Organized freethought—now organized very like organized religion—reached its apogee about 1883–85, after which it began a slow decline, very like organized religion.[18]

After Bradlaugh's death in 1891 the *National Reformer*, continuing to the end its tradition of atheism and radicalism, was edited by John M. Robertson, the future historian of freethought. In 1893 he replaced it with the *Free Review* (1893–97; then *University Magazine*, 1897–98), a monthly that was not specifically atheist but rather open to all advanced opinions, "with a view to getting a hearing for good independent criticism all around" and breaking the "conspiracy of silence" in the religious field.[19] This position was truly ecumenical irreligion: during its brief existence the review included among its contributors such unexpected names as Bernard Berenson, J. A. Hobson, and Ernest Newman.

In the last decades of the century, the pivotal figure in the heretical press was C. A. Watts, son of the printer (and sometime coeditor) of the *National Reformer* but "inheritor of the Holyoake tradition."[20] He had already succeeded Holyoake in the *Secular Review* (later *Agnostic Journal*); in 1884 he took over Charles Watts' printing, publishing, and bookselling business, the only London outlet for the freethought press. Though he published journals of his own, such as the monthly *Agnostic* during 1885, the younger Watts was primarily concerned to serve as a clearinghouse for freethought periodicals. In 1884 he commenced the *Agnostic Annual* (1884–1907; continued under other titles), "to aid in uniting all liberal thinkers on one common platform."[21] His first issue contained a remarkable symposium led by T. H. Huxley (who had coined the term *agnostic*)[22] and including Francis Newman and Ernst Haeckel. In the next year Watts commenced a monthly publisher's circular, *Watts' Literary Guide* (1885–94; then *Literary Guide*, 1894–1956; now the *Humanist*), a "different type of periodical, with the direct aim of establishing and developing contact with readers of heretical literature."[23] In effect, it was an advertiser for "liberal and advanced publications," offered for sale by Watts & Co. and including nonfreethought radical publications.[24] Watts consolidated his coordinating role in 1899 with the founding of the Rationalist Press Association, with himself as secretary. This was freethought's equivalent to the Society for Promoting Christian Knowledge or the Religious Tract Society or the Methodist Book Room, a remarkable achievement for the small rationalist press.

Closely connected with the secularist movement, though not strictly a part of it, was the National Sunday League, which sought to break the shackles of the British Sunday by pressing for Sunday opening of museums and art galleries. It published the *National Sunday League Record* (1856–59) and the *Free Sunday Advocate* (1869–1939).

14

MOVEMENTS

THE MISSIONARY PRESS

Of the various religiously inspired movements or causes, the missionary movement stimulated by the evangelical revival was the first to develop a specialized press of its own, the largest of its kind until it was surpassed by the temperance press in the second half of the century. Because the accreditation of missionaries was denominational, most of the missionary enterprise and of the missionary press was the work of denominational societies or of societies serving a group of denominations, and its periodicals are therefore to be studied under those headings. But evangelical supporters of missions recognized a commonality of purpose and interest, and their periodicals, beginning with the *Missionary Register* of the Church Missionary Society, often reported the work of other societies. There was a common pattern to the societies' publications. Each had a basic magazine, with a title such as "Missionary Record" (in Scotland often prefixed by "Home and Foreign"). Recognizing the importance of building up the next generation of supporters, each had at least one juvenile magazine for younger readers, often illustrated; whatever other functions they may have had, these journals supplied much of the Victorians' geographical knowledge and contributed to interest in the Empire. There might also be annual or quarterly reports (but these might also be included in general periodicals); sometimes there were cheaper journals for a popular audience; and there might be periodicals for ladies' auxiliaries. As the missionary enterprise developed, periodicals (and often societies) emerged to serve missions in particular regions; when medical missions were developed, they came to have a distinct press of their own. With all these specializations, the quantity, if not the primacy, of the missionary press grew throughout the century.

Only a few of these submovements need be mentioned here. The medical missions, in addition to their denominational organizations, had a nondenominational Medical Missionary Association, which published the quarterly *Medical Missions at Home and Abroad* (1878–1924; then *Conquest by Healing*, 1924–). The China Inland Mission, a "faith mission" of volunteers without formal denominational support, drew English backers who first published *Occasional Papers* (1866–75) and then a full-fledged monthly, *China's Millions* (1875–).

One missionary movement was unique in that it was the only type of evangelization entirely in the hands of women: the zenana missionaries who worked with Indian women secluded in purdah. This effort began in 1852, at first nondenominational though largely Anglican, publishing the *Indian Female Evangelist* (1872–93). It later divided along denominational lines,[1] with a Church of England Zenana Missionary Society, the nondenominational Zenana Bible and Medical Mission, two other societies, and a ladies' mission connected with the Baptist Missionary Society, all in the field and publishing periodicals.

ANTISLAVERY

The antislavery movement, at first directed against the slave trade, began among Quakers and Anglican evangelicals in the 1780s. In those early days, it was possible for the Society for the Abolition of the Slave Trade to achieve its object in 1806 without the aid of a periodical organ. But the Anti-Slavery Society, formed in 1823 to abolish slavery altogether, felt "the want of a regular medium of communication"[2] among its branches. The resulting journal was the *Anti-Slavery Monthly Reporter* (1825–30; then *Anti-Slavery Reporter*, 1831–36; then *British Emancipator*, 1837–40; then *British and Foreign Anti-Slavery Reporter*, 1840–45; then *Anti-Slavery Reporter*, 1846–1909; then *Anti-Slavery Reporter and Aborigines' Friend*, 1910–). Slavery in the British colonies was abolished in 1833, but the struggle continued to abolish the slave trade and slavery in other countries. A British adjunct to the American abolitionist movement was the Anglo-American Anti-Slavery Association, which published the *Anti-Slavery Advocate* (1852–63) "to direct the attention of the British public to the institution of slavery in the United States."[3] The increasing success of the anti-slavery campaigns served to highlight the problem of the exploitation of aborigines, for whose benefit was formed the British and Foreign Aborigines' Protection Society, whose *Annual Report* (1838–47) was merged in the *Colonial Intelligencer or Aborigines' Friend* (1847–54; title and subtitle reversed three times, 1855–1909). The two causes, societies, and journals were merged in 1909.

PEACE

The international peace movement, largely but not exclusively Quaker in inspiration, was launched after the end of the Napoleonic Wars with the founding of the Peace Society (Society for the Promotion of Permanent and Universal Peace) in 1816. For many years it limited itself to publishing literature: "The object of the Society shall be to print and circulate Tracts,"[4] of which several series were published. It also printed its annual reports from 1817 and issued a monthly periodical, the *Herald of Peace* (1819–1930), as a "medium of correspondence."[5] The Society and its *Herald* took a high pacifist line, condemning war abstractly as anti-Christian: "The cause is a *religious*, not a *political* one."[6] This attitude tended to limit the appeal of the movement. During the Crimean War, which it had failed to prevent, the political leaders of the peace movement, John Bright and Richard Cobden, founded the daily *Morning Star* (1856–69) to reach a wider audience. Rich Quakers provided backing, and Henry Richard, secretary of the Peace Society, was the first editor; "but when it appeared in danger of turning into a second *Herald of Peace*, Bright's brother-in-law, Samuel Lucas, became editor."[7] Neither periodical could be effective against the popular enthusiasm for the war, and the peace movement was set back for a generation.

TEMPERANCE

The temperance movement was a social crusade that was religiously motivated (mostly but not entirely Nonconformist) and conducted largely as a religious activity, eventually producing the largest and most ramified sector of the religious press. The movement started somewhat feebly in 1829 as a crusade against spirit drinking, partly stimulated by Wesley's prohibition of spirituous liquors. This partial abstinence received much respectable support and produced several periodicals,[8] but it was soon elbowed aside by the total abstinence or teetotal movement, drawing its somewhat rude strength from the middle and artisan classes.

The total abstinence movement was never united under one central organization and therefore generated not one set of periodicals but several. The first group originated in Preston and was always specific to the North of England. It started as the Preston Temperance Society in 1833, becoming regional in 1835 as the British Association for the Promotion of Temperance, renamed British Temperance League in 1854. Periodicals were supplied ready-made for its use by the Preston cheesemonger Joseph Livesey, an activist in several radical causes, whose *Moral Reformer* (1831-33), a general reformist monthly, was increasingly devoted to the temperance cause. Livesey founded the official organ, the *Preston Temperance Advocate* (1834-37; then *Temperance Advocate and Herald*, 1838; then *British Temperance Advocate and Journal*, 1839-41; then *National Temperance Advocate and Herald*, 1842-49; then *British Temperance Advocate*, 1850-), a penny monthly serving as a forum for temperance news from local societies.[9] Livesey also published temperance and other periodicals of his own, down to the *Staunch Teetotaler* (1867-68).

London-oriented temperance advocates formed a number of bodies that merged in 1842 as the National Temperance Society, renamed National Temperance League in 1856, more moderate and respectable than its northern counterpart. Journalistically, although it sought a higher-class audience, the result was not much different: the *National Temperance Chronicle* (1843-56). Its next journal, however, was a weekly newspaper, the *Weekly Record of the Temperance Movement* (1856-69; then *Temperance Record*, 1870-1907), originally a private venture of the London temperance publisher William Tweedie but taken over by the League in 1864, more lively than its predecessor.[10]

These two leagues and their periodicals served the temperance cause proper, that is, the cause of individual decisions for total abstinence. By 1853 there had developed a more advanced movement for legislative prohibition of drinking, a Manchester-based organization known as the United Kingdom Alliance. This became the spearhead of the temperance movement as a political force. It soon produced a weekly, the first and most important temperance newspaper, the *Alliance* (1854–55; then *Alliance Weekly News*, 1855–61; then *Alliance News*, 1862–). The changes in title reflected expansions of size, format, and circulation consequent upon the repeal of the stamp tax and paper duties. Edited from 1854 to 1898 by H. S. Sutton, the *Alliance News* served, especially after 1872, as a link between the London and provincial sides of the movement and as a coordinating force in temperance politics, supplying local activists with instructions and materials for propaganda.[11] Despite efforts to expand its circulation to win new converts, it remained largely an in-house journal, copies being distributed free to subscribers, the paper running at a loss.[12] So effective was journalism in the scheme of temperance politics that the Alliance formed its own press agency in 1889 to supply temperance news to over two hundred local newspapers. The Alliance Press Agency represents the highest level of professionalism displayed by any portion of the religious press.

The most ambitious literary effort of the Alliance was the quasi-scholarly *Meliora* (1858–69), "a quarterly review of Social Science in its ethical, economical, political, and ameliorative aspects." Omitting any mention of its sponsorship, *Meliora* was aimed at the intellectuals and philanthropists who were forming the Social Science Congress, publishing articles from many points of view on a variety of social topics, requiring only that they mention the great social evil of intemperance. Despite bad editing and an annual loss,[13] *Meliora* was a creditable effort by the prohibitionists to reach outside their own ranks.

Besides these nondenominational (though largely Nonconformist) periodicals, denominational journals and organizations appeared. One is not surprised to find a successful *Methodist Temperance Magazine* (1868–1906; other titles, 1907–). Less expected was the formation in 1862 of the Church of England Total Abstinence Society, mostly evangelical lower clergy; its founding received so little press notice that it was stimulated to produce its own organ, the *Church of England Temperance Magazine* (1862–72), edited by a London incumbent, Robert Maguire. Total abstinence, intemperately pressed, received little encouragement from bishops and prelates. To win wider support, the body was reorganized in 1872 as the Church of England Temperance Society, with the two archbishops as presidents, adopting the uniquely temperate policy of admitting moderate drinkers as well as abstainers. Maguire withdrew on this issue, and the magazine was renamed the *Church of England Temperance Chronicle* (1873-88; then *Temperance Chronicle*, 1888-1914), becoming a weekly from 1878. In all its forms, the journal was designed to win support for the temperance cause from the clergy and educated classes; it became "one of the four major late-Victorian temperance periodicals," though "literary rather than popular in character."[14] The Society also published two popular periodicals. One should also note a Roman Catholic temperance body, the League of the Cross, sponsored by Cardinal Manning, himself an abstainer, and briefly issuing a magazine.

The temperance cause in Scotland was represented by the Scottish Temperance League, which published a *Weekly Journal* under various titles from 1857 and a monthly organ from 1847 that became the quarterly *Scottish Review* (1853-63). Its children's magazine, the *Adviser* (1847-?), was said to have a circulation over 50,000.[15] There was a Belfast-centered Irish Temperance League with a *Journal* (1863-1906).

It was not necessary to have a sponsoring organization in order to have a temperance periodical; the numerous temperance publishers (ninety-eight in 1867) freely issued their own. Publishing empires sometimes grew from these. G. W. M. Reynolds' *Teetotaler* (1840-41) started him on a career that led to *Reynolds' News* (1850-); John Cassell started as a teetotal publisher before building his empire of family and educational publications; and Thomas Cook was a temperance publisher who, in meeting the need for drink-free holiday trips, created a great travel agency.[16] The profitable proliferation of temperance periodicals was facilitated by advertising for the penumbra of supporting services needed by the temperance subculture: alternative beverages, coffeehouses instead of pubs, temperance hotels and boardinghouses, and insurance societies. The most notable of the independent temperance periodicals were the London-based weekly *Temperance Star* (1857-76), later monthly, and an illustrated monthly for families, the *National Temperance Mirror* (1881-1907).[17]

The temperance movement was also noted for organizations and periodicals designed to reach specialized groups. Of these the largest was the children's organization, the Band of Hope, in which young people were induced to "take the pledge." The leading periodical of the Band of Hope, and in its 250,000 circulation the largest temperance journal of all, was the half-penny monthly *Band of Hope Review*

(1851–1937). The subtitle ("and Sunday scholar's friend") indicated the close relationship between the Band of Hope and Nonconformist Sunday schools, the *Review* being specifically religious as well as temperance and embracing other causes favored in those circles: Sabbath observance, peace, antislavery, and prevention of cruelty to animals. But total abstinence was the primary cause: "We wish you (*with the consent of your parents*) to promise by God's help, never to drink any of those intoxicating drinks which lead to Intemperance."[18] There were other Band of Hope periodicals at the regional and local levels, the most notable being published by the Sheffield and Lancashire and Cheshire Sunday School Band of Hope Unions, *Onward* (1865–1909; then *Workers Onward*, 1910–).

Among other specialties, the most striking was the National Temperance League's effort to reach the medical profession, the quarterly *Medical Temperance Journal* (1869–92; then *Medical Pioneer*, 1892–97; then *Medical Temperance Review*, 1898–1919). For insurance purposes, abstainers were served by the friendly society of Rechabites, organized in 1835, issuing publications such as the *Rechabite Magazine* (1840–50) and another of the same title (1864–69; then *Rechabite and Temperance Magazine*, 1870–). Later there was a fraternal organization, the Good Templars, with a host of periodicals both national and local. Besides all these, the basic temperance bodies had regional and local affiliates, many of which published periodicals.

It has been suggested that this proliferation of publications may have been "dysfunctional" in that it confirmed the "inbred character" of the temperance press.[19] But the press merely confirmed the character of the temperance movement, which, after the initial wave of conversions, was largely devoted (except for its political arm) to serving the needs of the converted. This was no inconsequential task. Abstinence in a nonabstaining society is a nonnatural behavior that requires repeated "reinforcement" and "ego-stroking," to the extent of forming a self-contained subculture. The multiplicity of temperance organizations and periodicals and their combination of national, local, and specialized units, provided a great network of sources of reinforcement. A professed abstainer probably had a greater chance of seeing his name in print than any other ordinary person. Temperance groups and journals served their subculture well, even if they made its further expansion unlikely.

BRITISH ISRAEL

We may conclude with a movement that had all the attributes of a religious movement except religion. The British Israel movement asserted that the British nation was the descendant of the lost ten tribes of Israel and therefore the heir of the biblical promises made to Israel (not to Judah, that is, the Jews). This movement was really a variety of British nationalism, though buttressed by biblical references; it drew support from military officers and some evangelical clergy. Several periodicals advocated the cause from the 1870s, bearing titles apparently religious and sometimes indistinguishable from Jewish publications or those of the missions to the Jews. A major figure was Edward Hine, whose principal journal was a monthly, *Life from the Dead* (1873-80), "being a national bell-ringing journal advocating the identity of the British nation with the lost ten tribes of Israel." Another activist, "a retired Indian civilian"[20] under the pseudonym of Philo-Israel, published a weekly, the *Banner of Israel* (1877-1925; originally *Israel's Identity Standard* in 1876). The movement is mentioned here as a mimic of religion and as a caution against relying on titles alone for identification. (Another mimic of religion, astrology, is readily identifiable.)

15

Specialities

PROFESSIONAL JOURNALS

It was only in the nineteenth century that the Protestant ministry in Britain became a profession in the modern sense. The clergy of the Church of England, to be sure, were members of a profession in the historic sense of the term, meaning that their occupation was compatible with gentility; but a clergyman was only "a different kind of gentleman,"[1] not distinguished by specialized education, knowledge, or skill. The Old Dissent, particularly the Congregationalists and Presbyterian-Unitarians, maintained the tradition of a learned ministry, but their numbers were few; new denominations started from scratch. The evolution of the profession, only partly accomplished by formal education, required periodicals to guide ministers in biblical exegesis, the higher realms of theology, and the techniques of homiletics.

The first learned journal of the profession (indeed, one of the first of any profession, other than Proceedings and Transactions of societies) was the *Journal of Sacred Literature* (1848–68), a quarterly founded by Dr. John Kitto, who had edited the *Cyclopedia of Biblical Literature*. The evangelical Kitto and his successors, Dr. Henry Burgess in 1854 and B. Harris Cowper in 1861, produced a nondenominational but conventionally orthodox journal whose biblical criticism never rose above the textual level, though (with S. P. Tregelles as a contributor) this was often quite good. Kitto was original in insisting upon signed or initialed articles to achieve "limitation of responsibility"[2] to the author alone. He was venturesome only once in admitting articles by the Essayist-and-Reviewer Baden Powell in his first two numbers; but he insisted that no heresy had been admitted to the journal, and his successors ensured that *Essays and Reviews* received hostile reviews.[3] Foreign literature was covered, and some articles were translated from the German. With all its limitations, the journal may have been too rich for the blood of the profession: "It existed below subsistence level: articles were unpaid for and losses were incurred."[4] The situation was not unusual, but it could not go on indefinitely.

The *Journal of Sacred Literature* was joined by two other serious journals in the 1850s. The Scottish-based *British and Foreign Evangelical Review* has already been noted for its role in bringing to Britain the theology of Germany and America; it was not exclusively professional, but its goal was the "cultivation of the higher departments of Theological Literature."[5] The more specialized *Journal of Classical and Sacred Philology* (1854-59) was the first academic journal in the field, published by Cambridge University Press and edited by Cambridge scholars. The contributors (signed or initialed) included some great names, such as F. J. A. Hort, J. B. Lightfoot (later bishop of Durham), and J. E. B. Mayor. Two-thirds of the journal was on the classical side; but Greek is also a sacred language. Philology, however, was too rarefied a subject for the non-academic audience, and the academic profession was itself in its infancy.

More practically useful to the clergy was the *Expositor* (1875-1925), a monthly founded by the Reverend Samuel Cox to publish essays by eminent scholars of all denominations to provide "the stuff of which sermons are made." Cox professed belief in "the supernatural character of the Biblical revelation" but significantly warned that "of course, men of the calibre of those who write for THE EXPOSITOR cannot be tied down to any forms of words";[6] articles were therefore signed. Cox's warning was shown to be prescient when, in 1884, he was dismissed by the publishers, Hodder and Stoughton, ostensibly on the grounds that his "personal views on eschatology and inspiration offended and alarmed a section of his readers."[7] The real purpose was to have the editor enforce orthodoxy on the contributors, which Cox had explicitly renounced in his prospectus:[8]

> Their demands settled into this: the exclusion (1) of Robertson Smith & all who share his "loose views of Inspiration": (2) of all allusions to "the larger hope," & even of the general tone of thought wch it carries with it: and (3) a public pledge to exclude those objectionable elements from the Magazine. . . . I don't like seeing a Magazine which I have tried to make liberal & catholic humbled into the organ of a sect or party. . . . I have determined to accept the £1000 which wch the Publishers are eager to buy off my opposition.[9]

The publishers replaced Cox with William Robertson Nicoll, whom they were later to make editor of the *British Weekly*. The change, however motivated, proved beneficial to the *Expositor*: a new series was begun, published also in America, and the magazine became at once more scholarly (Lightfoot contributed) and more literary (the editor solicited an article from Edmund Gosse and himself reviewed *Mark Rutherford*). Robertson Nicoll, who had joined as a Scottish Free Kirk minister in condemning Robertson Smith, eventually became broader in his own views, and his magazine rendered great service to the profession.[10]

Even more practically useful was the *Expository Times* (1889-), a monthly founded as a venture by James Hastings, then a Scottish country minister but later famous as the editor of the *Dictionary of the Bible* and the *Encyclopedia of Religion and Ethics*. Soon taken over by an Edinburgh publisher, T. & T. Clark, the *Expository Times* under Hastings's editorship was designed to assist ministers in preparing sermons and conducting Bible classes. Writings of eminent scholars were published, or more usually republished, in the journal.[11]

A quarterly review at the highest level of academic theology appeared only at the end of the century, when the faculties of theology at Oxford and Cambridge jointly founded and directed the *Journal of Theological Studies* (1899-) as "a regular organ of communication between students whose lives are spent at the Universities and elsewhere, in the pursuit of scientific Theology."[12] The *Journal* "from the first maintained high standards of scholarship."[13]

The expository and theological journals provided material for sermons, but a homiletic press was of more practical service to sermon-writers. The *Homilist* (1852–92) started "as an organ of *spoken* thought on Biblical subjects,"[14] a minister's journal for other ministers. It had "no *finish* . . . no *denominationalism* . . . no *polemical theology*. . . . Systematic theology is but a means to an end. *Spiritual morality is that end.*"[15] Most of the articles were written by the Congregationalist editor, Rev. David Thomas, to 1872 and thereafter his son Urijah Rees Thomas. This unpretentious journal "sold an aggregate of over 200,000 copies."[16]

More pretentious but nonetheless practical was the *Homiletic Quarterly* (1877–81; then *Homiletic Magazine*, 1882–91; merged into the *Thinker*, 1892–95). Each issue included a sermon by a great preacher and sermon outlines, but there were also articles on biblical exegesis and pastoral theology, nonsectarian but orthodox. This was one of a number of such journals,[17] such as the cheap *Contemporary Pulpit* (1884–93), another of Robertson Nicoll's projects.[18]

There was another profession, or subprofession, connected with organized religion: the church musicians. Periodicals abounded for organists and choirmasters. The Society for Promoting Church Music sponsored the *Parish Choir or Church Music Book* (1846-51); the *Choir* (title varies, 1863–80), edited by E. F. Rimbault, was another important journal. In 1844 the music publishing house of Novello bought the *Musical Times* (title varies, 1842–), the leading general music periodical, which later emphasized church music.[19]

TRACT AND SERMON PERIODICALS

One genre of religious publication that for long rivaled periodicals was the tract, beloved of evangelicals. A predecessor of the religious magazines, the *Spiritual Magazine* (1752–56?) of John Allen, a Baptist preacher, was in fact not a magazine but a serialized tract.[20] Hannah Moore's *Cheap Repository Tracts* (1795–98) demonstrated that tracts could be issued periodically with convenience and success.[21] Her success stimulated the formation in 1799 of the Religious Tract Society, which, however, did not immediately make use of this discovery. Its partial effort at periodicalizing tracts was the *Tract Magazine* (1824–46). However, much of the contents of this and other periodicals aimed at the lower classes consisted of what may be called mini-tracts embedded in miscellanies. The idea of periodicalized tracts, never really implemented on a large scale, nonetheless died hard: Newman sought to have the *Tracts for the Times* issued at regular periodical intervals (but he could not impose regularity on his contributors),[22] and the Christian Socialist *Politics for the People* (1848) could only be described as periodical tracts.

The sermon, often printed in pamphlet form, was another potential rival of the religious periodical. Religious people had a great hunger for sermons, the only unobjectionable form of entertainment on Sundays, and printed sermons allowed them to "hear" a variety of preachers besides their own. Almost from the first, religious magazines included sermons in their miscellanies, thus serving this public. "The sermon market was effectively ended by the growth of religious periodicals, because they printed weekly sermons for devotional reading. . . . The cheapening of periodicals in the eighteen-sixties, after the end of the paper duty, meant the end of sermon publishing in volume form."[23] In addition to the printing of sermons within magazines, there were periodicals solely devoted to sermons. The *Pulpit* (1823-71), a weekly, may stand for the type, which also appeared in denominational, regional, and local forms. One doesn't need to know Welsh to recognize in *Y Pwlpud Wesleyaidd* (1876-77) an example of the extensibility of the type. Many of the sermon periodicals were short-lived ventures, and none achieved eminence except for Spurgeon's *Metropolitan Tabernacle Pulpit.* The vogue of sermon periodicals led one of the Pitman family, who tried to popularize their shorthand or phonography by publishing a series of phonographic journals, to offer the *Phonographic Pulpit* (1869-76), a monthly consisting of facsimile stenographic transcripts of three sermons by eminent preachers, enabling adepts to improve simultaneously their skills and their souls.

PERIODICALS FOR THE LOWER CLASSES

An outgrowth of the vogue of religious tracts was the production of periodicals for the same audience—described as cottagers and indeed rural, notwithstanding the fact of urbanization—and distributed by the same "'cottage visitors,' essentially superiors descending from an alien culture."[24] This movement was also a response to the growth of literacy, which raised fears that the newly literate might read the wrong things, whether revolutionary or irreligious. This fear motivated the first of this type, Mrs. Trimmer's *Family Magazine* (1788-89) for servants and cottagers; a similar fear prompted the responses to the secular penny magazines of 1832: the *Christian's Penny Magazine*, the *Visitor* (later *Weekly Visitor*) of the RTS, and *Zion's Trumpet*, significantly subtitled the *Penny Spiritual Magazine.* The genre was established by evangelical Anglicans with the *Cottage Magazine*

(1811/2–47) and Carus Wilson's *Friendly Visitor* in 1819, followed by the old High Church with the *Cottager's Monthly Visitor* (1821–56), the Wesleyans (themselves moving into the middle classes) with their *Cottager's Friend* (1837–45) and the new High Church with the *Penny Post* (1851–96). Written in a condescendingly preachy style, bought in bulk by their "betters" for free distribution, these publications were unlikely to effect any real contact with their readers' minds.[25] Probably the best of the type was the first addressed to an audience not necessarily rural, the *Servant's Magazine* of the London Female Mission, which made the best of a relationship necessarily de haut en bas by trying to be practically useful to its readers. The first magazine addressed to urban workingmen was John Cassell's *Working Man's Friend* (1850–53); perhaps the best was the *British Workman* (1855–1921), a social and moral monthly with a temperance slant founded by a man who knew something of his audience, T. B. Smithies, also editor of the *Band of Hope Review*. The Religious Tract Society moved into this market in 1861 with the archaically named *Cottager in town and country*, renamed *Cottager and Artisan* in 1865. While some of these journals survived into the twentieth century, they represented a type that was becoming obsolescent with the further advance of literacy and the availability of cheap publications that provided sensationalism and gratified the hunger for excitement; the religious press could not match this.

WOMEN'S PERIODICALS

Periodicals for women had existed since the *Lady's Magazine* was founded in 1770. Most of the early examples and many of the later ones were addressed to upper- and middle-class women in their primary role as present or future wives, with a heavy emphasis on fashion. Practical Victorians added the all-purpose domestic magazine, such as the Beetons' *Englishwoman's Domestic Magazine*. By contrast, specifically religious magazines for women were few and insignificant. Of those whose titles proclaim their religious character, only Charlotte Elizabeth Tonna's *Christian Lady's Magazine* was important and successful. There was, however, in the 1840s a vogue for mothers' magazines, always instructive rather than fashionable and often pietistic, such as Mrs. Mary Milner's *Christian Mother's Magazine* (1844–45) and its successors. A religious character was evident in some of the few periodicals specifically addressed to women of the lower classes. The *Servant's Magazine* was in fact addressed to female domestics (there was no *Christian Footman's Magazine*; perhaps they were irredeemable). The *British Workwoman* (1683–1913) was addressed to women of the working classes whether "out or at home"; it was the female counterpart of the *British Workman*. In view of (or perhaps because of) the prevailing assumption that women were the more religious sex, this list of periodicals is rather thin.[26] We may add the official journals produced by the ladies' auxiliaries of evangelical societies, the zenana missionary press, and the organs of charities with a special appeal for women (though often managed by men), such as the *Female Missionary Intelligencer* (1853–99), the journal of the Society for the Promotion of Female Education in China, Africa and the East.

FAMILY MAGAZINES

A possible reason for the relative paucity of women's religious periodicals was the abundant sale of family magazines. The premise of the family magazine is paterfamilias reading to the assembled family, a stereotype that often was a reality, but the genre had a special appeal to women, who had more time on their hands for reading. Again, the religious entry into this field was a response to the success of secular journals deemed unsuitable, in this case the *Family Herald* in 1842 and the *London Journal* in 1845, noted for their melodramatic fiction. Their success stimulated the Religious Tract Society to offer the monthly *Leisure Hour* in 1852 and the more sober *Sunday at Home* in 1854. More effective were the efforts of individual entrepreneurs, of whom the nonconformist John Cassell was the ablest and most successful. His greatest success (over 250,000 circulation) came with *Cassell's Illustrated Family Paper* (1853–67, weekly; then monthly: *Cassell's Magazine*, 1867–74; *Cassell's Family Magazine*, 1874–97; *Cassell's Magazine*, 1897–1930), not explicitly religious. His best overtly religious magazine was the weekly *Quiver* (1861–), "a religious journal of a high standard of literary merit at a very low price"[27] (one penny). The most creative entrepreneur of popular religious periodicals was Alexander Strahan, with his weeklies *Good Words* (1860–1911) and the *Sunday Magazine* (1864–1906). *Good Words*, edited by the broad-minded Norman Macleod, was attacked by the *Record* for being insufficiently evangelical in tone and for publishing novels;[28] but these features were the very preconditions of success for popular magazines, even if they were religious. In 1881 it was said that eight religious weeklies sold between 1.25 million and 1.5 million copies; one of these was properly a newspaper, the *Christian World*—but even the *Christian World* serialized novels.[29]

CHILDREN'S PERIODICALS

Children's literature, especially children's periodical literature, was virtually invented in the nineteenth century. Until past mid-century, it may be said that children's periodicals were all religious in tone and intent. Early examples are the *Youth's Magazine* (1805–67), the Wesleyan *Youth's Instructor* (1817–55),[30] and Carus Wilson's dismal but cheap and successful *Children's Friend* from 1824. The Sunday school movement prompted the issuance of several periodicals from the 1820s: the Religious Tract Society offered the *Child's Companion* from 1824, and the Wesleyans responded with the *Child's Magazine* (1824–45). Such magazines had large circulations, being distributed through the Sunday schools; they "formed the most accessible literature for most children for about the first three-quarters of the nineteenth century. . . . a literature that was overloaded with precocious goodness, morbid piety and sickly sentiment."[31] There were also children's missionary magazines, to cultivate interest in the missionary enterprise; most Scottish denominations had one, and the Methodists offered the *Wesleyan Juvenile Offering* (1844–78), "affording our juvenile Subscribers and Collectors some Missionary Information, as an acknowledgment of their past services, and as an incentive to future exertion."[32] The Anglican High Church contribution was Charlotte Yonge's pastoral *Monthly Packet* from 1851. A second round of Sunday school magazines was produced by societies in the 1850s: the dreary *Child's Own Magazine* (1852–), published by the nonconformist Sunday School Union, and the *Sunday Scholar's Companion* (1855–82; then *Boys' and Girls' Companion*, 1883–1903) of the Church of England Sunday School Institute. There were also many private-venture magazines for children, and the American "Peter Parley" was widely pirated and imitated in England.

From the 1850s the children's periodical press was no longer the monopoly of religious interests, and from the 1860s (the age of cheap paper) it could no longer be assumed that children's literature was edifying, with the advent of the penny dreadfuls for boys. The Derby vicar J. Erskine Clark—who had earlier started a conventional

Sunday school magazine, the *Children's Prize* (1863–75; then *Prize*, 1875–)–determined to respond to what he called the "blood-and-thunder" journals with a half-penny weekly, the *Chatterbox* (1866–). The nonreligious title concealed a good deal of old-fashioned piety, but it was lively enough to wean the young J. M. Barrie from the penny dreadfuls.[33] There also appeared some children's magazines of quality. *Good Words*, having shown that a religious magazine could be readable, offered *Good Words for the Young* (1868–72), edited by George MacDonald, the writer of fairy tales, with contributions from Charles Kingsley and W. S. Gilbert. MacDonald's fairy tales were too good as literature to be appreciated by children, and perhaps this was the problem with his magazine; it failed. More practical was a journal specifically for younger children, *Little Folks* (1871–1933), published by the ubiquitous Cassell.

The most glaring sin of omission by the religious juvenile press was the failure to realize that children are divided into girls and boys and that boys will be boys. The failure to make separate provision for the more active literary interest of boys, especially older boys who might have the odd penny to spend, opened the door to the penny dreadfuls, which long had the boys' market to themselves. The religious response was belated but hugely successful: the *Boy's Own Paper*, published from 1879 by the Religious Tract Society, concealing its religious parentage and offering what boys actually wanted to read, free of immorality but stressing manliness rather than moralism. The "B.O.P." was the great redeeming feature both of the RTS and of the children's religious periodicals.

A periodical press for girls was slower to emerge than that for boys; it was assumed that girls, when they outgrew generalized children's periodicals, would read the magazines that their mothers read. A few magazines were addressed to young women by societies formed for their aid. The deficiency of periodicals for girls was finally and amply remedied by the *Girl's Own Paper* from 1880.

16

Conclusion: Heralds and Witnesses

Heralds and Witnesses, Advocates and Remembrancers, Guardians and Banners—the litany of titles of periodicals is eloquent testimony to the fecundity, vigor, and earnestness of the nineteenth-century religious press. It perhaps testifies also to a certain lack of originality, but this serves all the more to authenticate religious periodicals as the most extensive and indispensable entry for scholars into the minds of those by or for whom they were published. Through their periodicals the Victorians witnessed their faith, and we witness them.

Bearing witness was indeed the main function of religious periodicals. They recorded the achievements of denominations, organizations, and leaders; they defended general morality or specific doctrines. These are inward-directed functions; and in fact most of the religious press was written for and sold to those who were already adherents of the cause. The function of the herald—proclaiming a message to those who had not yet received it—was much less significant, even when it provided the ostensible purpose of the periodical. Controversial literature was written not to persuade an opponent but to defend and confirm existing faith against perceived assaults. The defensive motive often underlay even the most aggressive advocacy.[1] Periodicals addressed to the lower classes, seemingly designed to redeem the unchurched, had political motives of heading off social discontent or were designed as a defense "in the hope of stemming the torrent of moral poison with which the Penny Press is inundating the land."[2] Denominational journals were bought by members of the denomination and stimulated their denominational consciousness. The missionary press was published not for the use of missionaries but rather to build up their home base of recruits and contributors. The even larger temperance press was designed less to win new abstainers than, at the national level, to coordinate a political campaign and, in the plethora of organizational and local publications, to encourage and give support to recent converts. Children's periodicals were at first adjuncts of the Sunday schools and later safe alternatives to the penny dreadfuls. Almost the only periodicals really intended to win converts were those put out by new denominations, such as the Mormons or Christadelphians, or by freethinkers. Few converts were actually won by the periodical press.[3]

Religious periodicals also served to promote the religious self-identification of their readers as adherents of religious bodies and particularly of movements within denominations. By taking the *Record* or the *Guardian*, the *Rambler* or the *Dublin Review*, the *Watchman* or the *Wesleyan Times*, or (in the case of two Strict Baptist groups not otherwise identifiable) the *Earthen Vessel* (1845–?) or the *Gospel Standard* (1835–), one proclaimed one's religious identity more clearly even than by formal membership. Subscribing to a periodical was something like subscribing to the Thirty-Nine Articles, and subscriptions were liable to be cancelled if the periodical deviated from the approved line. The relation between readers and their periodicals of choice was almost intimately personal.

Religious periodicals were, for the most part, preaching to the converted. So were most preachers. This function, which psychologists in their despicable jargon call reinforcement, is not to be despised. No religious movement can long continue without it. The faith of the Victorians was much and powerfully reinforced by their religious press. That fact cannot be quantified, but it must be recognized. The continued and expanding use of the press by religious spokesmen is itself proof that periodicals met a need. When addressing their own people, they knew their audience.

The religious press, then, was not a cause of the religious revival of the nineteenth century but serves rather as evidence that it was happening. But sometime in the course of the century that revival began to wane and turn into a process of decline still at work in the twentieth century. By some point in the 1880s, the churches fell behind in the effort to keep up with population growth, to reach a working class that (with select exceptions) had evolved a life-style that did not include active religion, and to counter the growing attractiveness of secular activities.[4] The religious press provides little evidence that this decline had commenced. Perhaps a detailed content analysis on a scale unfeasible for a solitary researcher might reveal something, but one may doubt this. The religious press was still expanding as the century ended. No type or form of publication was given up: the Religious Tract Society was still offering tracts in the 1890s and even *Gospel Emblems* and *Gospel Handbills.* But the most successful periodicals were also the most technically proficient, with full-time editors and even staffs, better-written stories and higher-quality illustrations. Great editors such as Robertson Nicoll were at the height of their power.

It was in the elements of its greatest success that the religious press gave signs that something might have been lost. The early and mid-Victorian press had a hard-edged quality; it not only defended the faith but defended it *against* something; it made demands upon its readers. Hugh Price Hughes' *Methodist Times* was a belated recrudescence of that type; the temperance press continued it on a restricted theme; but the vigorous editorial stands of such as Robertson Nicoll tended to be taken on issues rather political than strictly religious, more Liberal than evangelical. The more successful periodicals sought to attract the willing interest of their readers; amusement was supplanting instruction. This tendency towards creeping pleasantness can sometimes be seen in changes of title. What are we to make of the metamorphosis of the *Church Missionary Juvenile Instructor* (1842–90) to *Children's World* (1891–1900) and finally to the *Round World and they that dwell therein* (1901–)? These changes are most common in children's magazines;[5] but even the *British Women's Temperance Journal* (1883–92) sprouted *Wings* (1892–1925). The decline of hard-edged religious journalism may indicate a loss of the hard edge in religion itself. Early Victorian journals liked to characterize themselves as manly; late Victorian periodicals appealed to families.

In an age of mass journalism, the religious press could succeed in keeping a large audience only by diluting its religion.[6] In religion, nothing fails like success.

Appendix

The following "Dictionary of Representative Organs" from *May's British and Irish Press Guide* (London, 1883), p. 34, shows a Victorian attempt to categorize religious periodicals:

Religious—(see under following heads):—Anglo-Catholic, Anti-Ritualistic, Baptist, Bible Christians, Book Hawking, Calvinistic Baptist, Calvinistic Methodist, Charitable Institutions, China Missions, Church Guilds, Church of Scotland, Church Reform, Congregational, Convocation, Destitute Children, District Visiting, Foreign Churches, Free Church of England, Free Church of Scotland, Free Gospel Churches, General Baptist, German Baptist, Indian Missions, Irish Missions, Jewish, Juvenile Literature, Large-type Readings, Methodist, Methodist New Connexion, Mission Work, Moravian, Mothers (reading for), New Jerusalem Church, Original Secession Church, Peace Movement, Plymouth Brethren, Presbyterian, Primitive Methodist, Prison Missions, Prophetic, Ragged Schools, Reformatories, Religious Family & General Readings, Religious Free Enquiry, Religious Newspapers, Religious Revival, Roman Catholic, Salvation Army, Scottish Congregational, Scottish Episcopal Church, Scripture Readers, Sermons, Society of Friends, Soldiers & Sailors (religious literature for), Strict Baptist, Sunday Schools, Sunday School Teachers, Theology, Unitarian, United Methodist Free Churches, United Presbyterian, Welsh Baptist, Welsh Church Magazines, Welsh Congregational, Welsh Presbyterian, Welsh Wesleyan, Wesleyan Methodist.

Notes

CHAPTER 1

1. Owen Chadwick, *The Victorian Church*, 2 vols. (London, 1966-70), 1:1.

2. G. Kitson Clark, *The Making of Victorian England* (London, 1962), 20.

3. See Chadwick, *Victorian Church*, 2:177.

4. Michael Wolff, John S. North, and Dorothy Deering, eds., *The Waterloo Directory of Victorian Periodicals 1824-1900* (Waterloo, Ont., 1976).

5. John W. Dodds, *The Age of Paradox* (New York, 1952), 111, drawn from the *Tercentenary Handlist of English and Welsh Newspapers, Magazines and Reviews* (London, 1920).

6. The exception, in part, is the section on "Newspapers and Magazines" (by Henry and Sheila Rosenberg) in vol. 3 of *The New Cambridge Bibliography of English Literature*, ed. George Watson (Cambridge, 1969). This section provided an initial list of periodicals to be studied.

7. Walter E. Houghton, ed., *The Wellesley Index to Victorian Periodicals 1824-1900*, 4 vols. (Toronto, 1966, 1972, 1979, 1988). Individual periodicals or authors are occasionally attributed in articles in *Victorian Periodicals Review* (formerly *Newsletter*), the organ of the Research Society for Victorian Periodicals (RSVP). This will henceforth be cited as *VPR* or *VPN*.

8. Albert Peel, *These Hundred Years* (London, 1931), 414. He desiderated "a list of periodicals with facts about their editorship or ownership."

9. There is a model study of 1700-1825 in chapter 2 of Francis E. Mineka, *The Dissidence of Dissent* (Chapel Hill, 1944). For the 1860s, Alvår Ellegård, *The Readership of the Periodical Press in Mid-Victorian Britain* (Göteborg, 1957), sketches the religious periodicals, among others. There are general chapters in L. E. Elliott-Binns, *Religion in the Victorian Era* (London, 1936), and by E. E. Kellett in *Early Victorian England*, ed. G. M. Young (London, 1934). P. G. Scott

has contributed "The Business of Belief: The Emergence of 'Religious' Publishing" in *Studies in Church History*, 10, ed. Derek Baker (Oxford, 1973), and "Victorian Religious Periodicals: Fragments That Remain" in ibid., 12 (Oxford, 1975). The most recent study is Louis Billington, "The Religious Periodical and Newspaper Press, 1770-1870," in Michael Harris and Alan Lee, eds., *The Press in English Society From the Seventeenth to Nineteenth Centuries* (London, 1986), 113-32.

CHAPTER 2

1. The *Tercentenary Handlist*, also known as the *Times Tercentenary Handlist*, lists periodicals by date of commencement, though with omissions and errors.

2. Francis E. Mineka, *The Dissidence of Dissent: The Monthly Repository, 1806-1838* (Chapel Hill, NC, 1944), 30. Mineka's chapter, "'News From Heaven': English Religious Periodicals to 1825," is the first general study of the religious press. It is an invaluable source, which I use frequently in this chapter.

3. See ibid., 27, 31-33, and T. M. Hatfield, "John Dunton's Periodicals," *Journalism Quarterly*, 10 (1933), 209-25.

4. See Josef L. Altholz, "The First Religious Magazines," *Notes & Queries*, 32 (June 1985), 223-24, for this and other precursors of the form or name of the magazine.

5. "To the Reader," prefaced to vol. 1 of the *Arminian Magazine* (1778), iii. Quotations from the *Christian's Magazine* in this paragraph are taken from "The Design," prefaced to vol. 1 (1760).

6. See J. C. Whitebrook, *Ann Dutton: A Life and Bibliography* (London, 1921). The uncertainty is due to the rarity of copies. The British Library has the first three volumes bound as [Ann Dutton], *Divine, Moral, and Historical Miscellanies* (London, 1761 etc.). The *British Union Catalogue of Periodicals* reports "no holdings" but ventures that it continued to 1784 and absorbed the *Gospel Magazine.*

7. "The Life of John Calvin," *Gospel Magazine*, 1 (April 1766), 171. See also Mineka, *Dissidence of Dissent*, 37-39.

8. John Blacket, "The Oldest Religious Periodical in the World," *Methodist Magazine*, 150 (January-March 1927), 54-57, 120-22, 186-89. The phrase appears on the masthead. The *Waterloo Directory* calls the *Gospel Magazine* (1796-) "the oldest of the religious magazines," but this statement is an error.

9. Mineka, *Dissidence of Dissent*, 48; Richard D. Altick, *The English Common Reader* (Chicago, 1957), 318-19.

10. Country readers of papers such as the *Record* advertised for used copies to be posted to them; they wanted the news, but it need not be fresh.

11. If there was an exception that proved the rule, it was the *Daily Express* (May 1-August 25, 1877), an Anglican paper.

12. Prospectus, *Record*, January 1, 1828, p. 1.

13. See Chapter 7.

14. See P. G. Scott, "Richard Cope Morgan, Religious Periodicals, and the Pontifex Factor," *VPN*, no. 16 (1972), 1-14.

CHAPTER 3

1. See chapter 2.

2. Peter Roger Mountjoy, "The Working-Class Press and Working-Class Conservatism," in G. Boyce, J. Curran, and P. Wingate, eds., *Newspaper History from the Seventeenth Century to the Present Day* (London, 1978), 270.

3. *Zion's Trumpet*, "Preface" to vols. 1-3, p. v. *Zion's Trumpet* was published at Bristol, the *Christian Guardian* in London.

4. The *Christian Guardian* is incorrectly listed in standard bibliographical sources; its survival until 1853 is demonstrated by James Ellis and Michael Wolff, "The *Christian Guardian* in 1853: An Unrecorded Volume," *VPN*, no. 16 (June 1972), 51-52. Carus Wilson resigned in 1849 because of ill health but expressed his opinion that a more frequent periodical was better suited to the times; his successors concurred in 1853.

5. Jane M. Ewbank, *The Life and Work of William Carus Wilson* (Kendal, 1959), 4. Examples of his style are given by Ford K. Brown, *Fathers of the Victorians* (Cambridge, 1961), 464-73.

6. John Clive, *Macaulay: The Shaping of the Historian* (New York, 1973), 33. The first three numbers had been edited by Josiah Pratt (secretary of the Church Missionary Society); then Macaulay (1802-16), Rev. Samuel C. Wilks (1816-50), J. W. Cunningham, vicar of Harrow (1850-58), and J. B. Marsden (1859-69).

7. G. R. Balleine, *A History of the Evangelical Party in the Church of England* (London, 1909), 152-153.

8. Owen Chadwick, *The Victorian Church*, 1: 448. For the circulation, see Alvar Ellegård, *The Readership of the Periodical Press in Mid-Victorian Britain* (Göteborg, 1957); Part 2 reprinted in *VPN*, no. 13 (September 1971), 3-22.

9. See "Preface" to vol. 1. The editors were Walter Purton (1879-92) and W. M. Sinclair (1892-1901).

10. Prospectus, *Record*, January 1, 1828, p. 1; originally issued 1827.

11. For the full story, see Josef L. Altholz, "Alexander Haldane, The *Record*, and Religious Journalism," *Victorian Periodicals Review*, 20 (Spring 1987), 23-31.

12. Balleine, *History of the Evangelical Party*, 207.

13. [W. J. Conybeare], "Church Parties," *Edinburgh Review*, 98 (October 1853), 284.

14. Letter of E. B. Pusey, *Record*, February 19, 1864, p. 3.

15. Balleine, *History of the Evangelical Party*, 272.

16. Ibid., 292-93. See *English Churchman*, November 27, 1884, p. 582.

17. The phrase is taken from Brown, *Fathers of the Victorians.*

18. Balleine, *History of the Evangelical Party*, 161.

19. Eugene Stock, *The History of the Church Missionary Society*, 4 vols. (London, 1899-1916), 1: 148.

20. At the end of 1840 it claimed a circulation of 3,150, "which we believe exceeds that of any other newspaper published in Ireland." *Achill Missionary Herald*, December 31, 1840, p. 1.

21. For the general story, see Desmond Bowen, *The Protestant Crusade in Ireland* (Dublin, 1977). Dallas had previously published the *Pastor's Assistant* (1842-1844) and one of the earliest parish papers, the *Wonston Weekly Calendar.*

CHAPTER 4

1. The pre-Tractarian High Church has generally been slighted. The best account is in Yngve Brilioth, *The Anglican Revival* (London, 1925).

2. This account is based on the editorial matter prepared for the *Wellesley Index* by Esther R. Houghton but not published. But see her "A 'New' Editor of the *British Critic*," *VPR*, 12 (Fall 1979), 102-05.

3. See Newman to R. H. Froude, February 1, 1835, in *The Letters and Diaries of John Henry Newman*, ed. Thomas Gornall (Oxford, 1981), 5: 222-23. This and subsequent volumes of the series are filled with references to the affairs of the *British Critic*, superseding Anne Mozley, ed., *Letters and Correspondence of John Henry Newman during his life in the English Church*, 2 vols. (London, 1891).

4. William Palmer, *A Narrative of Events Connected with the Publication of Tracts for the Times* (London, 1883; originally 1843), 87.

5. Ibid., 242-43.

6. "Introduction," *Christian Remembrancer*, 1 (January 1819), 2. There were several references to "the well known power of the periodical press": ibid, 5, 7.

7. Ellegård, *Readership of the Periodical Press*, 15.

8. There is a quaint account of Rose and the *British Magazine* in J. W. Burgon, *Lives of Twelve Good Men*, 2 vols., 2nd ed. (London, 1891), 2: 139-49. I am indebted to my student David Heughins for this reference.

9. "Address," *British Magazine*, 1 (March 1, 1832), 1-10. Rose's statements concerning editorial responsibility are of interest. He held himself responsible "for the *general tenour* of the religious and moral opinions in the original articles" but not for "opinions in communications and letters" or "the literary opinions delivered in Reviews" (10). This seems to be the source for Newman's use of "communicated" to disclaim responsibility in the *British Critic* and later the Roman Catholic *Rambler.* See Josef L. Altholz, "On the Use of 'Communicated' in the *Rambler*," *VPN*, 1: 28-29.

10. See numerous references in Newman, *Letters and Diaries*, vols. 4-5. See also Chadwick, *Victorian Church*, 1: 170-71, which notes that Rose first used the word "Anglicanism" in 1837.

11. "Introduction," *Church of England Quarterly Review*, 1 (January 1837), 31, 1.

12. Bibliographical reference sources such as the *Union List of Serials* or the *British Union Catalogue of Periodicals* list the *English Review* as an appendage of the *British Critic*, treating it as the successor under a new name. The only connection between the two distinct periodicals was the publisher, who undoubtedly sought to promote it as a revival of the *British Critic*.

13. "Newman's Sermons on Subjects of the Day," *English Review*, 1 (July 1844), 334.

14. *Ecclesiologist*, no. 2 (December 1841), 26. The story of this movement is given fully in J. F. White, *The Cambridge Movement* (Cambridge, 1962), and summed up in Chadwick, *Victorian Church*, 1: 212-14, 221.

15. Balleine, *History of the Evangelical Party*, 243. The editor from 1843 to 1863 was D. W. Godfrey. From 1864 to 1868 the title was shortened to the *Churchman*, thereafter again *English Churchman*.

16. Ellegård, *Readership of the Periodical Press*, 11.

17. See Chapter 3.

18. Ellegård, *Readership of the Periodical Press*, 16. The *Ecclesiastic* merged with the *Theologian* (1845-47) to form the *Theologian and Ecclesiastic* (1847-50), then *Ecclesiastic and Theologian* (1850-62) and again the *Ecclesiastic* (1862-68).

19. Joseph Hatton, *Journalistic London* (London, 1882), 211.

20. Charles Smyth, "'The Guardian' 1846-1883: The Years of Endurance," *Guardian* (January 18, 1946), 32. This centenary number also contains A. C. Headlam, "'The Guardian': The Beginning."

21. Chadwick, *Victorian Church* 1: 238. See *Guardian*, November 17, 1847. High Church leaders such as Keble and E. B. Pusey wrote for the *Guardian*.

22. The difference in style was captured by Benjamin Jowett, predicting to Florence Nightingale the probable reception of her theological work: "Imagine the Record with its female Atheist . . . or the Guardian with more pretence of . . . feeling in sorrow rather than anger requiring that that once honoured name should be banished from Christian households." Jowett to Nightingale, "until July 21st" (1862), Balliol College Library. The characteristic elegiac strain is deftly parodied.

23. "Advertisement," *Guardian* (January 21, 1846), 16.

24. "Dr. Hooker's Address," *Guardian* (August 26, 1868), 952, acknowledging "the rare union in Mr. Darwin of brilliant genius with patient research" but criticizing Hooker's "attack upon the clergy." See also *Guardian* (August 2, 1871), 937: "Nor is there any reason why a man may not be an Evolutionist and

yet a Christian." The review (probably by Church) opposed the mechanism of natural selection but warned against the "misuse" of Scripture to attack it (936). See also the appreciation of "Cardinal Newman," *Guardian* (May 21, 1879), 700 (probably by Rogers): "there are in the Christian Church bonds of affinity, subtler, more real, and more prevailing than even the fatal legacies of the great schisms."

25. B. A. Smith, *Dean Church: The Anglican Response to Newman* (London, 1958), 301.

26. Chadwick, *Victorian Church*, 2: 215. See the "Introductory Letter," *Monthly Packet*, 1 (January 1851), i-iv.

27. Advertisement on cover, *Literary Churchman*, December 29, 1855. The *Literary Churchman* is useful to historians who wish to study pamphlet controversies.

28. See C. B. Mortlock, *The People's Book of the Oxford Movement* (London, 1933), 87.

29. "The Church Press," *Union Review*, 1 (January 1863), 40.

30. See H. R. T. Brandreth, *Dr. Lee of Lambeth* (London, 1951).

31. "Our First Number," *Church Review*, 1 (January 1, 1861), 1. See also "To Our Readers," ibid. (January 4, 1862). It was never "popular." Ellegård gives a circulation of 1,000.

32. "Review of Position," *Church and State Review*, 1 (June 1, 1862), 3. Denison frequently criticized the *Guardian* for being too judicious in its condemnation of the biblical critics.

33. Mortlock, *People's Book of the Oxford Movement*, 94.

34. For reflections on this, see Billington, "Religious Periodical and Newspaper Press," 130-32.

35. "Story of Our First Beginnings," *Church Times*, February 8, 1963, p. 12.

36. See Josef L. Altholz, "The *Church Quarterly Review*, 1875-1900: A Marked File and Other Sources," *VPR*, 17 (Spring-Summer 1984), 52-57, with a correction in the next number. There are retrospective articles in 1900 and 1907.

37. Ronald C. D. Jasper, "The Church Quarterly Review 1875-1968," *Church Quarterly*, 1 (October 1968), 137. In 1968 the *Church Quarterly Review* merged with the *London Quarterly and Holborn Review*, itself a merger of two Methodist reviews, as the *Church Quarterly* (1968-71).

38. Letter by "Rector," *Newbery House Magazine*, 1 (July 1889), 127. See also "Newbery House and its Founder," ibid., 1-6.

39. The first article was by Charles (later Bishop) Gore, the High Church leader. Art criticism was provided by Roger Fry. Another unlikely contribution was an obituary article by Sir Frederick Pollock on Henry Sidgwick: *Pilot*, September 15, 1900, pp. 325-26.

40. Mortlock, *People's Book of the Oxford Movement*, 90.

CHAPTER 5

The title is taken from the splendid mistranslation of *Non Angli, sed Angeli* in chapter 3 of W. C. Sellar and R. J. Yeatman, *1066 and All That* (New York, 1931).

1. [W. J. Conybeare], "Church Parties," *Edinburgh Review*, 98 (October 1853), 334.

2. The *Wellesley Index*, 1: 1097, shows Stanley publishing in both the Tory/orthodox *Quarterly Review* and the Whig/liberal *Edinburgh Review*.

3. See Mark Francis, "The Origins of *Essays and Reviews*: An Interpretation of Mark Pattison in the 1850's," *Historical Journal*, 17 (December 1974), 797-811, and Josef L. Altholz, "Periodical Origins and Implications of *Essays and Reviews*," *VPN*, 10 (September 1977), 140-54.

4. *Wellesley Index*, 1: 554-55.

5. Ibid., 210-12.

6. Chadwick, *Victorian Church*, 2: 123. See also William Beach Thomas, *The Story of the Spectator* (London, 1928).

7. Cited in Chadwick, *Victorian Church*, 1: 355.

8. N. C. Masterman, *John Malcolm Ludlow: The Builder of Christian Socialism* (Cambridge, 1963), especially 114-29. See also Torben Christensen, *Origin and History of Christian Socialism 1848-54* (Aarhus, 1962).

9. "Our Platform," *Church Reformer*, 1 (January 1882), 1. Headlam's specific "socialism" was Henry George's single tax.

10. Chadwick, *Victorian Church*, 2: 277-78n.

11. Ibid., 2: 278. See also "Prologue," *Christian Socialist*, 1 (June 1883), 1-2.

12. Peter d'A. Jones, *The Christian Socialist Revival 1877-1914* (Princeton, 1968), 28.

13. The Mauricians were Hughes and Llewellyn Davies. Holland was a contributor at first. High Churchmen included Charles Gore, Percy Dearmer, and "Father" Dolling. Others were Canon Barnett, Bishop Wilberforce's son Basil, and the archbishop's son A. C. Benson.

14. Chadwick, *Victorian Church*, 2: 279. Contributors included Ludlow, Gore and Barnett, Bishop Stubbs, the economist J. A. Hobson, and the Fabian Mrs. Webb.

15. There is a full account in the *Wellesley Index*, 2: 522-28. All the reference lists (epitomized in the *Waterloo Directory*) list the *London Review* as two volumes, 1829-30, some even listing holdings of vol. 2; but there was only vol. 1 of two numbers.

16. "Introduction," *Church of England Quarterly Review*, 1 (January 1837), 1.

17. "Address," *Ecclesiastical Gazette*, 1 (July 11, 1838), 1.

18. "Notice," *Church and State Gazette* (December 26, 1856), 822.

19. "To Readers," *Clerical Journal*, 1 (July 22, 1853), 83.

20. For Cox, see Charlotte C. Watkins, "Edward William Cox and the Rise of 'Class Journalism,'" *VPR*, 15 (Fall 1982), 87-93.

21. "Preface," *Clerical Directory* (1858), n.p. See Josef L. Altholz, "Mr. Serjeant Cox, John Crockford, and the Origins of *Crockford's Clerical Directory*," *VPR*, 17 (Winter 1984), 153-58.

22. See the Preface to vol. 1 and the announcements in the June, 1859 number. An advertisement identifies the proprietors as Messrs. Paul and Bee, shorthand reporters. The statement that speakers revised the reports of their speeches may help to answer a vexed question about the literal accuracy of *Hansard's*.

23. W. K. Lowther Clarke, *A History of the S.P.C.K.* (London, 1959), 181-82. R. K. Webb, *The British Working Class Reader* (London, 1955), 74, 77-78, notes that sales were only 20,000 in 1836; the magazine was transferred to the publisher, J. W. Parker, in 1837; and the Committee devoted itself thereafter chiefly to educational publishing.

24. Only the Welsh edition (in part) is listed in the *Waterloo Directory*, which suggests that this paper, distributed to members, was not formally "published." It is given here from the listing in C. F. Pascoe, *Two Hundred Years of the S.P.G.*, 2 vols. (London, 1901), 2: 814.

25. This too is omitted from the *Waterloo Directory*; it was offered for sale but not copyrighted. The British Library file lacks 1847-63.

26. See Brian Harrison, "'A World of Which We Had No Conception': Liberalism and the Temperance Press, 1830-1872," *Victorian Studies*, 13 (December 1969), 140-41.

27. J. J. Jones, "The Welsh Church Periodical Press," *National Library of Wales Journal*, 4 (Summer 1945), 94. This section is based on this source.

28. "The State of Ireland," *Christian Examiner*, 1 (July 1825), 7.

29. Stephen J. M. Brown, *The Press in Ireland* (Dublin, 1957), 98. See also the "Preface" to vol. I of the *Christian Examiner*.

30. P. M. H. Bell, *Disestablishment in Ireland and Wales* (London, 1969), 162. See also "Prospectus," *Irish Ecclesiastical Gazette*, 1 (March 1856), 5.

31. "Editor's Address," inside front cover of *Parish Magazine*, 2 (December 1860); similarly in December, 1861. See also Chadwick, *Victorian Church*, 2: 426-27.

32. There is a list in *Sell's Dictionary of the World's Press* (London, 1887), 483.

33. The British Library has single numbers of W. Emery Stark's lists, generally treated as trade circulars rather than periodical publications. They are mostly 1885 numbers; the *Church Preferment Gazette* for December, 1885 is copyrighted. Perhaps Stark copyrighted a single number of each to protect the titles. The *Waterloo Directory* has other entries, but never a complete run.

34. *Report of the Select Committee of the House of Lords on Church Patronage*, H. C. 289 (1874), 7: 301ff. (note the comments on "Clerical Agents" in the Index); *Report of the Commissioners appointed to inquire into the Law and*

Existing Practice as to the Sale, Exchange, and Resignation of Ecclesiastical Benefices (C. 2375), H. C. (1878-1879), 20: 595ff., and especially *Minutes of Evidence and Appendix* (C. 2507), H. C. (1880), 20: 373ff.

35. *Church Preferment Gazette* (December 1885), 37. The inside front cover lists Stark's other periodicals.

36. Chadwick, *Victorian Church*, 2: 208-13; Alan Haig, *The Victorian Clergy* (London, 1984), chapter 6, which treats the matter in terms of an increasing number of curates chasing a limited number of livings.

CHAPTER 6

1. "The Preface," *Evangelical Magazine*, 1 (July 1793), 3.

2. Ibid., 4. The December 1800 number published a "spiritual barometer" that has become famous as a self-caricature of evangelical attitudes.

3. For these matters, see Albert Peel, *These Hundred Years*, and R. Tudur Jones, *Congregationalism in England, 1662-1962* (London, 1962). See also Billington, "Religious Press," 117-18.

4. Preface to vol. 14, *Spiritual Magazine* (1838). The nonconformist control is suggested by this passage: "We are conscientious dissenters from a form of worship, but we do not dissent from the *truths* contained in that form of worship; and therefore we will continue to pray for the welfare of our country in connection with a national church."

5. Preface to vol. 13, ibid. No copies or dates of *Zion's Casket* are listed.

6. "Appeal to the British People," *Christian's Penny Magazine*, 1 (June 9, 1832), 1.

7. The "Preface" to vol. 1 refers to 2,938 copies and a first year's profits of £12. 3s. 2d. For these journals, see Patrick Scott, "'Zion's Trumpet': Evangelical Enterprise and Rivalry, 1833-35," *Victorian Studies*, 13 (December 1969), 199-203.

8. Cited in Monica Correa Fryckstedt, "Charlotte Elizabeth Tonna and *The Christian Lady's Magazine*," *VPR*, 14 (Summer 1981), 44.

9. "Preface," *Christian Lady's Magazine*, 1 (1834), i-ii.

10. "Introduction," ibid., 1 (January 1834), 3.

11. Ibid., 5.

12. "Preface," *Servants' Magazine*, 1 (1838), iv.

13. "Editor's Address," ibid., 1.

14. See John Cassell's testimony on religious and temperance periodicals, May 16 and 20, 1851, Select Committee on Newspaper Stamps, H. C. 558 (1851), 17. There is a history, Simon Nowell-Smith, *The House of Cassell, 1848-1958* (London, 1958).

15. "Preface," *Quiver*, 1 (1861), n.p.

16. See Patricia Thomas Srebrnik, *Alexander Strahan: Victorian Publisher* (Ann Arbor, 1986).

17. "Projected Change in the Basis of the Periodical," *British and Foreign Evangelical Review*, 1 (1853), iii.

18. Ellegård, *Readership of the Periodical Press*, 15-16.

19. P. G. Scott, "Richard Cope Morgan, Religious Periodicals, and the Pontifex Factor," *VPN*, no. 16 (June 1972), 8. This article is valuable both for Morgan's periodicals and the subculture for which he published.

20. *Prospectus of a newspaper, designed for serious families, academies, etc.* (London, 1798). This was the *Weekly Register.*

21. "Prospectus," *Christian Reporter*, January 3, 1820, 1-2.

22. *General Baptist Magazine*, 1 (April 1798).

23. Thomas Williams, "The Editor to the Reader," *Philanthropic Gazette*, January 1, 1817, p. 1. On January 15, a department of "Philanthropic Intelligence" was added.

24. *Christian Cabinet*, August 2, 1855, p. 3.

25. Leading article, *London Christian Times*, October 14, 1863, p. 6.

26. "Exclusion of Papists from Parliament," *Protestant Magazine*, 1 (February 1, 1839), 1. See also the "Notice" and "Address" in the January 1 number, 1-2. Charlotte Elizabeth Tonna was editor, 1841-45.

27. G. I. T. Machin, *Politics and the Churches in Great Britain 1832 to 1868* (Oxford, 1977), 98.

28. The *Protestant Magazine* had opposed the previous smaller Maynooth grant as early as 1839.

29. "Preface" to vol. 1, *Bulwark*, v. The subtitle was *Reformation Journal*; the editor, 1851-72, was James Begg, a Free Kirk minister. See also E. R. Norman, *Anti-Catholicism in Victorian England* (London, 1968), 65-66.

30. There is a capsule history of the society and its organ in the January 1898 issue. See also Machin, *Politics and the Churches 1832 to 1868*, 254.

31. See G. I. T. Machin, *Politics and the Churches in Great Britain 1869 to 1921* (Oxford, 1987), 208, 234-35.

32. Peter Roger Mountjoy, "The Working-Class Press and Working-Class Conservativism," in George Boyce, James Curran, and Pauline Wingate, eds., *Newspaper History from the Seventeenth Century to the Present Day* (London, 1978), 271.

33. There is some confusion about the full list of RTS periodicals. The *Waterloo Directory* attempts to correct its confusion by giving a list in "Addenda," 1186-87, still not complete. The Society regularly listed its periodicals in advertisements in May's *British and Irish Press Guide.* It came to publish, among other things, at least six annuals, mostly almanacs. By the end of the century, only one-quarter of its pieces were tracts.

34. Sheila A. Egoff, *Children's Periodicals of the Nineteenth Century* (London, 1951), 11.

35. From an advertisement of another journal, cited in Mountjoy, "Working-Class Press," 274.

36. The *Weekly Visitor* (1851-54), edited by Robert Bickersteth, later bishop of Ripon, would appear to be a revival of the weekly version of this, but there is no evident connection.

37. "Address to our Readers," inside cover, *Sunday at Home* (December 1854). The journal is described as a "companion" to the *Leisure Hour.*

38. "Address to our Subscribers," inside cover, *Sunday at Home* (May 1854). There is a strikingly realistic sentence that suggests another audience for the journal: "Among our middle and educated classes there are many, especially young people, on whom the Lord's day unhappily rises rather as a day of weariness."

39. Listings of this periodical are confused, as is often the case with RTS journals, perhaps because they were not copyrighted. I have used the running titles of the early volumes. See also Mountjoy, "Working-Class Press," 277.

40. Egoff, *Children's Periodicals*, 24-25. There is a popular history: Jack Cox, *Take a Cold Tub, Sir! The Story of the Boy's Own Paper* (Guildford, 1982).

41. Both these journals stated only that they were published at "'The Leisure Hour' Office."

42. "Preface" to vol. 1, *Ragged School Union Magazine* (1849), iii.

43. *Ragged School Children's Magazine* (1850-51), then *Our Children's Magazine* (1852-68).

44. "Editorial Address," *Sunday School Times*, January 6, 1860, p. 4.

45. Continuing as *New Chronicle of Christian Education* (1928-).

46. "Editorial," *Night and Day*, 1 (January 1877), 2.

47. *Father William's Stories* (1866-67); then *Children's Treasury* (1868-81); finally *Our Darlings* (1881-).

48. William Tuckniss, "The Agencies at Present in Operation within the Metropolis for the Suppression of Vice and Crime," in Henry Mayhew, *London Labour and the London Poor* (1861-62 edition), ed. Victor Neuburg (Harmondsworth, 1985), 471-72.

CHAPTER 7

1. "Preface" to vol. 1, *Protestant Dissenter's Magazine* (1794), 3.

2. Ibid., 6.

3. "Prospectus of a Review of Books on a New Plan, adapted to general utility. To be published 1st January, 1805, and continued Monthly, Price One Shilling and Sixpence, the *Eclectic Review*" (n.p., n.d. [1804]).

4. "Preface," *Eclectic Review*, 1 (January 1805), iii.

5. Elie Halévy, *Victorian Years 1841-95* [History of the English People in the Nineteenth Century, IV] (New York, 1951), 389. See also the account by James E. Basker in Alvin Sullivan, ed., *British Literary Magazines* (Westport, CT, 1983), 2: 124-33.

6. One of the most inexplicable gaffes by a great historian is Halévy's remark (*Victorian Years*, 390) that Miall "drove Vaughan from the editorial chair of the

Eclectic Review and replaced him by Dr. Price." Vaughan never was editor, and Price already was. The error was pointed out by Norman Gash, *Reaction and Reconstruction in English Politics 1832-1852* (Oxford, 1965), 74 n. 2.

7. In a review of "Gilfillan's Literary Portraits," *Eclectic Review*, n.s. 27 (February 1850), 174-87, especially 184-85.

8. Cited in *The British Banner versus the Eclectic Review* (London, n.d.). The British Library dates this 1855, but it seems to include Linwood's reply of 1850.

9. There is a racy short account in Chadwick, *Victorian Church*, 1: 406, and a long and detailed treatment in Albert Peel, *These Hundred Years: A History of the Congregational Union of England and Wales* (London, 1931), 217-34. See also R. Tudur Jones, *Congregationalism in England*, 250-51. Campbell was supported (on grounds of Calvinist orthodoxy) by Alexander Haldane of the Anglican *Record* and by James Grant, editor of the *Morning Advertiser* (the organ of the Licensed Victuallers). See *The Controversy on Important Theological Questions; between the 'Eclectic Review'. . . on the one side, and Mr. James Grant, Editor of the 'Morning Advertiser,' on the other* (London, 1856), published by the *Morning Advertiser* and claiming seventy editions. The original review of *The Rivulet* was in the *Eclectic Review* for January 1856, 86-87; see also the "Editorial Postscripts" in the February and March issues.

10. Cited in Joseph Thompson, *Lancashire Independent College* (London, 1895), 96.

11. See the useful edition of Allon's correspondence, Albert Peel, ed., *Letters to a Victorian Editor* (London, 1929), 76, 105.

12. Baines to Allon, March 11, 1886, ibid., 25.

13. *Wellesley Index*, 4: 122.

14. Halévy, *Victorian Years*, 390. Ellegård, *Readership of the Periodical Press*, concurs: "the leading political organ of Dissent, giving considerably more space to politics than to religion and literature" (12). For Miall, see Chadwick, *Victorian Church*, 1: 151-52, and Arthur Miall, *Life of Edward Miall* (London, 1884).

15. See Machin, *Politics and the Churches 1832 to 1868*, 186.

16. *World*, May 4, 1827, p. 1; June 27, 1827, p. 3.

17. Leading article, *Christian Times*, August 12, 1848, p. 8.

18. "To our Subscribers," ibid., December 29, 1848, p. 1.

19. "A Word to our Readers," *Christian World*, April 9, 1857, p. 4.

20. Marianne Farningham [pseud. of Hearn], "Some Personal Reminiscences," *Christian World*, April 11, 1907, p. 25. This was the jubilee issue.

21. Editorial, *Christian World*, April 11, 1957, p. 1. This is a valuable centennial issue.

22. T. H. Darlow, *William Robertson Nicoll: His Life and Letters* (London, 1925), 67. There is a capsule history of the religious press on pp. 57-65.

23. Nicoll to Marcus Dods, August 7, 1886, in ibid., 70.

24. Chadwick, *Victorian Church*, 2: 426. See the evaluation of the religious census on pp. 233-34.

25. Nicoll to J. Macniven, November 9, 1886, in Darlow, *Robertson Nicoll*, 73.

26. See Stephen Koss, *Nonconformity in Modern British Politics* (Hamden, CT, 1975), 41.

27. "The Creed and the Hope of Progress," *British Weekly*, November 5, 1886, p. 1.

28. Publisher's notice, ibid., p. 16. There was a parallel Scottish edition.

29. See the jubilee number of the *British Weekly*, November 12, 1936.

30. This history is traced in "To the Members and Friends of the London Missionary Society," *Missionary Magazine and Chronicle*, 1 (June 1836), 1-2, and the "Preface" to vol. 1, iii.

31. Hugh Price Hughes, "An Appeal to the Free Churches," *Free Churchman*, 1 (October 1897), 1. Hughes' own newspaper was the *Methodist Times*.

CHAPTER 8

1. See J. F. Maclear, "The Idea of 'American Protestantism' and British Nonconformity, 1829-1840," *Journal of British Studies*, 21 (Fall 1981), 73. Nonconformists had a lively interest in their American counterpart denominations; Maclear mentions also the *Evangelical* and *Baptist Magazines*, the *Eclectic Review*, and the *Patriot*.

2. Peel, *These Hundred Years*, 129. See also 16, 18. Blackburn founded the *Congregational Year Book* in 1846.

3. See J. Nicoll Cooper, "Dissenters and National Journalism: *The Patriot* in the 1830s," *VPR*, 14 (Summer 1981), 58-65. See also "Address to the Public," *Patriot*, February 22, 1832, p. 4.

4. Peel, *These Hundred Years*, 129.

5. Quoted, ibid., 137.

6. "Dedication," *Christian Witness*, 1 (January 1844), viii.

7. "To the People of England," preface to the bound vol. 1 of the *Christian's Penny Magazine*.

8. "Sink rhetoric. . . . Commence with your leading thought, and avoid irrelevant digressions. . . . Your article at the first is four-fifths too long. . . . Begin by crossing out all explanatory sentences. Leave nothing but simple propositions." Campbell, "How to Write for Periodicals," *Christian Witness*, 1 (June 1844), 277.

9. For these controversies, see Peel, *These Hundred Years*, 171-72, 218-34. A separate body of trustees was set up for the magazines and the fund.

10. Campbell commented: "The expulsion of the Editor of the *Christian Witness* is the reward it is proposed to make to the Editor of the *British Banner* for the stand which he has made in that journal against the increase of German error." Peel, *These Hundred Years*, 232. The journalistic ethics of conflict of interest had not yet been considered.

11. Tudur Jones, *Congregationalism in England*, 234.

12. "Preface" to the bound vol. 1 of the *British Banner*, signed by Campbell.

13. Halévy, *Victorian Years*, 391.

14. "The British Banner: Reasons for Resignation," *British Banner*, December 12, 1856. Campbell also edited a penny weekly, the *British Ensign* (1859-64).

15. One should note two Welsh-language Congregationalist monthlies: *Y Dysgedydd* (1821-) and the more political *Y Diwigiwr* (1836-).

16. W. T. Whitley, *A History of British Baptists* (London, 1923), 273. (This is an excellent source generally for Baptist periodicals.) The opening number of the *Baptist Magazine* stated that "the work is not given to the *Public*, nor even to the *religious* Public; it is intended to be a Magazine for the use and benefit of the Baptists." It denied, however, that it was in opposition to the *Evangelical Magazine.* "Dialogue between an Editor and his Friend," *Baptist Magazine*, 1 (January 1809), 2. The opening date is often wrongly listed.

17. Chadwick, *Victorian Church*, 1: 415. However, the *Baptist Manual* (1845-59; then *Baptist Handbook*, 1860-) is an important denominational record. Billington, "Religious Press," 125, discusses some lesser Particular Baptist periodicals.

18. Ellegård, *Readership of the Periodical Press*, 12.

19. Spurgeon, "Our Aims and Intentions," *The Sword and the Trowel*, 1 (January 1865), 1.

20. See R. J. Helmstadter, "Spurgeon in Outcast London," in P. T. Phillips, ed., *The View from the Pulpit* (Toronto, 1978), 161-85.

21. There is an extensive survey in Herbert McLachlan, *The Unitarian Movement in the Religious Life of England* (London, 1934), 165-223. The splendid introductions to the *Prospective, National, Theological* and *Modern Reviews* in vol. 3 of the *Wellesley Index* form a nearly complete history of Unitarian higher journalism. The *Monthly Repository*, the exception, has a history of its own, Mineka, *Dissidence of Dissent.*

22. "Preface," *Monthly Repository*, 1 (January 1806), vi.

23. There is a frank avowal in "Junius Redivivus on the Conduct of the Monthly Repository," ibid., n.s. 6 (December 1832), 793-97. Mineka, *Dissidence of Dissent*, 249-51, traces the decline of the religious element. To serve the denomination, Fox started the *Unitarian Chronicle* (1832-33; then *Unitarian Magazine and Chronicle*, 1834-35).

24. "Editor's Address to the Reader," *Christian Reformer*, 1 (January 1815), 1-2.

25. *Christian Teacher*, n.s. 5 (October 1843), 443; cited in *Wellesley Index*, 3: 339.

26. "Prefatory Note" to vol. 1, *Prospective Review*, i-ii; cited in ibid., 3: 340-41. The *Wellesley Index* is the best source for the *Prospective Review.* There is also an account in Alvin Sullivan, ed., *British Literary Magazines*, 3: 322-25.

27. James Martineau, quoted in McLachlan, *Unitarian Movement*, 194. For Thom, who was executive editor, see R. K. Webb, "John Hamilton Thom: Intellect and Conscience in Liverpool," in Phillips, ed., *The View from the Pulpit*, 211-43.

28. *Wellesley Index*, 3: 342.

29. The Prospectus was separately published; quoted in *Wellesley Index*, 3: 139.

30. Greg's phrase; quoted in ibid., 3: 143.

31. Ibid., 3: 145. This introduction, *British Literary Magazines*, 3: 237-42, and McLachlan, *Unitarian Movement*, 194-97, are the only full treatments of the subject.

32. *Wellesley Index*, 3: 510.

33. R. A. Armstrong, "The Story of Nineteenth Century Reviewing," *Modern Review*, 1 (January 1880), 31, 30. This article (1-33) is a remarkable history of the higher journalism, especially the religious press. The *Wellesley Index*, 3: 94-99, has a full treatment of the *Modern Review*.

34. McLachlan, *Unitarian Movement*, 202-04. McLachlan also lists numerous other Unitarian magazines, many of them local. The denomination's periodicals were less London-based, more frankly provincial, than most.

35. See Hutton's delightful memoir in McLachlan, *Unitarian Movement*, 216-17.

36. Ibid., 217.

37. "The Time and the Work," *Unitarian Herald*, May 4, 1861, p. 1. The "respectful" hearing accorded to *Essays and Reviews* was cited as evidence that the time was right for liberal theology!

38. McLachlan, *Unitarian Movement*, 225. See also R. K. Webb, "Flying Missionaries: Unitarian Journalists in Victorian England," in J. M. W. Bean, ed., *The Political Culture of Modern Britain* (London, 1987).

39. There is an index: *Quaker Records*, ed. Joseph J. Green (London, 1894).

40. "Circular," *British Friend*, First Month, 31st, 1843, p. 1. Both this and the *Friend*, although in fact magazines, paid stamp tax as if they were newspapers.

41. Chadwick, *Victorian Church*, 1: 434.

42. Elizabeth Isichei, *Victorian Quakers* (London, 1970), 32. This superb denominational history has a bibliography of Quaker periodicals, publications, and sources.

43. W. C. Westlake, "Opening Remarks," *Friends' Examiner*, 1 (First Month, 1867), 1-11. See also "Editorial," ibid. (Fourth Month, 1867), 173-76.

CHAPTER 9

1. "To the Reader," preface to vol. 1, *Arminian Magazine* (January 1778), vi, dated November 1, 1777. See Samuel J. Rogal, "A Survey of Methodist Periodi-

cals Published in England, 1778-1900," *VPR*, 14 (Summer 1981), 66-69, with an inadequate list of periodicals.

2. John Blacket, "The Oldest Religious Periodical in the World," *Methodist Magazine*, 150 (January-March 1927), 56-57.

3. "Prospectus of the Third Series," *Wesleyan-Methodist Magazine*, 1 (January 1822), 1-6. Both of the new series were subheaded "being a continuation of the Arminian Magazine"; vol. 1 of the 3rd series was double-numbered vol. 45 "from the commencement." In 1811 a half-priced abridged edition was issued. See W. R. Ward, ed., *The Early Correspondence of Jabez Bunting 1820-1829* [Camden 4th ser., 11] (London, 1972), and *Early Victorian Methodism* (Oxford, 1976); also Billington, "Religious Periodical and Newspaper Press," 116.

4. *Missionary Notices*, 1 (December 1818), 292. The *Wesleyan Juvenile Offering* (1844-78) was the missionary magazine for children.

5. Ward, *Early Correspondence of Bunting*, 44.

6. "Prospectus," *Christian Advocate*, January 7, 1830, p. 1.

7. "Prospectus," *Watchman*, January 7, 1835, p. 1, and leading article, p. 4.

8. "The Anti-Wesleyan Movement," ibid., p. 7.

9. "And Now the Recorder Story," *Methodist Recorder*, April 6, 1961, p. 19. This was the centenary number of the *Methodist Recorder.*

10. W. J. Noble, "One Hundred Years of Editorship," ibid., p. 16.

11. "Our Address to Methodists," *Wesleyan Times*, January 15, 1849, p. 24. This was in the second number; the first had an address exalting the role of newspapers.

12. Further confusion is caused by a pirated American edition of *The Quarterly Review* under the title *London Quarterly Review.* A shelf check is needed at all libraries claiming either review.

13. Barbara J. Dunlap, "The London Quarterly and Holborn Review," *British Literary Magazines*, 3: 203-09. The *London Quarterly Review* is listed in the *Wellesley Index*, vol. 4, which was not available at the time of writing. The basic source is William Strawson, "The London Quarterly and Holborn Review, 1853-1968," *Church Quarterly*, 1 (July 1968), 40-52.

14. See the opening number, *Methodist*, January 1, 1874.

15. "The Methodist Times," ibid., December 24, 1884, p. 378. See also "The Methodist Times," ibid., December 17, 1884, p. 366. The subscriber list was transferred to the new journal.

16. "Our Raison d'Etre," *Methodist Times*, January 1, 1885, p. 1.

17. Ibid.

18. John Kent, "Hugh Price Hughes and the Nonconformist Conscience," in *Essays in Modern English Church History in Memory of Norman Sykes*, ed. G. V. Bennett and J. D. Walsh (London, 1966), 204.

19. Julia Stewart Werner, *The Primitive Methodist Connexion* (Madison, WI, 1984), especially 95. This is an excellent history of the early years.

20. Billington, "Religious Periodical and Newspaper Press," 117. Billington notes that the Primitives eventually owned their press and publishing business.

21. Werner, *Primitive Methodist Connexion*, 160-61.

22. Strawson, "London Quarterly and Holborn Review," 42-43.

23. This is from the preface to the 1852 volume, significantly an exhortation to increase the circulation. This is the first volume extant at the British Library, which also lacks two denominational children's magazines.

24. Controversies within the Association forced the resignation of the long-time editor, Robert Eckett, in 1854. See Eckett's "Editorial Statement, and Farewell," *Wesleyan Methodist Association Magazine* (December 1854), 555-60. The magazine was enlivened in 1855 by adding new sections.

25. This material is inaccessible to those who do not read Welsh. There are hints to *A Bibliography of the History of Wales*, 2nd ed. (Cardiff, 1962), and Kenneth O. Morgan, *Wales in British Politics 1868-1922*, 3rd ed. (Cardiff, 1980).

26. "The War Cry," *War Cry*, December 27, 1879, p. 1. Bibliographical citations of "1880" are incorrect.

27. [William Booth], "A Retrospect of the Work of the Army during the year 1880," ibid., December 30, 1880, p. 1. See also the jubilee number, December 28, 1929.

28. No copy of this well-attested journal is listed either in the *British Union Catalogue of Periodicals* or the *Union List of Serials*, perhaps because the religious libraries that hold it were not queried. I am indebted for information to A. Lawrence Marshburn, director of the Biola Library (whose Brethren holdings have been moved to Emmaus Bible College, Dubuque, Iowa), and to my student Shih-An Deng.

29. Arnold Ehlert, *Brethren Writers* (Grand Rapids, MI, 1969), contains a checklist of Brethren periodicals.

30. See the announcement in the *Ambassador*, September 1865. The *Ambassador* claimed (October 1865, back cover) to print 1,000 copies, but it did not sell more than 800. Roberts has an autobiography and a biography. For another American denomination represented by British periodicals, see Louis Billington, "The Churches of Christ in Britain: A study in nineteenth-century sectarianism," *Journal of Religious History*, 8 (1974), 21-48.

CHAPTER 10

1. See "Notes to Correspondents," *Edinburgh Christian Instructor*, n.s. 1 (September 1832), 656-60.

2. "Abuses in the Church," ibid. (December 1832), 805.

3. A bimonthly intended for paid articles supplied by the clergy: "Advertisement" to vol. 1, *Presbyterian Review* (July 1831), 1-2.

4. Published in Glasgow. See "Importance of the Subject," *Church of Scotland Magazine*, 1 (March 1834), 1-4.

5. There is a mystery here. All recorded files begin with July 1839; but the lead article in this number, p. 1, calls this a "new series" of the journal; the "Preface" to the bound vol. 1, p. v, refers to a first series; and the *Church of Scotland Magazine*, 5 (June 1838), 223, actually reviews the first number, dated May, 1838, with a "Postscript" (September 1838), 344, noting four other issues. Presumably, there was an earlier series, now lost or misfiled.

6. W. M. Mackenzie, *Hugh Miller: A Critical Study* (London, 1905), 222-23.

7. "To our Readers," *Witness*, December 29, 1841, p. 2. Miller noted one earlier religious newspaper, the *Scottish Guardian* (1832-61).

8. See A. H. Charteris, "Introductory Note," *Life and Work*, 1 (January 1879), 1, and "Editorial Note," ibid. (December 1879), 177.

9. "Remarks," *Home and Foreign Missionary Record for the Free Church of Scotland*, 1 (June 1843), 1.

10. "To Advertisers. Circulation of the 'Record,'" 1 (May 1844), 133.

11. Mackenzie, *Hugh Miller*, 225; see also 228.

12. Ibid., 238-39.

13. It would be unknown except that W. G. Blaikie was editor, 1849-53. See William Gordon Blaikie, *An Autobiography*, ed. Norman L. Walker (London, 1901), 124-28.

14. "Prospectus," *North British Review* (1844), quoted in Mark A. Weinstein's article in Sullivan, *British Literary Magazines*, 3: 275-81, which is ampler than the introduction in *Wellesley Index*, 1: 663-66.

15. Joanne Shattock, "Problems of Parentage: The *North British Review* and the Free Church of Scotland," in Shattock and Michael Wolff, eds., *The Victorian Periodical Press: Samplings and Soundings* (Leicester, 1982), 146. Besides this article (pp. 145-66), Shattock also published "Spreading It Thinly: Some Victorian Reviewers at Work," *VPN*, 9 (1976), 84-87, and "Editorial Policy and the Quarterlies: The Case of the *North British Review*," ibid., 10 (1977), 130-39.

16. In 1854 Fraser arranged for simultaneous publication in America. Shattock, "Problems of Parentage," 153.

17. Blaikie, *Autobiography*, 139.

18. Shattock, "Problems of Parentage," 163. These writers drew praise from the London *Times*, December 31, 1864, cited in *British Literary Magazines*, 3: 279.

19. Their prospectus (evidently by Acton) was "Note to the 100th Number of THE NORTH BRITISH REVIEW," *North British Review*, 50 (July 1869), 602-05.

20. The *Covenanter* is not listed in the *Waterloo Directory* or its sources. The author was allowed to make a shelf check of the religious journals at Edinburgh New College Library, which has been helpful generally in this chapter. One should

also note the *Reformed Presbyterian Witness* (1864-), founded by a secession from the Reformed Presbytery that still exists.

21. "Address to the Public" bound in vol. 1, *Christian Magazine* (1797), i-iii.

22. MS. note bound in front of the British Library copy of ibid. This is a marked file.

23. From January to May 1847 it was called the *United Secession and Relief Magazine*, the name of the united group not having been determined. See the notice in the inside front cover of the *Missionary Record of the United Secession Church* (December 1846). The proper title commences in June 1847.

24. "Prospectus of a New Religious Periodical," bound in vol. 1 of the *Voluntary Church Magazine* (1833); also "To Our Readers," ibid. (March 1833), 1-9.

25. This, and indeed nearly everything in this paragraph, is based on A. Albert Campbell, *Irish Presbyterian Magazines, Past and Present. A Bibliography* (Belfast, 1919). Many of these periodicals are missing from the libraries whose holdings are listed in the bibliographies conflated in the *Waterloo Directory* (Phase I), and the bibliographic listings are often wanting or erroneous. This problem is largely rectified by John S. North, *The Waterloo Directory of Irish Newspapers and Periodicals, 1800-1900* (Waterloo, Ont., 1986). Similar problems with Scottish periodicals may be resolved by North's *Waterloo Directory of Scottish Newspapers and Periodicals, 1800-1900*, which was published too late to be consulted.

26. Campbell, *Irish Presbyterian Magazines*, 6.

27. Stephen J. M. Brown, *The Press in Ireland* (Dublin, 1937; reprint New York, 1971), 97.

28. *Weekly Review*, April 26, 1862, p. 1. An article in this issue on the *Essays and Reviews* controversy, "The Faith: Its Aids and its Assailants," is at once orthodox and sensitive, recognizing the issue to be "the ethics of the atonement."

29. Balleine, *Evangelical Party*, 208. Alexander Haldane of the *Record* was a strenuous opponent of Irving. See *Record*, January 11, 1830, to which "Religious Periodicals," *Morning Watch*, 2 (December 1830), is a scathing response.

CHAPTER 11

1. J. G. Snead-Cox, *The Life of Cardinal Vaughan*, 2 vols. (London, 1910), 1: 181.

2. John R. Fletcher, "Early Catholic Periodicals in England," *Dublin Review*, 198 (April 1936), 284-310, is the best source. It is based on F. C. H[usenbeth], "Catholic Periodicals," *Notes & Queries*, 3rd s. 2 (January 5, 1867), 2-4, (January 12, 1867), 29-31, and Joseph Gillow, *A Literary and Biographical History, or Bibliographical Dictionary of the English Catholics*, 5 vols. (London, 1855-1902). Gillow also published a series of articles and letters on "Early Catholic Periodicals" in the *Tablet* between January 22 and March 5, 1881.

3. Joseph P. Chinnici, *The English Catholic Enlightenment* (Shepherdstown, WV, 1980), 41. The *Orthodox Journal* was for Milner "a magazine devoted almost exclusively to his own tirades." Joan Connell, *The Roman Catholic Church in England 1780-1850* (Philadelphia, 1984), 77.

4. For Andrews's journals, see Fletcher, "Early Catholic Periodicals," 286-90. Andrews's children carried on the *London and Dublin Orthodox Journal.*

5. Fletcher, "Early Catholic Periodicals," 293-94, citing contradictory accounts by Husenbeth and Gillow.

6. Ibid., 297-98, again citing contradictory evidence for the resignation of the editor, Matthew P. Hayes.

7. See *Wellesley Index*, 2: 19.

8. This had been founded by a convert, James Smith, whom Dolman kept as editor through 1842. Fletcher, "Early Catholic Periodicals," 295-96.

9. This incorporated the *Weekly and Monthly Orthodox*, founded earlier in 1849 by Andrews's daughter Mary. Ibid., 303. The confusing relationships among these periodicals require a genealogical chart: ibid., 305.

10. Ibid., 291.

11. Ibid., 291-92, relying heavily upon Gillow.

12. Lingard, feeling that he had outlived his age, became disgusted with the magazine: Chinnici, *English Catholic Enlightenment*, 136-48. Fletcher, "Early Catholic Periodicals," 295, refers to "the secession of its clerical proprietors."

13. O'Connell contributed financially, especially in the crisis of the first year, but exercised no control. After his death in 1847, Wiseman acted as sole proprietor. Quin was also a proprietor but was forced out after he quit the editorship. See Josef L. Altholz, "Daniel O'Connell and the *Dublin Review*," *Catholic Historical Review*, 74 (January 1988), 1-12.

14. See *Wellesley Index*, 2: 11-12.

15. John Henry Newman, *Apologia pro vita sua*, ed. Martin J. Svaglic (Oxford, 1967), 109-11. The article was "Tracts for the Times (Part III)," *Dublin Review*, 7 (August 1839), 139-80. Wiseman had hoped the *Dublin* would affect the Tractarians.

16. *Wellesley Index*, 2: 12-13, is the best account of this arrangement.

17. See Josef L. Altholz, *The Liberal Catholic Movement in England* (London, 1962), 34-39, 72-73, 182-84.

18. See Josef L. Altholz, "The Redaction of Catholic Periodicals," in Joel H. Wiener, ed., *Innovators and Preachers: The Role of the Editor in Victorian England* (Westport, CT, 1985), 157-58n.

19. Quoted by Wilfrid Ward, *William George Ward and the Catholic Revival* (London, 1912), 223. Manning and a theological censor kept Ward narrow.

20. *Wellesley Index*, 2: 19. See also J. J. Dwyer, "The Catholic Press, 1850-1950," in *The English Catholics 1850-1950*, ed. G. A. Beck (London, 1950), 475-514, and the *Dublin*'s sixtieth and hundredth anniversary issues, April, 1896 and April, 1936.

21. Fletcher, "Early Catholic Periodicals," 299.

22. Lucas's language was often immoderate, for example, "a large portion of Sir Robert Peel's followers are not sane." Dwyer, "The Catholic Press," 483.

23. For this conflict, see Josef L. Altholz, "The *Tablet*, the *True Tablet*, and Nothing but the *Tablet*," *VPN*, 9 (June 1976), 68-72.

24. Lucas thought that the *Rambler* had been started against him in 1848: Altholz, *Liberal Catholic Movement*, 13.

25. Vaughan's control of the *Tablet* is summarized by Edward Norman, *The English Catholic Church in the Nineteenth Century* (Oxford, 1984), 360-61. The later history of the *Tablet* is told in Dwyer, "Catholic Press," 484-89.

26. Altholz, *Liberal Catholic Movement*, is the most detailed history of the *Rambler* and its successor; see Chapter 1 for the early phase. See also *Wellesley Index*, 2: 732-41.

27. The right of laymen to discuss theology was a major concern of Simpson, but his own major contributions were in Elizabethan history and literature. See Damian McElrath, *Richard Simpson 1820-1876* (Louvain, 1972).

28. [Nicholas Wiseman], "The Present Catholic Dangers," *Dublin Review*, 41 (December 1856), 441-70. The *Rambler*'s phrase was in a review of its American counterpart, *Brownson's Quarterly Review*, in *Rambler*, 2nd s. 6 (October 1856), 315-16.

29. See Altholz, *Liberal Catholic Movement*, and Acton's correspondence with his mentor, *Ignaz von Döllinger / Lord Acton: Briefwechsel 1850-1890*, ed. Victor Conzemius, Band I (München, 1963).

30. For a remark about Augustine, see Acton's review of Chéruel, *Rambler*, 2nd s. 10 (August 1858), 135. The education articles were written by Scott Nasmyth Stokes, a Catholic inspector of schools.

31. Under Simpson's influence the *Rambler* ceased to publish serialized novels. With Acton's entry, the articles became heavier, and more short reviews were published.

32. *Rambler*, 3rd s. 1 (July 1859), 198-230. This was published as "communicated," a device Newman borrowed from the *British Critic* to allow the publication of articles for which the editor assumed no responsibility. See Altholz, *Liberal Catholic Movement*, 91-112, and Newman, *Letters and Diaries*, vol. 19.

33. Wetherell was Newman's choice. He thought he was not subeditor but coeditor. See Altholz, "Redaction of Catholic Periodicals," 151.

34. See *The Correspondence of Lord Acton and Richard Simpson*, ed. Josef L. Altholz, Damian McElrath, and James C. Holland, 3 vols. (Cambridge, 1971-75), 2: 163-77.

35. Among the contributors were Germans such as the church historian Döllinger and the economist Wilhelm Roscher, a French Jewish economist, Maurice Block, as well as English Protestants such as Robert Lowe, MP, and a young High Churchman, D. C. Lathbury, who actually joined the staff in April, 1863.

36. Acton's phrase; cited in *The Life-Work of Sir Peter le Page Renouf*, ed. W. H. Rylands, G. Maspero, and E. Naville, 4 vols. (Paris, 1902-07), 4: lviii. Renouf, an Egyptologist and Assyriologist, became subeditor of the review in 1863.

37. Acton, "Conflicts with Rome," *The History of Freedom and Other Essays*, ed. J. N. Figgis and R. V. Laurence (London, 1907), 489; orig. *Home and Foreign Review*, 4 (April 1864), 667-90. Acton's colleagues concurred.

38. Matthew Arnold, "The Function of Criticism at the Present Time" (1865); reprinted in *Essays in Criticism* (London, 1928), 20.

39. Finances were supplied by Sir Rowland Blennerhasset, a former pupil of Döllinger, later an Irish MP. The Anglican D. C. Lathbury was subeditor. The *Chronicle*'s political character was stated by Wetherell to Gladstone, February 4, 1868, British Library Add. MS. 44414 ff. 73-76. See also Guy Ryan, "The Acton Circle and the 'Chronicle'," *VPN*, 7 (June 1974), 10-24.

40. See *Wellesley Index*, 1: 664.

41. Mary Griset Holland, *The British Catholic Press and the Educational Controversy, 1847-1863* (New York, 1987), 114-15. This work discusses other Catholic journals during its period.

42. The full title was the *Weekly Register and Catholic Standard.*

43. Fletcher, "Early Catholic Periodicals," 304.

44. See *Acton-Simpson Correspondence*, 2: 73, 153, 159, 189. See also David Newsome, *The Parting of Friends* (London, 1966), 405.

45. The *Weekly Register* was put up for sale in 1863, but Professor James C. Holland informs me that the first sign of a transfer was in the issue of April 2, 1864.

46. Dwyer, "Catholic Press," 505.

47. Ibid. Other contributors included Wilfrid Scawen Blunt, Coventry Patmore, and Lionel Johnson. Hilaire Belloc first published in *Merry England.* Lord Ripon and Charles (later Chief Justice) Russell were sleeping partners.

48. The Modernists had no organ of their own. See David G. Schultenover, *George Tyrrell: In Search of Catholicism* (Shepherdstown, WV, 1981), 152, 382, 385. Dell also edited the short-lived *New Era* (1899-1900).

49. Cited in Fletcher, "Early Catholic Periodicals," 305.

50. Ibid., 305-06, and Dwyer, "Catholic Press," 503-04.

51. Dwyer, "Catholic Press," 506-07. See also the centenary number of the *Universe*, December 8, 1960.

52. See Josef L. Altholz, "*The Month*, 1864-1900," *VPR*, 14 (Summer 1981), 70-72.

53. Schultenover, *George Tyrrell*, 470.

54. An example of this is given by Lawrence F. Barmann, *Baron Friedrich von Hügel and the Modernist Crisis in England* (Cambridge, 1972), 97 n. 2.

55. Dwyer, "Catholic Press," 506-07, and Fletcher, "Early Catholic Periodicals," 307-08.

56. Dwyer, "Catholic Press," 508-09, and Fletcher, "Early Catholic Periodicals," 309-10.

57. Chadwick, *Victorian Church*, 2: 409, observes that the *Downside Review* and the *Month* "were marked by a humane breadth and depth derived partly from the cherishing of the recusant past and partly from the consciousness of a European inheritance."

58. Brown, *Press in Ireland*, 263.

59. Information kindly supplied by Professor Emmet Larkin. On the *Pilot*, see *The Correspondence of Daniel O'Connell*, ed. Maurice O'Connell, 8 vols. (Dublin, 1972-80), 7: 10.

60. Emmet Larkin, *The Roman Catholic Church in Ireland and the Fall of Parnell, 1888-1891* (Chapel Hill, NC, 1979), 238. See Hugh Oram, *The Newspaper Book* (Dublin, 1983), 87-88, for a similar case in Belfast.

61. Brown, *Press in Ireland*, 32, giving the dates as 1857-66. The chief editor of the *Catholic Telegraph* was William Bernard MacCabe.

62. Ibid., 78-80.

63. Ibid. Brown lists some other Catholic journals on p. 84.

64. On an interim basis Newman edited the *Catholic University Gazette* (1854-56). It published his lectures on *The Idea of a University*.

65. Newman, *Letters and Diaries*, 17: 547.

66. See the Introduction to *Atlantis* in *Wellesley Index*, 3: 53-58. Newman withdrew as editor when he resigned as rector in 1861; Sullivan and Renouf carried on through 1863. The 1870 number was edited by the rector, Bartholomew Woodlock.

67. Brown, *Press in Ireland*, 69.

68. A history of the *Lyceum*, with attributions, is in *A Page of Irish History: Story of University College, Dublin, 1883-1909* (Dublin, 1930), 289-332.

69. Brown, *Press in Ireland*, 70-72.

70. Earlier styled *Catholic Ireland* and the *Irish Monthly Magazine* (1873).

71. See Brown, *Press in Ireland*, 72-75.

72. Information supplied by Professor Larkin. Both Moran and Conroy rose in the hierarchy.

73. See Brown, *Press in Ireland*, 80-81.

74. One was the *Irish Catholic Directory*, from 1835. The other appeared as the *Complete Catholic Directory, Almanac and Registry*, 1837-45; *Battersby's Registry for the Catholic World*, 1846-57; *Battersby's Catholic Directory*, 1858-64; simply *Catholic Directory* from 1865.

CHAPTER 12

1. "Prospectus," *Intellectual Repository for the New Church*, 1 (January-April 1812), 3-4.

2. Chadwick, *Victorian Church*, 1: 439. Pp. 436-39 are a capsule history. See also "Prospectus," *Latter-Day Saints Millennial Star*, 1 (May 1840), 5-6.

3. The history of the Jewish press is chronicled in the *Jewish Chronicle*'s centenary volume: *The Jewish Chronicle 1841-1941: A Century of Newspaper History* (London, 1949). Although the volume is anonymous, the publishers acknowledge that almost all of the material was prepared by Cecil Roth. It is a detailed history of the Jewish press in general. This section is based upon it unless another source is cited.

4. Leading article on the refounding of the *Jewish Chronicle*, October 18, 1844, p. 1.

5. Vallentine had withdrawn in 1846.

6. The *Jewish Chronicle* so styled itself in its advertisement in *Sell's Dictionary of the World's Press* (London, 1890), 1212.

7. Ibid., 1214.

8. There was a fourth newspaper in 1889-91, the somewhat scurrilous *Jewish Society*.

9. "Introductory," *Jewish Quarterly Review*, 1 (October 1888), 1-2.

10. See Leonard Prager, "A Bibliography of Yiddish Periodicals in Great Britain (1867-1967)," *Studies in Bibliography and Booklore*, 9 (Spring 1969), 3-32.

11. H. J. Hanham, ed., *Bibliography of British History 1851-1914* (Oxford, 1976), 462.

12. [W. T. Stead], "Seeking Counsel of the Wise," *Borderland*, 1 (July 1893), 7.

13. He briefly succeeded Beesley as editor. See Martha S. Vogeler, "Frederic Harrison and the Higher Journalism: A Review," *VPR*, 17 (Spring-Summer 1984), 61-62.

14. The best account is in Henry Pelling, *The Origins of the Labour Party 1880-1900*, 2nd ed. (Oxford, 1965), 132-44.

15. John Trevor, "A Statement," *Labour Church Record* (January 1901), 5. There is life after editorship.

16. See the listings in R. Harrison, G. B. Woolven, and R. Duncan, *The Warwick Guide to Labour Periodicals: A Check List* (Hassocks, 1977).

CHAPTER 13

1. A useful survey of the subtle distinctions within freethought is Shirley A. Mullen, *Organized Freethought: The Religion of Unbelief in Victorian England* (Westport, CT, 1987).

2. Patricia Hollis, *The Pauper Press: A Study in Working-class Radicalism of the 1830s* (London, 1970), 136.

3. Ibid., 137. Papers "containing only matters of devotion, piety, or charity" were exempted: Altick, *English Common Reader*, 328. Did this cover denominational news?

4. Unstamped religious fortnightly and weekly magazines are listed among the "unstamped" journals in Hollis, *Pauper Press*, and in Joel H. Wiener, *A Descriptive Finding List of Unstamped British Periodicals 1830-1836* (London, 1970). That religious magazines were sincere in denying that they were newspapers is attested by the fact that professed religious newspapers invariably sought to pay the tax. The Stamp Office, though it did not prosecute, maintained that all were liable. See the discussion before the Select Committee on Newspaper Stamps, *Parliamentary Papers* 1851 (558) vol. 17.

5. See Joel H. Wiener, *The War of the Unstamped: The Movement to Repeal the British Newspaper Tax, 1830-1836* (Ithaca, NY, 1969), and Hollis, *Pauper Press.*

6. The most recent study is Joel H. Wiener, *Radicalism and Freethought in Nineteenth-Century Britain: The Life of Richard Carlile* (Westport, CT, 1983).

7. Wiener, *Finding List*, paraphrased in *Waterloo Directory*, 412.

8. Ibid., 210.

9. Ibid., 224. The *Waterloo Directory* attributes this prosecution to "failure to pay church rates," but churchwardens prosecuted for this, not the Stamp Office, which was concerned with failure to pay stamp tax. The change to a monthly was designed to evade the definition of a newspaper. Wiener's *Finding List* includes more such periodicals than can be named here.

10. Chadwick, *Victorian Church*, 1: 487-88.

11. Advertisement, *Reasoner*, August 26, 1826, p. 208. The *Reasoner* claimed to revive both the *Movement* and the *New Moral World.*

12. Charles William F. Goss, *A Descriptive Bibliography of the Writings of George Jacob Holyoake with a brief sketch of his life* (London, 1908), 68.

13. Ibid., 68-71. Goss provides an accurate listing of Holyoake's periodicals.

14. Quoted in ibid., 71.

15. "Preface" to vol. 4 (1857-58) of the *Investigator*, a bitter attack on Holyoake. For continuing financial problems, see "Address to the Friends of Freethought," ibid. (February 1858), 139-40. Mullen, *Organized Freethought*, has much to say about the split of the freethinkers.

16. "Our Policy," *Investigator*, 5 (November 1, 1858), 124-25.

17. Hanham, *Bibliography of British History*, 457. For the editorial history, see Stephen Coltham, "English Working-Class Newspapers in 1867," *Victorian Studies*, 13 (December 1969), 165-66.

18. Owen Chadwick, *The Secularization of the European Mind in the Nineteenth Century* (Cambridge, 1975), 88-93.

19. Editorial, "Concerning Magazines in General and This One in Particular," *Free Review*, 1 (October 1, 1893), 3, 4. Editorial responsibility was disclaimed.

20. J. M. Robertson, *History of Freethought in the Nineteenth Century*, cited in A. Gowans Whyte, *The Story of the R.P.A. 1899-1949* (London, 1949), 13.

21. But Watts was opposed to "dogmatic Atheism" as well as religion. "Introduction," *Agnostic Annual*, 1 (1884), 3-4.

22. Huxley's remarks on this are worth noting: "Some twenty years ago, or thereabouts, I invented the word 'Agnostic' to denote people, who, like myself, confess themselves to be hopelessly ignorant concerning a variety of matters, about which metaphysicians and theologians, both orthodox and heterodox, dogmatise with the utmost confidence; and it has been a source of some amusement to me to watch the general acceptance of the term and its correlate, 'Agnosticism' (I think the *Spectator* first adopted and popularised both)." Ibid., 5.

23. Whyte, *R.P.A.*, 21, noting in both periodicals "the absence of the militant, aggressive quality."

24. Along with lists of publications, there were correspondence and reviews. The British Library has only no. 23 (September 15, 1887), which lists the following "Liberal Newspapers and Magazines" (p. 3): *Secular Thought*, ed. Watts, weekly [not listed elsewhere]; *Secular Review*, ed. "Saladin" [W. Stewart Ross], weekly; *National Reformer*, ed. Bradlaugh and Annie Besant, weekly; *Progress*, ed. G. W. Foote, monthly [Darwinian and freethought]; *Our Corner*, ed. Annie Besant, monthly; *Knowledge*, ed. Richard A. Proctor, monthly [Darwinian]; *Democrat*, monthly [labour]; *Church Reformer*, ed. Stewart Headlam, monthly. The latter seems odd in this context; but the 1884 *Agnostic Annual* had accepted an advertisement for the *Christian Socialist.*

CHAPTER 14

1. Balleine, *History of the Evangelical Party*, 264-65. The various societies and their periodicals can be found in the *Waterloo Directory.*

2. "Address to Anti-Slavery Associations," *Anti-Slavery Monthly Reporter*, 1 (June 1825), 1. The original *Reporter* was published by the London society.

3. "Anti-Slavery an English Question," *Anti-Slavery Advocate* (November 1859), 9.

4. Cited in Isichei, *Victorian Quakers*, 220.

5. "Remarks on the Objects of the '*Herald*'," *Herald of Peace*, 1 (February 1819), 33.

6. Ibid., 34.

7. Isichei, *Victorian Quakers*, 224.

8. Four periodicals, one of them a *Temperance Penny Magazine* (1836-48), are noticed in Brian Harrison, "'A World of Which We Had No Conception.' Liberalism and the English Temperance Press: 1830-1872" (hereafter cited as "A World"), *Victorian Studies*, 13 (December 1969), 132-35. This article is fundamental to the history of the temperance press.

9. Ibid., 133, 135-36. The place of publication varied: Preston in 1834, Leeds in 1838 (absorbing the *Leeds Temperance Herald*), Douglas on the Isle of Man (for cheaper postage throughout the United Kingdom), 1839-42, Bolton in 1850. The *National Temperance Advocate*, January 15, 1842, p. 1, refers to the

gratuitous distribution of 4,000 copies to doctors and ministers and cities six other temperance monthlies (three for children).

10. Harrison, "A World," 133, 136, 139-40. There was general news on the front page; the rest was temperance news.

11. Ibid., 137-39; A. E. Dingle, *The Campaign for Prohibition in Victorian England* (London, 1980), 211-13.

12. In normal times, circulation averaged 15,000 copies, perhaps 10,000 being gratuitous: Dingle, *Campaign*, 213. Harrison, "A World," stresses the substantial losses; but the *Alliance* accepted these losses, largely because of free copies for subscribers, and eventually overcame them by advertisements. For the temperance press as a paradigm of pressure-group journalism, see Brian Harrison, "Press and Pressure Group in Modern Britain," in Joanne Shattock and Michael Wolff, eds., *The Victorian Periodical Press: Samplings and Soundings* (Leicester, 1982), 261-95.

13. Harrison, "A World," 156.

14. Ibid., 141. There is a full treatment in Gerald Wayne Olsen, "The *Church of England Temperance Magazine*, 1862-1873," *VPN*, 11 (June 1978), 38-49.

15. Harrison, "A World," 140.

16. Ibid., 148-49.

17. Ibid., 149-50, for the *Temperance Star*. The *National Temperance Mirror* purported to be published by the "National Temperance Publication Depot."

18. "To the Boys and Girls of All Nations," *Band of Hope Review*, 1 (January 1851), 1. The first volume was dedicated to Samuel Gurney and bore a testimonial from Lord Shaftesbury on its cover.

19. Harrison, "A World," 145.

20. Cited in "Anglo-Israelism," *Church Quarterly Review*, 10 (July 1880), 318-39, a review of the British Israel periodicals at that time.

CHAPTER 15

1. The title of Brian Heeney's study of the profession (Hamden, CT, 1976).

2. "Introductory Article," *Journal of Sacred Literature*, 1 (January 1848), 7.

3. "Introductory Article. On the Domain and Principles of this Journal," ibid., 14 (October 1861), 3. This was a transitional article between Burgess and Cowper, with an apologia for Kitto and a declaration of belief in the divine inspiration of Scripture.

4. Ellegård, "Readership of the Periodical Press," 16.

5. "Projected Change in the Basis of the Periodical," prefatory note to vol. 1, *British and Foreign Evangelical Review*, iii.

6. "Preface" to vol. 1, *Expositor* (1875), v, vii.

7. Darlow, *William Robertson Nicoll*, 45.

8. Signed articles not only enforced the individual responsibility of authors but also prevented any attempt by the editor "to constrain them to uniformity whether of conception or of utterance." "Preface," vii.

9. Samuel Cox to Henry Allon, August 30, 1884, in Albert Peel, *Letters to a Victorian Editor* (London, 1929), 292-93. William Robertson Smith had been dismissed from his professorship for heretical criticism by the Scottish Free Kirk. The "larger hope" probably referred to the possibility of eventual salvation for the damned.

10. Owen Chadwick notes that this "intelligent nonconformist journal" by 1887 "allowed a fairly free discussion of the difficulty" of biblical criticism. Chadwick, *Victorian Church*, 2: 98.

11. See the jubilee number (October 1939) of the *Expository Times.*

12. H.B.S., "Introductory Statement," *Journal of Theological Studies*, 1 (October, 1899), 1.

13. Chadwick, *Victorian Church*, 2: 452.

14. Inside front cover, *Homilist*, 1 (June 1852).

15. Preface to vol. 2 (1853), iii.

16. Tudur Jones, *Congregationalism in England*, 305n.

17. The inside front cover of the *Homiletic Quarterly* for October, 1877, quotes a "blurb" from the *Liverpool Mercury*: "It has evidently been suggested by '*The Homilist*,' of Dr. Thomas, of Stockwell, and '*The Clergyman's Magazine*,' recently introduced for the benefit of incumbents in the Church of England."

18. Darlow, *Robertson Nicoll*, 45.

19. I am indebted to Leanne Langley of the University of Notre Dame London Program for this information. See Imogen Fellinger's article on "Periodicals" in *The New Grove Dictionary of Music and Musicians*, ed. Stanley Sadie (London, 1980).

20. See Altholz, "First Religious Magazines," 223.

21. Richard D. Altick, *The English Common Reader* (Chicago, 1957), 76.

22. Numerous references in vols. 4-5 of Newman, *Letters and Diaries*, beginning with 4: 178.

23. Patrick Scott, "The Business of Belief: The Emergence of 'Religious' Publishing," in Derek Baker, ed., *Studies in Church History*, 10 (Oxford, 1973), 217-18. Scott's general theme is the separation of religious from general publishing (books as well as periodicals).

24. Peter Roger Mountjoy, "The Working-Class Press and Working-Class Conservatism," in G. Boyce, J. Curran and P. Wingate, eds., *Newspaper History from the Seventeenth Century to the Present Day* (London, 1978), 273.

25. See the comments on tracts, which apply also to periodicals, in R. K. Webb, *The British Working Class Reader* (London, 1955), 27-28, especially his suggestion as to the uses to which such things, "being paper," might have been put.

26. This section is largely based on E. M. Palmegiano, "Women and British Periodicals 1832-1867: A Bibliography," *VPN*, 9 (March 1976), especially 4-5, a pioneering effort in this field.

27. "To Our Readers," *Quiver*, 1 (September 21, 1861), 30.

28. Altick, *English Common Reader*, 125. Even Macleod had limits to his broadmindedness: he turned down Trollope's *Rachel Ray*.

29. Ibid., 361.

30. At three- to sixpence, this was not for the poor. Circulation reached 12,250 in 1827 and sank to 3,500 in 1855. Louis Billington, "The Religious Periodical and Newspaper Press, 1770-1870," in Michael Harris and Alan Lee, eds., *The Press in English Society from the Seventeenth to Nineteenth Centuries* (London, 1986), 234 n. 53.

31. Sheila A. Egoff, *Children's Periodicals of the 19th Century: A Survey and Bibliography* (London, 1951), 11-12. This is the fundamental work on the subject, though it may be supplemented by Diana Dixon's essay on "Children and the Press, 1866-1914" in *The Press in English Society*.

32. "To Our Young Readers," *Wesleyan Juvenile Offering*, 1 (January 1844), 1.

33. Egoff, *Children's Periodicals*, 20-21.

CHAPTER 16

1. See Walter L. Arnstein, *Protestant versus Catholic in Mid-Victorian England* (Columbia, MO, 1982).

2. Advertisement for the *True Briton* in *Englishwoman's Magazine* (April 1851), 260, cited in Mountjoy, "Working-Class Press and Working-Class Conservatism," 274.

3. One thinks of Newman's "first real hit from Romanism" in the *Dublin Review*. Edmund Bishop, the liturgical historian, had his intellectual difficulties removed by the *Home and Foreign Review* and converted; see Nigel Abercrombie, *The Life and Work of Edmund Bishop* (London, 1959). One must search a vast literature to find a few such cases.

4. See Owen Chadwick, *Victorian Church*, 2: 232-33, and generally the chapter on "The Town Church," for a moderate view. See also K. S. Inglis, *Churches and the Working Class in Victorian England* (London, 1963).

5. Other examples are the *Juvenile Missionary Magazine* (1844-87), then *Juvenile* (1888-94), then *News from Afar* (1895-); *Wesleyan Juvenile Offering* (1844-78), then *At Home and Abroad* (1879-); *Juvenile Instructor and Companion* (1850-93), then *Golden Link Between Church and Home* (1894-98), then *Young People* (1899-1907). The growing appreciation of the uniqueness of childhood was, of course, a factor.

6. A similar conclusion is reached by Billington, "Religious Periodical and Newspaper Press," 131-32.

Selected Bibliography

BOOKS

Altick, Richard D. *The English Common Reader.* Chicago, 1957.

Balleine, G. R. *A History of the Evangelical Party in the Church of England.* London, 1908; new ed., 1951.

A Bibliography of the History of Wales. 2nd ed. Cardiff, 1962.

Brown, Lucy M., and Ian R. Christie. *Bibliography of British History, 1789-1851.* Oxford, 1977.

Brown, Stephen J. M. *The Press in Ireland.* Dublin, 1937; repr. New York, 1971.

Campbell, A. Albert. *Irish Presbyterian Magazines, Past and Present: A Bibliography.* Belfast, 1919.

Chadwick, Owen. *The Victorian Church.* 2 vols. London, 1966, 1970.

Darlow, T. H. *William Robertson Nicoll: His Life and Letters.* London, 1925.

Egoff, Shelia A. *Children's Periodicals of the Nineteenth Century.* London, 1951.

Ellegård, Alvår. *The Readership of the Periodical Press in Mid-Victorian Britain.* Göteborg, 1957. Part 2 repr. *Victorian Periodicals Newsletter* (September 1971), 3-22.

Elliot-Binns, L. E. *Religion in the Victorian Era.* London, 1936; 3rd ed., 1953.

Fox Bourne, H. R. *English Newspapers.* Vol. 2. London, 1887.

Gillow, Joseph. *A Literary and Biographical History, or Bibliographical Dictionary of English Catholics, from the Breach with Rome in 1534 to the Present Time.* 5 vols. London, 1885-1902.

Goss, C. W. F. *A Descriptive Bibliography of the Writings of George Jacob Holyoake.* London, 1908.

Hanham, H. J. *Bibliography of British History, 1851-1914.* Oxford, 1976.

Hollis, Patricia. *The Pauper Press.* London, 1970.

Houghton, Walter E., ed. *The Wellesley Index to Victorian Periodicals 1824-1900.* 3 vols. Toronto, 1966, 1972, 1979. Vol. 4, ed. Jean Slingerland, 1988.

The Jewish Chronicle, 1841-1941: A Century of Newspaper History. London, 1949.

Madden, Lionel, and Diana Dixon. *The Nineteenth Century Periodical Press in Britain: A Bibliography of Modern Studies 1901-1971.* Supplement to *Victorian Periodicals Newsletter* (September 1975).

McLachlan, Herbert. *The Unitarian Movement in the Religious Life of England.* Vol. 1. London, 1934.

Mineka, Francis E. *The Dissidence of Dissent: The Monthly Repository, 1806-1838.* Chapel Hill, NC, 1944. Includes a chapter on English religious periodicals to 1825.

Overton, J. H. *The English Church in the Nineteenth Century*. London, 1894. Includes a chapter on "Church Literature."

Palmegiano, E. M. *Women and British Periodicals 1832-1867: A Bibliography.* Supplement to *Victorian Periodicals Newsletter* (1976).

Peel, Albert. *These Hundred Years: A History of the Congregational Union of England and Wales, 1831-1931.* London, 1931.

Shattock, Joanne, and Michael Wolff, eds. *The Victorian Periodical Press: Samplings and Soundings.* Leicester, 1982.

Sullivan, Alvin, ed. *British Literary Magazines: The Romantic Age, 1789-1836.* Westport, CT, 1983. Vol. 2 in series.

———. *British Literary Magazines: The Victorian and Edwardian Age, 1837-1913.* Westport, CT, 1984. Vol. 3 in series.

Tercentenary Handlist of English and Welsh Newspapers, Magazines and Reviews. London, 1920. Also known as *Times Tercentenary Handlist.*

Vann, J. Don, and Rosemary T. VanArsdel. *Victorian Periodicals: A Guide to Research.* New York, 1978. Another volume to be published.

The Waterloo Directory of Victorian Periodicals 1824-1900. Edited by Michael Wolff, John S. North, and Dorothy Deering. Waterloo, Ont., 1976.

Whitley, W. T. *A History of British Baptists.* London, 1923.

Whyte, A. Gowans. *The Story of the R.P.A.* London, 1949. The Rationalist Press Association.

Wiener, Joel H. *A Descriptive Finding List of Unstamped British Periodicals 1830-1836.* London, 1970.

ARTICLES AND CHAPTERS

Altholz, Josef L. "The First Religious Magazines." *Notes & Queries*, n.s. 32 (June 1985), 223-24.

———. "The Redaction of Catholic Periodicals." In Joel H. Wiener, ed. *Innovators and Preachers: The Role of the Editor in Victorian Periodicals.* Westport, CT, 1985, pp. 143-60.

Billington, Louis. "The Religious Periodical and Newspaper Press, 1770-1870." In Michael Harris and Alan Lee, eds. *The Press in English Society from the Seventeenth to Nineteenth Centuries.* London, 1986, pp. 113-32, 231-39.

Briggs, J. H. Y. "Press, Religious." In Sally Mitchell, ed. *Victorian Britain: An Encyclopedia.* New York, 1988, pp. 632-33.

Dwyer, J. J. "The Catholic Press." In G. A. Beck, ed. *The English Catholics 1850-1950.* London, 1950, pp. 475-514.

Fletcher, John R. "Early Catholic Periodicals in England." *Dublin Review*, 198 (April 1936), 284-310.

Harrison, Brian. "'A World of Which We Had No Conception': Liberalism and the Temperance Press 1830-1872." *Victorian Studies*, 13 (December 1969), 125-58.

Jones, J. J. "The Welsh Church Periodical Press." *National Library of Wales Journal*, 4 (Summer 1945), 92-94.

Kellett, E. E. "The Press." In G. M. Young, ed. *Early Victorian England.* 2 vols. London, 1934, 2: 1-97.

Mountjoy, Peter Roger. "The Working-Class Press and Working-Class Conservatism." In George Boyce, James Curran and Pauline Wingate, eds. *Newspaper History from the Seventeenth Century to the Present Day.* London, 1978, pp. 265-280.

Rosenberg, Henry M. and Sheila K. "Newspapers and Magazines." In George Watson, ed. *The New Cambridge Bibliography of English Literature.* Vol. 3: *1800-1900.* Cambridge, 1969, cols. 1755-1884.

Scott, Patrick. "The Business of Belief: The Emergence of 'Religious' Publishing." In Derek Baker, ed. *Studies in Church History.* Oxford, 1973, 10: 213-24.

———. "Victorian Religious Periodicals: Fragments That Remain." In Derek Baker, ed. *Materials, Sources and Methods of Ecclesiastical History.* Oxford, 1975, pp. 325-39.

PERIODICALS

Victorian Periodicals Newsletter. 1968-1981. Cited as *VPN.* Then: *Victorian Periodicals Review.* 1981- . Cited as *VPR.*

Victorian Studies. 1958- .

Index of Religious Periodicals, 1760–1900

Entries in this reference section provide information in the following order: title; publication dates (under that title, in years); sponsor (denomination or movement) or category; frequency; type (e.g., magazine); page references; "see also" followed by related titles, antecessors or successors. Items may be omitted where unknown or inappropriate. The absence of a terminal date indicates either that the periodical still continues or that its termination is not known. Two entries in a category separated by a comma are successive; if separated by a slash, they are joint. Abbreviations for sponsoring societies are spelled out in the General Index.

The following abbreviations are used for sponsors or categories: AssocPre, Associate Presbyterian; Ba, Baptist; BiChr, Bible Christian; brCoE, broad Church of England; BrIs, British Israel; CalMe, Calvinistic Methodist; CoE, Church of England (general); CoI, Church of Ireland; CoS, Church of Scotland; Con, Congregational; Chrdel, Christadelphian; ChrSo, Christain Socialist; EpCoS, Episcopal Church of Scotland; Eth, Ethical; ev, evangelical (general); evCoE, evangelical Anglican; Fr, Friends; Fr (in combination), Free; frtht, freethought, GenBa, General Baptist; hiCoE, high Church of England; Hunt, Huntingdonian; Jew, Jewish; juv, juvenile; LabCh, Labour Church; Me, Methodist (general); MeNC, Methodist New Connexion; miss, missionary; ncon, nonconformist (general); n-denom, nondenominational; PlBr, Plymouth Brethren; Pre, Presbyterian (general); PrMe, Primitive Methodist; RC, Roman Catholic; Ref (in combination), Reformed; RelPre, Relief Presbyterian; SaAr, Salvation Army; Sec (in combination), Secession; Soc, Society; Spir, Spiritualist; Swed, Swedenborgian; temp, temperance; Theos, Theosophist; U (in combination), United; Un, Unitarian; Univ, Universalist; WesMe, Wesleyan Methodist; WesRef, Wesleyan Reformed; WMeAs, Wesleyan Methodist Association. Frequencies are abbreviated: ann, annual; dai, daily; fort, fortnightly; irr, irregular; mo, monthly; qu, quarterly; sem, semiannual; wk, weekly; 2mo, bimonthly; 2/wk, twice weekly; 3/wk, thrice weekly. Types are: dir, directory; expo, expository; mag, magazine; new, newspaper; obit, obituary; pol, political; prof, professional; proph, prophecy; rep, report; rev, review; ser, sermon; tra, tract; theol, theological; yrbk, yearbook.

Aborigines' Friend or Colonial Intelligencer (1855-58, 1874-1909) ev irr rep, 125. *See also Colonial Intelligencer or Aborigines' Friend*

Achill Missionary Herald (1837-69) CoI mo mag, 21, 43, 52. *See also Irish Church Advocate; Church Advocate*

Adviser (1847-?) temp/juv mo mag, 128

Agnostic (1885) frtht mo mag, 121

Agnostic Annual (1884-1907) frtht ann mag, 122

Agnostic Journal (1889-1907) frtht wk mag, 120, 121. *See also Secular Review; Secularist*

Aldersgate Primitive Methodist Magazine (1899-1932) PrMe mo mag, 84. *See also Methodist Magazine; Primitive Methodist Magazine*

Alliance (1854-55) temp wk new, 127. *See also Alliance News; Alliance Weekly News*

Alliance News (1862-) temp wk new, 127. *See also Alliance; Alliance Weekly News*

Alliance Weekly News (1855-61) temp wk new, 127. *See also Alliance; Alliance News*

Ambassador of the Coming Age (1864-68) Chrdel mo mag, 88. *See also Christadelphian*

Andrews' Penny Orthodox Journal (1832-34) RC wk mag, 98. *See also London and Dublin Orthodox Journal of Useful Knowledge; Weekly Orthodox Journal of Entertaining Christian Knowledge*

Annals of the Propagation of the Faith (1837-) RC mo, qu rep, 108

Annual Monitor (1813-) Fr ann obit, 78

Annual Report (1811-) SPCK ann rep, 40

Annual Report (1838-47) ev (Aborigines Soc) ann rep, 125. *See also Aborigines' Friend or Colonial Intelligencer; Colonial Intelligencer or Aborigines' Friend*

Anti-Patronage Reporter (1833-34) CoS mo rep, 90. *See also Church Patronage Reporter*

Anti-Slavery Advocate (1852-63) ev mo mag, 125

Anti-Slavery Monthly Reporter (1825-30 ev mo mag, 124. *See also Anti-Slavery Reporter; British and Foreign Anti-Slavery Reporter; British Emancipator*

Anti-Slavery Reporter (1831-36, 1846-1909) ev mo mag, 124. *See also Anti-Slavery Monthly Reporter; British and Foreign Anti-Slavery Reporter; British Emancipator*

Arminian Magazine (1778-97) WesMe mo mag, 9, 10, 80, 85. *See also Methodist Magazine; Wesleyan Methodist Magazine*

At Home and Abroad (1879) WesMe mo mag, 175n. *See also Wesleyan Juvenile Offering*

Atlantis (1858-70) RC qu, irr rev, 107-8
Authorised Report (1861) CoE ann rep, 40

Band of Hope Review (1851-1937) temp mo mag, 128-29, 136
Banner of Israel (1877-1925) BrIs wk mag, 3, 130. *See also Israel's Identity Standard*
Banner of the Truth in Ireland (1851-93) CoI mo mag, 21. *See also Banner of Truth*
Banner of Truth (1893-) CoI mo mag, 21. *See also Banner of the Truth in Ireland*
Banner of Ulster (1842-69) Pre 2/wk new, 95
Baptist Handbook (1860-) Ba ann rep, 160n. *See also Baptist Manual*
Baptist Magazine (1809-1904) Ba mo mag, 71
Baptist Manual (1845-59) Ba ann rep, 160n. *See also Baptist Handbook*
Baptist Times and Freeman (1899-) Ba wk new, 71. *See also Freeman*
Baptist Union Magazine (1892-95) GenBa sem mag, 71. *See also Church and Household; General Baptist Magazine; General Baptist Repository*
Battersby's Catholic Directory (1858-64) RC ann dir, 169n. *See also Battersby's Registry for the Catholic World; Catholic Directory; Complete Catholic Directory; Almanac and Registry*
Battersby's Registry for the Catholic World (1846-57) RC ann dir, 169n. *See also Battersby's Catholic Directory; Catholic Directory; Complete Catholic Directory; Almanac and Registry*
Battleaxe (1883-86) CoE mo mag, 41, 87. *See also Church Army Gazette*
Beacon (1858-59) ncon wk new, 62. *See also Christian Times*
Bible Christian Magazine (1822-1907) BiChr mo mag, 85
Bible of Reason (1836) frtht wk mag, 119
Bible Treasury (1856-1920) PlBr mo expo, 88
Biblical Review (1846-50) Con mo mag, 67. *See also Congregational Magazine; London Christian Instructor*
Borderland (1893-97) Spir qu mag, 115
Boys' and Girls' Companion (1883-1903) CoE mo mag, 138. *See also Sunday Scholar's Companion*
Boy's Own Paper (1879-1967) RTS wk new, 2, 55, 139
British and Foreign Anti-Slavery Reporter (1840-45) ev mo mag, 124. *See also Anti-Slavery Monthly Reporter; Anti-Slavery Reporter; British Emancipator*
British and Foreign Evangelical Review (1853-88) ev qu rev, 48, 89, 132. *See also Foreign Evangelical Review; Theological Monthly*
British Banner (1848-58) Con wk, 3/wk, 2/wk new, 12, 59, 61, 69-70. *See also British Standard*
British Critic (1793-1843) hiCoE mo, qu mag, rev, 11, 23-25, 26. *See also Quarterly Theological Review*
British Emancipator (1837-40) ev mo mag, 124. *See also Anti-Slavery Monthly Reporter; Anti-Slavery Reporter; British and Foreign Anti-Slavery Reporter*

British Ensign (1859-64) Con wk new, 160n
British Friend (1843-1913) Fr mo mag, 78
British Magazine (1832-49) hiCoE mo mag, 24, 25-26
British Protestant (1845-64) ev mo mag, 52. *See also Protestant Churchman*
British Quarterly Review (1845-86) ncon qu rev, 58, 59-60, 68, 70. *See also Congregational Review*
British Standard (1857-67) Con wk new, 12, 61, 70. *See also British Banner; English Independent; Independent and Nonconformist; Nonconformist and Independent*
British Temperance Advocate (1850-) temp mo mag, 126. *See also British Temperance Advocate and Journal; National Temperance Advocate and Herald; Preston Temperance Advocate; Temperance Advocate and Herald*
British Temperance Advocate and Journal (1839-41) temp mo mag, 126. *See also British Temperance Advocate; National Temperance Advocate and Herald; Preston Temperance Advocate; Temperance Advocate and Herald*
British Weekly (1886-) ncon wk new, 13, 63-64, 133
British Women's Temperance Journal (1883-92) temp mo mag, 143. *See also Wings*
British Workman (1855-1921) ev/temp mo mag, 136, 137
British Workwoman (1863-1913) ev mo mag, 137
Bulwark (1851-) ev mo mag, 50, 89

Cassell's Family Magazine (1874-97) n-denom mo mag, 137. *See also Cassell's Illustrated Family Paper; Cassell's Magazine*
Cassell's Illustrated Family Paper (1853-67) n-denom wk new, 48, 137. *See also Cassell's Family Magazine; Cassell's Magazine*
Cassell's Magazine (1867-74, 1897-1930) n-denom mo mag, 48, 137. *See also Cassell's Family Magazine; Cassell's Illustrated Family Paper*
Catholic Advocate (1820-21) RC wk new, 98
Catholic Directory (1838-) RC ann dir, 97
Catholic Directory (1865-) RC ann dir, 169n. *See also Battersby's Catholic Directory; Battersby's Registry for the Catholic World; Complete Catholic Directory; Almanac and Registry*
Catholic Directory for Scotland (1829-) RC ann dir, 108
Catholic Gentleman's Magazine (1818-19) RC mo mag, 99
Catholic Herald (1884-) RC wk new, 106
Catholic Ireland 1873 RC mo rev, 169n. *See also Irish Monthly; Irish Monthly Magazine*
Catholic Journal (1828-29) RC wk new, 98
Catholic Magazine (1831-36) RC mo mag, 98. *See also Catholicon*
Catholic Magazine (1837-44) RC mo mag, 98. *See also Edinburgh Catholic Magazine*
Catholic Magazine and Reflector (1801) RC mo mag, 98

Catholic Miscellany (1822-30) RC mo mag, 98
Catholic Opinion (1867-76) RC wk new, 105. *See also Catholic Times*
Catholic Register and Magazine (1850) RC mo mag, 99
Catholic Spectator (1823-26) RC mo mag, 98. *See also Catholicon*
Catholic Standard (1849-55) RC wk new, 103-4. *See also Weekly Register*
Catholic Telegraph (1856-67) RC wk new, 107. *See also Weekly Telegraph*
Catholic Times (1870-) RC wk new, 105. *See also Catholic Opinion; Northern Press*
Catholic University Gazette (1854-56) RC wk mag, 169n
Catholicon (1816-18) RC mo mag, 98. *See also Catholic Spectator*
Catholicon (1836) RC irr mag, 98. *See also Catholic Magazine*
Chatterbox (1866-) CoE wk mag, 43, 139
Cheap Repository Tracts (1795-97) evCoE mo tra, 16, 53, 134
Child's Companion (1824-) RTS mo mag, 53, 138
Child's Magazine (1824-45) Me mo mag, 138
Child's Own Magazine (1852-) ncon mo mag, 138
Children's Friend (1824-1930) evCoE mo mag, 16, 53, 138
Children's Prize (1863-75) CoE mo mag, 139. *See also Prize*
Children's Treasury (1868-81) ev wk mag, 157n. *See also Father William's Stories; Our Darlings*
Children's World (1891-1900) CMS mo mag, 20, 143. *See also Church Missionary Juvenile Instructor*
China's Millions (1875-) miss mo mag, 124. *See also Occasional Papers*
Christadelphian (1869-) Chrdel mo mag, 88. *See also Ambassador of the Coming Age*
Christian (1870-1969) ev wk mag, 49. *See also Revival*
Christian Advocate (1830-39) WesMe wk new, 81
Christian Advocate (1861-74) evCoE mo mag, 18. *See also Christian Observer*
Christian Advocate (1885-1923) Me wk mag, 83. *See also Irish Christian Advocate*
Christian Ambassador (1863-78) PrMe qu rev, 84-85. *See also Primitive Methodist Quarterly Review*
Christian Cabinet (1855-64) ev wk new, 51
Christian Corrector (1831-32) frtht wk new, 119
Christian Examiner (1825-69) CoI mo mag, 42
Christian Freeman (1859-1909) Un mo mag, 77
Christian Guardian (1802-53) evCoE mo mag, 16. *See also Zion's Trumpet*
Christian Herald (1876-) ev wk proph, 49. *See also Signs of the Times*
Christian Irishman (1883-) Pre mo mag, 95. *See also Key of Truth*
Christian Journal (1833-45) RelPre mo mag, 94. *See also Relief Magazine*
Christian Life (1876-1929) Un wk new, 77. *See also Unitarian Herald*
Christian Magazine (1797-1820) AssocPre mo mag, 93-94. *See also Christian Monitor; Edinburgh Theological Magazine, United Secession Magazine*

Christian Mission Magazine (1869-78) Booth mo mag, 87. *See also East London Evangelist*

Christian Monitor (1821-25) AssocPre mo mag, 93. *See also Christian Magazine; Edinburgh Theological Magazine; United Secession Magazine*

Christian Mothers' Magazine (1844-45) n-denom mo mag, 136

Christian Observer (1802-77) evCoE mo mag, 16-17, 18, 19, 46

Christian Reformer (1815-63) Un mo mag, 73, 74, 75

Christian Reformer (1886-87) Un mo mag, 76

Christian Remembrancer (1845-68) hiCoE mo, qu rev, 25, 31

Christian Reporter (1820-22) WesMe wk new, 50, 80. *See also Philanthropic Gazette*

Christian Socialist (1850-51) brCoE wk mag, 35-36. *See also A Journal of Association*

Christian Socialist (1883-91) hiCoE, n-denom wk mag, 36, 172n

Christian Spectator (1838-56) RTS mo rep, 53. *See also Religious Tract Society Reporter; Religious Tract Society Record of Work at Home and Abroad*

Christian Teacher (1835-44) Un mo, qu mag, 73-74

Christian Times (1848-58) ncon wk new, 62. *See also Beacon*

Christian Times (1866-71) ev wk new, 51. *See also Illustrated Christian Times; London Christian Times*

Christian Witness (1834-41) PlBr mag, 88

Christian Witness (1844-71) Con mo mag, 59, 68-69

Christian Words (1866-) WesRef mo mag, 86. *See also Wesleyan Reform Union Magazine*

Christian World (1857-) ncon wk new, 13, 30, 51, 62-63, 64, 138

Christian World Family Circle Edition (1878-84) ncon wk mag, 62. *See also Family Circle; Fiction and Fact*

Christian World Pulpit (1871-) ncon wk ser, 62

Christian's Magazine (1760-67) CoE mo mag, 9, 23, 31, 37

Christian's Penny Magazine (1832-38) ev wk mag, 46

Christian's Penny Magazine (1846-81) Con mo mag, 68-69

Chronicle (1867-68) RC wk new, 103

Chronicle of Convocation (1859-) CoE ann rep, 39

Chronicle of the London Missionary Society (1867-) LMS mo rep, 64. *See also Missionary Magazine and Chronicle*

Church (1844-91) Ba mo mag, 71

Church Advocate (1879-91) CoI mo mag, 21. *See also Achill Missionary Herald; Irish Church Advocate*

Church and Household (1896-1901) GenBa sem mag, 71. *See also Baptist Union Magazine; General Baptist Magazine; General Baptist Repository*

Church and State Gazette (1842-56) CoE wk new, 29, 38. *See also Union; Union Review*

Church and State Review (1862-67) hiCoE mo rev, 29-30
Church Army Gazette (1886-) CoE mo mag, 41. *See also Battleaxe*
Church Examiner May-Dec. (1832) frtht wk, mo new, 119
Church Institution Circular (1862-64) CoE irr rep, 41
Church Intelligencer (1884-1938) evCoE mo rep, 22. *See also Monthly Intelligencer*
Church Journal (1853) CoE mo mag, 39. *See also Clerical Journal*
Church Missionary Gleaner (1841-70, 1874-1920) CMS mo mag, 20
Church Missionary Intelligencer (1849-1906) CMS mo mag, 20
Church Missionary Juvenile Instructor (1842-90) CMS mo mag, 20, 143. *See also Children's World*
Church Missionary Paper (1849-81) CMS qu rep, 20. *See also Quarterly Papers; Church Missionary Quarterly Paper*
Church Missionary Quarterly Paper (1882-) CMS qu rep, 20. *See also Church Missionary Paper; Quarterly Papers*
Church Missionary Record (1830-90) CMS mo mag, 20
Church of England Quarterly Review (1837-58) hiCoE qu rev, 26, 38
Church of England Temperance Chronicle (1873-88) temp mo, wk mag, 41, 128. *See also Church of England Temperance Magazine; Temperance Chronicle*
Church of England Temperance Magazine (1862-72) temp mo mag, 41, 127. *See also Church of England Temperance Chronicle; Temperance Chronicle*
Church of Ireland Gazette (1900-) CoI mo mag, 43. *See also Irish Ecclesiastical Gazette*
Church of Scotland Home and Foreign Missionary Record (1862-1900) CoS mo rep, 90, 91. *See also Home and Foreign Missionary Record*
Church of Scotland Magazine (1834-38) CoS mo mag, 90
Church Patronage Reporter (1829-32) CoS mo rep, 90. *See also Anti-Patronage Reporter*
Church Preferment Gazette (1866?-1894?) CoE mo adv, 44
Church Quarterly Review (1875-1968) hiCoE qu rev, 31, 82
Church Reformer (1882-95) hiCoE mo mag, 36, 172n
Church Review (1861-1902) hiCoE mo, wk mag, 29
Church Times (1863-) hiCoE wk new, 13, 30-31
Churchman (1879-) evCoE mo mag, 20
Circular (1863) FrCoE, 22
Clerical Guide (1817, 1822, 1829, 1836) CoE irr dir, 37
Clerical Journal (1853-69) CoE fort mag, 39. *See also Church Journal; Crockford's Clerical Directory*
Clergy List (1841-1917) CoE ann dir, 37, 39
Colonial Intelligencer or Aborigines' Friend (1847-54, 1859-66) ev irr rep, 125. *See also Aborigines' Friend or Colonial Intelligencer*
Commonwealth (1896-) ChrSo mo mag, 37

Complete Catholic Directory, Almanac and Registry (1837-45) RC ann dir, 169n. *See also Battersby's Catholic Directory; Battersby's Registry for the Catholic World; Catholic Directory; Compete Catholic Directory, Almanac and Registry*
Congregational Magazine (1825-45) Con mo mag, 67, 68. *See also Biblical Review; London Christian Instructor*
Congregational Review (1887-91) Con qu rev, 60, 70. *See also British Quarterly Review; Congregationalist*
Congregational Year Book (1846-) Con ann yrbk, 159n
Congregationalist Con mo mag, 60, 70. *See also Congregational Review*
Contemporary Pulpit (1884-93) n-denom mo ser, 134
Contemporary Review (1866-) brCoE (to 1882) qu rev, 13, 34
Cottage Magazine (1811/12-47) evCoE mo mag, 135
Cottager (1861-65) RTS mo mag, 54, 136. *See also Cottager and Artisan*
Cottager and Artisan (1865-1919) RTS mo mag, 54, 136. *See also Cottager*
Cottager's Friend (1837-45) Me mo mag, 136
Cottager's Monthly Visitor (1821-56) hiCoE mo mag, 136
Counsellor (1861) frtht mo mag, 120. *See also Herald of Progress; Reasoner*
Countess of Huntingdon's New Magazine (1850-51) Hunt mo mag, 86. *See also Evangelical Register; Harbinger*
Covenanter (1830-34?) RefPre mag, 93. *See also Reformed Presbyterian Magazine; Scottish Presbyterian*
Critical Review (1890-1904) FrCoS qu rev, 93. *See also Theological Review*
Crockford's Clerical Directory (1855-) CoE irr, ann dir, 39. *See also Clerical Journal*
Y Cyfaill Eglwysig (1862-) CoE mo mag, 42

Daily Express (1877) CoE dai new, 30, 148n
Darkest Russia, In (1891) Jew mo new, 112
Devil's Pulpit (1831-32) frtht wk new, 118
Y Diwigiwr (1836-) Con mo mag, 160n
Dolman's Magazine (1845-49) RC mo mag, 98
Downside Review (1880-) RC qu rev, 106
Y Drysorfa (1831-) CalMe mo mag, 86
Dublin Review (1836-1969) RC qu rev, 11, 98, 99-100, 101, 102, 103, 104
Y Dysgedydd (1821-) Con mo mag, 160n

Earthen Vessel (1845-?) Ba mo mag, 142
East London Evangelist (1868-69) Booth mo mag, 87. *See also Christian Mission Magazine*
Ecclesiastic (1846-47, 1862-68) hiCoE mo mag, 27, 151n. *See also Ecclesiastic and Theologian; Theologian; Theologian and Ecclesiastic*
Ecclesiastic and Theologian (1850-62) hiCoE mo mag, 151n. *See also Ecclesiastic; Theologian; Theologian and Ecclesiastic*

Ecclesiastical Gazette (1838-1900) CoE mo rep/adv, 38, 44
Ecclesiologist (1841-68) hiCoE mo rep/mag, 26-27
Echoes of Service (1885-) PlBr mo mag, 88. *See also Missionary Echo*
Eclectic Review (1805-1868) ncon mo rev, 11, 46, 58-59, 68
Edinburgh Catholic Magazine (1832-33) RC mo mag, 98. *See also Catholic Magazine*
Edinburgh Christian Instructor (1810-40) CoS mo mag, 90
Edinburgh Christian Magazine (1850-59) CoS mo mag, 91
Edinburgh Theological Magazine (1826-32) AssocPre mo mag, 93. *See also Christian Magazine; Christian Monitor; United Secession Magazine*
Yr Eglwysydd (1847-62) CoE mo mag, 42
English Churchman (1843-) hiCoE, evCoE wk new, 19, 27
English Independent (1867-79) ncon wk new, 61, 68. *See also British Standard; Independent and Nonconformist; Nonconformist and Independent; Patriot; World*
English Presbyterian Messenger (1845-67) Pre mo mag, 96
English Review (1844-53) hiCoE qu rev, 26
Englishwoman's Magazine (1846-54) n-denom mo mag, 175n
Evangelical Christendom (1847-) ev mo mag, 52
Evangelical Magazine (1793-1904) ev mo mag, 45-46, 57, 58, 71, 93
Evangelical Register (1824-43) Hunt qu mag, 86. *See also Countess of Huntingdon's New Magazine; Harbinger*
Evangelical Repository (1854-88) Pre qu, mo theol, 89
Evangelical Witness (1862-73) Pre mo mag, 95. *See also Witness*
Expositor (1875-1925) ncon mo exp, 63, 132-33
Expository Times (1889-) n-denom mo mag, 133

Family Circle (1885-97) ncon wk mag, 62. *See also Christian World Family Circle Edition; Fiction and Fact*
Family Magazine (1788-89) CoE mo mag, 10, 135
Father William's Stories (1866-67) ev wk mag, 157n. *See also Children's Treasury; Our Darlings*
Female Missionary Intelligencer (1854-99) ev mo rep, 137
Fiction and Fact (1898) ncon wk mag, 62. *See also Christian World Family Circle Edition; Family Circle*
Foreign Evangelical Review (1852-53) ev qu rev, 4-8. *See also British and Foreign Evangelical Review; Theological Monthly*
Free Church Chronicle (1899-1934) ncon mo mag, 65
Free Church Magazine (1844-53) FrCoS mo mag, 92
Free Church of England Magazine and Harbinger (1867-68) FrCoE/Hunt mo mag, 22. *See also Harbinger; Magazine*
Free Church of Scotland Monthly Record (1862-1900) FrCoS mo rep, 91. *See also Free Church of Scotland Weekly Record; Home and Foreign Missionary Record for the Free Church of Scotland; Home and Foreign Record*

Free Church of Scotland Weekly Record (1861-62) FrCoS wk rep, 91. *See also Free Church of Scotland Monthly Record; Home and Foreign Missionary Record for the Free Church of Scotland; Home and Foreign Record*

Free Churchman (1897-) ncon mo mag, 65

Free Review (1893-97) frtht mo mag, 121. *See also National Reformer; University Magazine*

Free Sunday Advocate (1869-1939) frtht mo mag, 122

Freeman (1855-99) Ba wk new, 71. *See also Baptist Times and Freeman*

Friend (1843-) Fr mo, wk mag, 78

Friendly Visitor (1819-1912) evCoE mo mag, 16, 136

Friend's Examiner (1867) Fr sem mag, 78. *See also Friends' Quarterly Examiner*

Friends' Quarterly Examiner (1867-1946) Fr qu mag, 78. *See also Friends' Examiner*

Gauntlet (1833-34) frtht wk new, 118

General Baptist Magazine (1798-1800) GenBa mo mag, 71

General Baptist Magazine (1860-91) GenBa sem mag, 71. *See also Baptist Union Magazine; Church and Household; General Baptist Repository*

General Baptist Repository (1802-59) GenBa sem mag, 71. *See also Baptist Union Magazine; Church and Household; General Baptist Magazine*

Girl's Own Paper (1880-1927) RTS wk mag, 55, 139

Glasgow Observer (1885-) RC wk new, 108

Golden Link Between Church and Home (1894-98) juv mo mag, 175n. *See also Juvenile Instructor and Companion; Young People*

Y Goleuad (1869-1918) CalMe mo mag, 86

Good Words (1860-1911) n-denom wk, mo mag, 13, 48, 90, 139

Good Words for the Young (1868-72) n-denom mo mag, 139

Goodwill (1894-) ChrSo mo mag, 37

Gospel Emblems (1898-99) RTS, 143

Gospel Handbills (1897-98) RTS, 143

Gospel Magazine (1766-1784) evCoE mo mag, 10, 15, 46, 79

Gospel Magazine (1796-) ev mo mag, 148n

Gospel Standard (1835-) Ba mo mag, 142

Grain of Mustard Seed (1881-98) SPG mo rep, 40. *See also Women in the Mission Field*

Guardian (1846-) hiCoE wk new, 27-28, 31, 44

Y Gwyleidydd (1822-37) CoE mo mag, 41

Y Gwyliedydd (1877-1909) WesMe wk new, 86

Harbinger (1852-66) Hunt mo mag, 22, 86. *See also Countess of Huntingdon's New Magazine, Evangelical Register, Free Church of England Magazine and Harbinger, Magazine*

Yr Haul (1836-) CoE wk mag, 41-42

Hebrew Intelligencer (1823) Jew mo mag, 110
Hebrew Observer (1853-54) Jew wk new, 111. *See also Jewish Chronicle*
Hebrew Review (1834-36) Jew mo rev, 110
Herald of Peace (1819-1930) peace mo mag, 123
Herald of Progress (1845-46) frtht wk mag, 120. *See also Counsellor; Reasoner*
Home and Foreign Missionary Record (1839-62) CoS mo rep, 90. *See also Church of Scotland Home and Foreign Missionary Record*
Home and Foreign Missionary Record for the Free Church of Scotland (1843-50) FrCoS mo rep, 91-92. *See also Free Church of Scotland Monthly Record; Free Church of Scotland Weekly Record; Home and Foreign Record*
Home and Foreign Record (1850-56) FrCoS mo rep, 91. *See also Free Church of Scotland Monthly Record; Free Church of Scotland Weekly Record; Home and Foreign Missionary Record for the Free Church of Scotland*
Home and Foreign Review (1862-64) RC qu rev, 11, 93, 100, 102-3. *See also Rambler*
Homiletic Magazine (1882-91) n-denom mo prof, 134. *See also Homiletic Quarterly; Thinker*
Homiletic Quarterly (1877-81) n-denom qu prof, 134. *See also Homiletic Magazine; Thinker*
Homilist (1852-92) n-denom mo prof, 133

Illuminator (1835-36) Me fort new, 81
Illustrated Christian Times (1865-66) ev wk new, 51. *See also Christian Times; London Christian Times*
In His Name (1888-1907) ev qu rep, 55. *See also Ragged School Union Magazine; Ragged School Union Quarterly Record*
Independent and Nonconformist (1890-1900) Con wk new, 61. *See also British Standard; English Independent; Nonconformist; Nonconformist and Independent; Patriot; World*
Indian Female Evangelist (1872-93) n-denom, 124
Inquirer (1842-) Un wk new, 73, 76-77
Intellectual Repository and New Jerusalem Magazine (1830-81) Swed mo mag, 109. *See also Intellectual Repository for the New Church; New-Church Magazine*
Intellectual Repository for the New Church (1812-29) Swed qu mag, 109. *See also Intellectual Repository and New Jerusalem Magazine; New-Church Magazine*
Investigator (1858-59) frtht mo mag, 120-21. *See also London Investigator*
Irish Catholic (1888-) RC wk new, 107
Irish Catholic Directory (1835-) RC ann dir, 169n
Irish Catholic Magazine (1847-48) RC mo mag, 107
Irish Christian Advocate (1883-85) Me wk mag, 83. *See also Christian Advocate*

Irish Church Advocate (1870-79) CoI fort mag, 21, 43. *See also Achill Missionary Herald; Church Advocate*

Irish Ecclesiastical Gazette (1856-99) CoI mo new/mag, 43. *See also Church of Ireland Gazette*

Irish Ecclesiastical Journal (1842-52) CoI mo mag, 43

Irish Ecclesiastical Record (1864-) Rc mo mag, 108

Irish Friend (1837-42) Fr mo mag, 78

Irish Missionary Magazine (1844-45) ev mo mag, 52. *See also Protestant Advocate*

Irish Monthly (1873-) RC mo rev, 108, 169n. *See also Catholic Ireland; Irish Monthly Magazine*

Irish Monthly Magazine (1873) RC mo rev, 169n. *See also Catholic Ireland; Irish Monthly*

Irish Presbyterian (1895-?) Pre mo mag, 95. *See also Plain Words; Presbyterian Churchman*

Irish Rosary (1897-) RC mo mag, 108

Irish Temperance League Journal (1863-1906) temp mo mag, 128

Israel's Identity Standard (1876) BrIs wk mag, 130. *See also Banner of Israel*

Jewish Chronicle (Sefer Zikkaron) (1841-42, 1844-) Jew wk, fort, wk new, 110-13. *See also Hebrew Observer*

Jewish Quarterly Review (1888-1907) Jew qu rev, 113

Jewish Record (1868-71) Jew wk new, 112

Jewish Society (1889-91) Jew wk new, 170n.

Jewish Standard (1888-91) Jew wk new, 113

Jewish World (1873-1934) Jew wk new, 113

Jewish Year Book (1896-) Jew ann yrbk, 113-14

Journal (1861) CoE (York Convo) irr rep, 39

Journal of Association (1851-52) ChrSo wk mag, 36. *See also Christian Socialist*

Journal of Classical and Sacred Philology (1854-59) n-denom 3/yr prof, 132

Journal of Convocation (1854-58) CoE ann rep, 39. *See also Synodalia*

Journal of Sacred Literature (1848-68) n-denom qu prof, 131-32

Journal of Theological Studies (1899-) n-denom qu rev, 133

Juvenile (1888-94) LMS mo mag, 64, 175n. *See also Juvenile Missionary Magazine; News from Afar*

Juvenile Instructor and Companion (1850-93) juv mo mag, 175n. *See also Golden Link Between Church and Home; Young People*

Juvenile Missionary Herald (1845-1908) Ba mo mag, 72

Juvenile Missionary Magazine (1844-87) LMS mo mag, 64, 175n. *See also Juvenile; News from Afar*

Juvenile Missionary Magazine (1846-47) USecPre mo mag, 94. *See also Juvenile Missionary Magazine of the United Presbyterian Church*

Juvenile Missionary Magazine of the United Presbyterian Church (1847-77) UPre mo mag, 94. *See also Juvenile Missionary Magazine*

Key of Truth (1880-82) Pre mo mag, 95. *See also Christian Irishman*
Knowledge (1881-1903) frtht mo mag, 172n

Labour Church Record (1899-1901) LabCh qu mag, 116. *See also Labour Prophet*
Labour Prophet (1892-98) LabCh mo mag, 116. *See also Labour Church Record*
Laity's Directory (1759-88) RC ann dir, 97
Laity's Directory (1768-) RC ann dir, 97
Lamp (1850-1905) RC mo mag, 104
Latter-Day Saints Millenial Star (1840-1945) LDS mo, fort, wk mag, 1, 109-10
Leeds Temperance Herald (1837) temp mo? mag, 172n. *See Temperance Advocate and Herald*
Leisure Hour (1852-1905) RTS mo mag, 48, 54, 137
Liberator (1855-) ncon mo mag, 61
Life and Work (1879-) CoS mo mag, 91
Life from the Dead (1873-80) BrIs mo mag, 130
Literary Churchman (1855-92) hiCoE fort rev, 28
Literary Guide (1894-1956) frtht mo adv, 122. *See also Watts' Literary Guide*
Little Folks (1871-1933) n-denom mag, 139
Y Llan a'r Dywysogaeth (1881-) CoE wk new, 42
London and Dublin Orthodox Journal of Useful Knowledge (1835-46) RC wk mag, 98. *See also Andrews' Penny Orthodox Journal; Weekly Orthodox Journal of Entertaining Christian Knowledge*
London Christian Instructor (1818-24) Con mo mag, 67. *See also Biblical Review; Congregational Magazine*
London Christian Times (1863-64) ev wk new, 51. *See also Christian Times; Illustrated Christian Times*
London Investigator (1854-57) frtht mo mag, 120. *See also Investigator*
London Quarterly Review (1853-1931) WesMe qu rev, 82, 85. *See also London Review*
London Review (1829) CoE qu rev, 37
London Review (1858-62) WesMe qu rev, 82. *See also London Quarterly Review*
Lucifer (1887-97) Theos mo mag, 114. *See also Theosophical Review*

Macphail's Edinburgh Ecclesiastical Journal (1846-63) CoS mag/rev, 91
Magazine of the Free Church of England and of Lady Huntingdon's Connection (1869-85) FrCoE/Hunt mo mag, 22. *See also Free Church of England Magazine and Harbinger; Harbinger*

Medical Missions at Home and Abroad (1878-1924) miss qu mag, 124
Medical Pioneer (1892-97) temp qu mag, 129. *See also Medical Temperance Journal; Medical Temperance Review*
Medical Temperance Journal (1869-92) temp qu mag, 129. *See also Medical Pioneer; Medical Temperance Review*
Medical Temperance Review (1898-1919) temp qu mag, 129. *See also Medical Pioneer; Medical Temperance Journal*
Medium (1870-95) Spir wk mag, 115
Meliora (1858-69) temp qu rev, 127
Methodist (1874-84) Me wk new, 82
Methodist Magazine (1798-1821) WesMe mo mag, 10, 80, 81. *See also Arminian Magazine; Wesleyan Methodist Magazine*
Methodist Magazine, A (1819-20) PrMe mo mag, 84. *See also Aldersgate Primitive Methodist Magazine; Primitive Methodist Magazine*
Methodist Monthly (1892-1907) UMeFr mo mag, 86. *See also United Methodist Free Churches Magazine; Wesleyan Methodist Association Magazine*
Methodist New Connexion Magazine (1798-1907) MeNC mo mag, 83
Methodist Recorder (1861-) Me wk new, 81
Methodist Temperance Magazine (1868-1906) Me mo mag, 83, 127
Methodist Times (1885-1937) Me wk new, 82-83, 143
Metropolitan Tabernacle Pulpit (1863-) Ba wk ser, 2, 72, 135. *See also New Park Street Pulpit*
Mission Field (1856-1941) SPG mo mag, 40. *See also Monthly Record of Church Missions*
Missionary Echo (1872-84) PlBr mo mag, 88. *See also Echoes of Service*
Missionary Herald (1819-21) Ba mo rep/mag, 71. *See also Missionary Herald of the Baptist Missionary Society*
Missionary Herald (1843-1946) Pre mo mag, 95. *See also Monthly Missionary Herald*
Missionary Herald of the Baptist Missionary Society (1821-1911) Ba mo rep/mag, 71. *See also Missionary Herald*
Missionary Magazine and Chronicle (1837-66) LMS mo mag, 64. *See also Chronicle of the London Missionary Society*
Missionary Notices (1816-38) Me mo rep, 80
Missionary Record (1846) USecPre mo mag, 94. *See also Missionary Record of the United Presbyterian Church*
Missionary Record of the United Presbyterian Church (1847) UPre mo mag, 94. *See also Missionary Record*
Missionary Register (1813-55) CMS mo mag, 20, 123
Missionary Transactions (1795-1836) LMS irr, qu rep, 64
Modern Review (1880-84) Un qu rev, 76
Month (1864-) RC mo mag, 105
Monthly Intelligencer (1867-84) evCoE mo rep, 22. *See also Church Intelligencer*

Monthly Messenger (1851-56, 1857-85) Pre/ev mo mag, 95
Monthly Missionary Herald (1837-43) Pre mo mag, 95. *See also Missionary Herald*
Monthly Packet (1851-99) hiCoE mo mag, 28, 138
Monthly Paper of the National Society (1847-75) CoE mo mag, 41. *See also School Guardian*
Monthly Record of Church Missions (1852-55) SPG mo mag, 40. *See also Mission Field*
Monthly Repository 1806-37 Un (to 1834) mo mag, 71. *See also Universal Theological Magazine; Universalist's Miscellany*
Moral Reformer (1831-33) temp mo mag, 126
Morning Star (1856-69) peace dai new, 125
Morning Watch (1829-33) Pre qu mag, 90, 96
Movement (1843-45) frtht wk mag, 119

National Church (1872-1919) CoE mo rep, 41
National Reformer (1860-93) frtht wk new, 120, 121. *See also Free Review; University Magazine*
National Review (1855-64) Un qu rev, 34, 74-75, 76, 77
National Sunday League Record (1856-59) frtht mo rep, 122
National Temperance Advocate and Herald (1842-49) temp mo mag, 126. *See also British Temperance Advocate; British Temperance Advocate and Journal; Preston Temperance Advocate; Temperance Advocate and Herald*
National Temperance Chronicle (1843-56) temp mo mag, 126. *See also Temperance Record; Weekly Record of the Temperance Movement*
National Temperance Mirror (1881-1907) temp mo mag, 128, 173n
National Waif's Magazine (1899-1906) ev mo mag, 56. *See also Night and Day*
New-Church Magazine (1881-) Swed mo mag, 109. *See also Intellectual Repository and New Jerusalem Magazine; Intellectual Repository for the New Church*
New Era (1899-1900) RC wk mag, 168n
New Moral World (1834-45) frtht wk mag, 119
New Park Street Pulpit (1856-62) Ba wk ser, 72. *See also Metropolitan Tabernacle Pulpit*
Newbery House Magazine (1889-94) hiCoE mo rev, 31
News from Afar (1895-) LMS mo mag, 64, 175n. *See also Juvenile; Juvenile Missionary Magazine*
Night and Day (1877-) ev mo mag, 56. *See also National Waif's Magazine*
Nonconformist (1841-80) ncon wk new, 4, 58, 59, 60-61, 68. *See also English Independent; Independent and Nonconformist; Nonconformist and Independent*
Nonconformist and Independent (1880-89) ncon/Con wk new, 61. *See also British Standard; English Independent; Independent and Nonconformist; Nonconformist; Patriot; World*

Nonconformist Elector (1847) ncon 2/wk pol, 61
North British Review 1844-71 FrCoS/RC qu rev, 92-93, 103
Northern Press (1860-70) RC wk new, 105. *See also Catholic Times*

Occasional Papers (1866-75) miss irr mag, 124. *See also China's Millions*
Onward (1865-1909) temp mo mag, 129
Oracle of Reason (1842-43) frtht wk mag, 119
Ordo Recitandi RC ann dir, 97
Original Secession Magazine (1847-50, 1852-?) SecPre mo mag, 94
Orthodox Journal (1813-20, 1823-24, 1829) RC mo mag, 97-98
Orthodox Presbyterian (1829-40) Pre mo mag, 95
Our Children's Magazine (1852-68) ev mo mag, 157n. *See also Ragged School Children's Magazine*
Our Corner (1883-88) frtht mo mag, 172n
Our Darlings (1881-) ev wk mag, 157n. *See also Children's Treasury; Father William's Stories*

Parish Magazine (1859-) CoE mo mag, 43
Pastor's Assistant (1842-44) CoE prof, 150n
Patriot (1832-66) ncon/Con wk new, 3, 12, 61, 68, 69. *See also English Independent; Independent and Nonconformist; Nonconformist and Independent; World*
Penny Catholic Magazine (1839-40) RC wk mag, 98
Penny Post (1851-96) hiCoE mo mag, 136
Penny Protestant Operative (1840-48) ev mo mag, 51
Penny Spiritual Magazine. See Zion's Trumpet
Periodical Accounts (1800-37) Ba irr, ann rep, 71
Philanthropic Gazette (1817-23) n-denom wk new, 50. *See also Christian Reporter*
Phonographic Pulpit (1869-76) n-denom mo ser, 2, 135
Pilot (1900-04) hiCoE wk rev, 28, 31
Plain Words (1862-76) Pre mo mag, 95. *See also Irish Presbyterian; Presbyterian Churchman*
Poilisher Yiddel (1884) Jew wk new, 114
Politics for the People (1848) brCoE wk tra, 35, 134
Positivist Review (1893-1923) Pos mo rev, 115
Presbyterian (1868-73) FrCoS mo mag, 92
Presbyterian Churchman (1877-94) Pre mo mag, 95. *See also Irish Presbyterian; Plain Words*
Presbyterian Magazine (1832-36) CoS mo mag, 90
Presbyterian Review (1831-48) CoS 2 mo rev, 90
Present Day (1883-86) frtht mo mag, 120
Present Testimony (1849-73) PlBr mo mag, 88

Preston Temperance Advocate (1834-37) temp mo mag, 126. *See also British Temperance Advocate; British Temperance Advocate and Journal; National Temperance Advocate and Herald; Temperance Advocate and Herald*
Primitive Methodist (1868-1905) PrMe wk new, 85
Primitive Methodist Children's Magazine (1824-51) PrMe mo mag, 84
Primitive Methodist Magazine (1821-98) PrMe mo mag, 84. *See also Aldersgate Primitive Methodist Magazine; Methodist Magazine*
Primitive Methodist Quarterly Review (1879-1909) PrMe qu rev, 84. *See also Christian Ambassador*
Primitive Methodist World (1883-1908) PrMe wk new, 85
Prize (1875-) CoE mo mag, 139. *See also Children's Prize*
Proceedings (1800-1922) CMS ann rep, 20
Progress (1883-87) frtht mo mag, 172n
Prospective Review (1845-55) Un qu rev, 34, 58
Protestant Advocate (1846) ev mo mag, 52. *See also Irish Missionary Magazine*
Protestant Alliance (1853-1930) ev mo lett, mag, 52
Protestant Churchman (1865-1907) ev mo rep/mag, 52. *See also British Protestant*
Protestant Dissenter's Magazine (1794-99) ncon mo mag, 57
Protestant Elector (1837) ev wk pol, 52
Protestant Magazine (1839-65) ev mo mag, 47, 51
Protestant Observer (1888-1917) ev mo mag, 53. *See also Protestant Times*
Protestant Times (1881-88) ev mo mag, 52. *See also Protestant Observer*
Publicist (1815) RC mo mag, 98
Pulpit (1823-71) n-denom wk ser, 135
Y Pwlpud Wesleyaidd (1876-77) Me ser, 135

Quarterly Papers (1816-49) CMS qu rep, 20. *See also Church Missionary Paper; Church Missionary Quarterly Paper*
Quarterly Messenger (1863-73) YMCA qu mag, 56
Quarterly Theological Review (1825-26) hiCoE qu rev, 11, 23. *See also British Critic*
Quiver (1861-1956) ev wk mag, 48, 137

Ragged School Children's Magazine (1850-51) ev mo mag, 157n. *See also Our Children's Magazine*
Ragged School Union Magazine (1849-75) ev mo mag, 55. *See also In His Name; Ragged School Union Quarterly Record*
Ragged School Union Quarterly Record (1876-87) ev qu rep, 55. *See also In His Name, Ragged School Union Magazine*
Rambler (1848-62) RC wk, mo, 2mo mag, 100, 101-2, 103, 104. *See also Home and Foreign Review*
Rationalist (1833) frtht mo mag, 119

Reasoner (1846-61) frtht wk mag, 120. *See also Counsellor; Herald of Progress*
Rechabite and Temperance Magazine (1870-) temp mo mag, 129. *See also Rechabite Magazine*
Rechabite Magazine (1840-50) temp mo mag, 129
Rechabite Magazine (1864-69) temp mo mag, 129. *See also Rechabite and Temperance Magazine*
Record (1828-) evCoE 2/wk, 3/wk, wk new, 12, 17-19, 27, 44, 51, 69, 137
Reformed Church Record (1881-91) RefCoE mo mag, 22
Reformed Presbyterian Magazine (1855-76) RefPre mo mag, 93. *See also Covenanter; Scottish Presbyterian*
Reformed Presbyterian Witness (1864-) RefPre fort mag, 165n
Relief Magazine (1845-46) RelPre mo mag, 94. *See also Christian Journal; United Presbyterian Magazine; United Secession Magazine*
Religious Tract Society Record of Work at Home and Abroad (1877-1900) RTS qu rep, 53. *See also Christian Spectator; Religious Tract Society Reporter*
Religious Tract Society Reporter (1857-75) RTS mo rep, 53. *See also Christian Spectator; Religious Tract Society Record of Work at Home and Abroad*
Republican (1819-26) frtht wk new, 118
Revival (1859-70) ev wk mag, 49. *See also Christian*
Revivalist (1853-64) PrMe mo mag, 84
Rock (1867-1905) evCoE wk new, 19, 27

Salvationist (1879) SaAr mo mag, 87
Saturday Magazine (1832-44) SPCK wk mag, 40
School Guardian (1876-1937) CoE wk new, 41. *See also Monthly Paper of the National Society*
Scottish Congregational Magazine (1835-80) Con mo mag, 70. *See also Scottish Congregationalist*
Scottish Congregationalist (1881-) Con mo mag, 70. *See also Scottish Congregational Magazine*
Scottish Guardian (1832-61) Pre wk new, 164n
Scottish Magazine (1849-54) EpCoS mo mag, 42
Scottish Missionary Chronicle (1832-39) Pre rep, 94
Scottish Missionary Register (1820-46) Pre rep, 94
Scottish Presbyterian (1835-54) RefPre mo mag, 93. *See also Covenanter; Reformed Presbyterian Magazine*
Scottish Review (1853-63) temp qu rev, 128
Scottish Standard Bearer (1890-) EpCoS mo mag, 42
Scripture Readers' Journal (1853-1907) evCoE qu mag, 21
Secular Review (1877-88) frtht wk rev/mag, 120, 121. *See also Agnostic Journal; Secularist*
Secular Thought (1887?) frtht wk, 172n
Secularist (1876-77) frtht wk rev, 120. *See also Agnostic Journal; Secular Review*

Sefer Zikkaron. See Jewish Chronicle
Seren Gomer (1818-1931) Ba wk new, 71
Servant's Magazine (1838-69) ev mo mag, 47-48, 136
Signs of the Times (1867-75) ev mo proph, 49. *See also Christian Herald*
Slap at the Church, A (1832) frtht wk new, 119
South Place Magazine (1895-1909) Eth mo mag, 116
Spectator (1861-) brCoE (to 1886) wk new/mag, 28, 34-35, 75
Spiritual Magazine (1761-84?) evCoE mo mag, 9, 10
Spiritual Magazine (1825-52) ncon mo mag, 46. *See also Zion's Casket*
Staunch Teetotaler (1867-68) temp mo mag, 126
Sunday at Home (1854-1940) RTS wk mag, 54, 137
Sunday Magazine (1864-1906) ev wk mag, 48, 90, 137
Sunday Scholar's Companion (1855-82) CoE mo mag, 138. *See also Boys' and Girls' Companion*
Sunday School Chronicle (1874-1928) ncon wk mag, 56, 64
Sunday School Times (1860-1925) ev wk mag, 56, 64
Sword and the Trowel (1865-) Ba mo mag, 72
Synodalia (1852-53) CoE ann rep, 39. *See also Journal of Convocation*

Tablet (1840-) RC wk new, 100-1, 104, 106. *See also True Tablet*
Teetotaler (1840-41) temp mag, 128
Temperance Advocate and Herald (1838) temp mo mag, 126. *See also British Temperance Advocate; British Temperance Advocate and Journal; Leeds Temperance Herald; National Temperance Advocate and Herald; Preston Temperance Advocate*
Temperance Chronicle (1888-1914) temp wk mag, 41, 128. *See also Church of England Temperance Magazine; Church of England Temperance Chronicle*
Temperance Penny Magazine (1836-48) temp mo mag, 172
Temperance Record (1870-1907) temp wk new, 126. *See also National Temperance Chronicle; Weekly Record of the Temperance Movement*
Temperance Star (1857-76) temp wk, mo mag, 128
Theologian (1845-47) hiCoE mo mag, 151n. *See also Ecclesiastic; Ecclesiastic and Theologian; Theologian and Ecclesiastic*
Theologian and Ecclesiastic (1847-50) hiCoE mo mag, 151n. *See also Ecclesiastic; Ecclesiastic and Theologian; Theologian*
Theological Monthly (1889-91) ev mo rev, 49. *See also British and Foreign Evangelical Review; Foreign Evangelical Review*
Theological Repository (1769-1771, 1784-1788) Un irr mag, 10, 72, 73
Theological Review (1864-79) Un 2mo rev, 75-76
Theological Review (1886-90) FrCoS qu rev, 93. *See also Critical Review*
Theosophical Review (1897-1907) Theos qu rev, 114. *See also Lucifer*
Thinker (1892-95) n-denom mo prof, 134. *See also Homiletic Magazine; Homiletic Quarterly*

Tract Magazine (1824-46) RTS mo mag, 53, 134
True Briton (1851-54) n-denom wk mag, 175n
True Tablet (1842) RC wk new, 100. *See also Tablet*
Truth-Teller (1824-29) Rc wk new, pamph, 98

Union (1857-63) hiCoE mo new, 29, 38. *See also Union Review; Church and State Gazette*
Union Review (1863-75) hiCoE 2mo rev, 29, 38. *See also Union; Church and State Gazette*
Unitarian Chronicle (1832-33) Un mo mag, 160n. *See also Unitarian Magazine and Chronicle*
Unitarian Herald (1861-89) Un wk new, 77. *See also Christian Life*
Unitarian Magazine and Chronicle (1834-35) Un mo mag, 160n. *See also Unitarian Chronicle*
United Methodist Free Churches Magazine (1858-91) UMeFr mo mag, 86. *See also Methodist Monthly; Wesleyan Methodist Association Magazine*
United Presbyterian Magazine (1847-1900) UPre mo mag, 93, 94. *See also Relief Magazine; United Secession Magazine*
United Secession and Relief Magazine (1847) Pre mo mag, 165n. *See also United Presbyterian Magazine*
United Secession Magazine (1833-47) AssocPre mo mag, 94. *See also Christian Magazine; Christian Monitor; Edinburgh Theological Magazine; Relief Magazine; United Presbyterian Magazine*
Universal Theological Magazine (1802-05) Univ mo mag, 72-73. *See also Monthly Repository; Universalist's Miscellany*
Universalist's Miscellany (1797-1801) Univ mo mag, 72. *See also Monthly Repository; Universal Theological Magazine*
Universe (1860-) RC wk new, 104-5, 106
University Magazine (1897-98) frtht mo rev, 121. *See also Free Review; National Reformer*

Vahan (1891-1920) Theos mag, 114
Visitor (1836-51) RTS mo mag, 54, 135. *See also Weekly Visitor*
Voice of Jacob (1841-47) Jew fort new, 111
Voluntary Church Magazine (1833-41) Pre mo mag, 94

War Cry (1879-) SaAr wk mag, 41, 87
Watchman (1835-84) WesMe wk new, 81
Watchman's Lantern (1834-35) WesMe fort new, 81
Watts' Literary Guide (1885-94) frtht mo adv, 122. *See also Literary Guide*
Weekly Journal (1857-) temp wk mag, 128
Weekly Orthodox Journal of Entertaining Christian Knowledge (1832-34) RC wk mag, 98. *See also Andrews' Penny Orthodox Journal; London and Dublin Orthodox Journal of Useful Knowledge*

Weekly Record of the Temperance Movement (1856-69) temp wk new, 126. *See also National Temperance Chronicle; Temperance Record*
Weekly Register (1798-99?) ev wk new, 11, 50
Weekly Register (1849-50, 1855-1902) RC wk new, 99, 104. *See also Catholic Standard*
Weekly Review (1862-81) Pre wk rev, 95
Weekly Telegraph (1852-56) RC wk new, 107. *See also Catholic Telegraph*
Weekly Visitor (1833-35) RTS wk mag, 53, 135. *See also Visitor*
Weekly Visitor (1851-54) evCoE wk mag, 157n
Wesleyan Juvenile Offering (1844-78) WesMe mo mag, 138, 162n, 175n. *See also At Home and Abroad*
Wesleyan Methodist Association Magazine (1838-57) WMeAs mo mag, 85. *See also Methodist Monthly; United Methodist Free Churches Magazine*
Wesleyan Methodist Magazine (1822-1914) WesMe mo mag, 80, 81. *See also Arminian Magazine; Methodist Magazine*
Wesleyan Missionary Notices (1839-1904) WesMe mo rep, 80
Wesleyan Reform Union Magazine (1861-65) WesRef mo mag, 86. *See also Christian Words*
Wesleyan Times (1849-67) WesMe wk new, 81-82
Wings (1892-1925) temp mo mag, 143. *See also British Women's Temperance Journal*
Witness (1840-64) CoS; FrCoS 3/wk new, 90-91, 92
Witness (1874-1941) Pre wk new, 95. *See also Evangelical Witness*
Women in the Mission Field (1899-1903) SPG mo rep, 40. *See also Grain of Mustard Seed*
Wonston Weekly Calendar (1835?-37?) CoE wk mag, 150n
Work and Worship (1897-1915) RefCoE mo mag, 22
Working Man's Friend (1850-53) n-denom mo mag, 136
World (1827-32) ncon wk new, 12, 51, 61. *See also English Independent; Independent and Nonconformist; Nonconformist and Independent; Patriot*

haYehudi (1898-1913) Jew wk mag, 114
Yiddish Express (1895-) Jew wk, dai new, 114
Young Israel (1897-1901) Jew mag, 113
Young People (1899-1907) juv mo mag, 175n. *See also Golden Link Between Church and Home; Juvenile Instructor and Companion*
Youth's Instructor (1817-55) Me mo mag, 138
Youth's Magazine (1805-67) ev mo mag, 138

Zion's Casket (?-1837) ncon mo mag, 46. *See also Spiritual Magazine*
Zion's Trumpet (1798-1801) evCoE mo mag, 16. *See also Christian Guardian*
Zion's Trumpet (Penny Spiritual Magazine) (1833-68) ev mo mag, 46-47

General Index

Abrahams, Israel, 113
Achill Island, 21
Acton, Sir John (later Lord), 93, 102-3
Adderley, James G., 37
Addison, Joseph, 8
Adler, Cyrus, 113
Advowson, 44
Aged Pilgrims' Friend Society, 47
Allen, John, 134
Alliance Press Agency, 127
Allon, Henry, 60
American Civil War, 63, 75
American Episcopal Church, 22
Andrews, William Eusebius, 97-98
Angel, Moses, 111
Anglican evangelicals, 15-22
Anglicanism, 9, 151n
Anglo-Catholicism, 18, 22, 29, 30, 52
Anglo-Jewish Association, 112
Anti-Catholic periodicals, 21, 51-52, 89
Anti-patronage movement (Scotland), 90, 91, 94
Anti-Persecution Union, 119
Anti-Roman Pacquet, 7
Anti-slavery movement, 124-25
Anti-Slavery Reporter and Aborigines' Friend, 124
Anti-Slavery Society, 124
Apologia pro vita sua (Newman), 35
Archbishop of Canterbury, 24, 26
Arians, 10
Arminianism, 37, 79
Arminius, Jacob, 79, 80
Armstrong, R. A., 76
Arnold, Matthew, 75, 103
Arnold, Thomas, 33
Ashley, Lord. *See* Shaftesbury, Earl of
Ashwell, A. R., 31
Aspland, Robert, 73
Aspland, Robert Brook, 73
Associate Presbytery, 93-94
Association for the Promotion of the Unity of Christendom (APUC), 29
Athenian Mercury, 8
Augustine, 99, 167n

Bagehot, Walter, 74, 75, 76
Bagshawe, H. R., 100
Baines, Edward, 60
Band of Hope, 128-29
Baptist General Union, 71
Baptist Missionary Society, 71-72

Baptists, 45, 57, 67, 70-72. *See also* General Baptists, Particular Baptists
Barker, Joseph, 121
Barnardo, T. J., 56
Barnett, Canon Samuel, 153n
Barrie, J. M., 63, 139
Baxter, Michael, 49
Beard, Charles, 76
Beard, J. R., 74, 77
Beesley, E. S., 115
Beeton, Mrs. (Isabella), 48, 136
Begg, James, 156n
Belfast, 78, 83, 95, 128
Belloc, Hilaire, 168n
Benedictines, 106
Benefices Act of 1898, 44
Benisch, Abraham, 111-12
Benson, A. C., 153n
Benson, Joseph, 80
Bensusan, S. L., 113
Berenson, Bernard, 121
Bernard, Montague, 27
Besant, Annie, 114, 121
Bible Christians, 85
Bible Monthly, 88
Bible Society, 20
Bickersteth, Robert, 157n
Birmingham, 56, 70, 88, 99
Bishop, Edmund, 175n
Blackburn, John, 67
Blaikie, W. C., 93
Blavatsky, Madame H. P., 114
Blennerhasset, Sir Rowland, 168n
Block, Maurice, 167n
Blunt, Wilfrid Scawen, 168n
Boer War, 83
Bombay, 114
Book of Mormon, 109, 110
Booker (booksellers), 98
Booker, Thomas, 98-99
Bookman, 63
Book Room (Methodist), 79, 84, 85, 122
Boone, J. S., 24
Booth, Bramwell, 87
Booth, William, 41, 87
Bourne, Hugh, 84
Bourne, Stephen, 61
Bradlaugh, Charles, 120-21
Bresslau, M. H., 111
Bright, John, 125
Bristol, 149n
British and Foreign Aborigines' Protection Society, 125
British and Foreign School Society, 64
British and Foreign Unitarian Association, 73
British and Irish Press Guide (May's), 156n
British Anti-State-Church Association, 61
British Association for the Promotion of Temperance, 126
British Israel, 3
British Library, 154n, 158n, 163n
British Temperance League, 126
British Union Catalogue of Periodicals, 151n, 163n
Broad Church, 18, 33-35, 93
Brontë, Charlotte, 16
Browning, Robert, 73
Brownson's Quarterly Review, 167n
Bunting, Jabez, 80, 81, 85
Burder, George, 46
Burgess, Henry, 131
Burke, Edmund, 60
Burns, James, 102
Butler, Charles, 99
Byron, Lady, 75

Calvinism, 9, 10, 67, 71, 79, 89
Calvinistic Methodists (Welsh Presbyterians), 86
Cambridge Camden Society, 26
Cambridge University, 133; Press, 132
Cameronians, 93

Campbell, John, 12, 13, 58-59, 61, 67, 68-70
Capes, Frederick, 102
Capes, John Moore, 101-2
Care, Henry, 7
Carlile, Richard, 118
Carlile, Wilson, 41
Caroline, Queen, 81
Carpenter, William, 119
Carter, T. T., 29
Cassell, John, 48, 128, 137, 139
Catholic Apostolic Church, 96
Catholic Association, 97
Catholic Emancipation, 51
Catholic University of Ireland, 107-8
Catholics. *See* Roman Catholics
Chadwick, Edwin, 37
Chadwick, Owen, 1
Chalmers, Thomas, 93
"Charlotte Elizabeth." *See* Tonna
Charles, Thomas, 86
Chartism, 35
Chatterbox, 43, 139
Cheshire, 129
Cheyne, T. K., 113
Children's periodicals, 3-4, 13, 16, 40, 43, 53, 54-55, 64, 72, 84, 138-139
China Inland Mission, 124
Christadelphians, 88, 142
Christian's Amusement, 8
Christian Social Union, 36-37
Christian Socialism, 33, 35-37
Christian Socialist Society, 36
Church, R. W., 27, 28, 31
Church Army, 41, 87
Church Association, 21-22
Church Congresses, 39
Church Institution, 41
Church Missionary Society (CMS), 20, 123
Church of England, 15, 33, 37-42, 43-44, 45, 57, 131; Sunday School Institute, 138
Church of England Scripture Readers' Association, 21
Church of England Temperance Society, 41, 127
Church of England Total Abstinence Society, 127
Church of Ireland (Anglican), 42-43
Church of Jesus Christ of Latter-Day Saints. *See* Mormons
Church (Kirk) of Scotland, 89, 90-91, 93; General Assembly, 90
Church of the New Jerusalem (New Church), 109
Church Pastoral Aid Society, 21
Church Quarterly, 152n
Church rates, 60
Clapham Sect, 16, 19, 23
Clark, G. Kitson, 1
Clark, T. & T. (publishers), 133
Clarke, J. Erskine, 43, 139
Clarke, James, 62
Class journalism, 7
Cleave, John, 119
Clough, Archdeacon, 42
Clowes, William, 84
Cobden, Richard, 125
Coghlan, Peter, 97
Colenso, J. W., 40
Coleridge, Henry, 105
Coleridge, S. T., 33
Collins, Anthony (pseud.). *See* Johnson, William H.
Commonweal, 36
Compleat Library, 8
Comte, Auguste, 115
Conder, Josiah, 58
Congregational Union, 59, 68, 69
Congregational Union of Scotland, 70
Congregationalists (Independents), 5, 45, 57, 67-70, 131
Connaught Patriot, 107
Conquest by Healing, 124
Conroy, George, 108

Contemporary Review, 13, 34, 48, 75
Convocation, Province of Canterbury, 29, 39
Convocation, Province of York, 39
Cook, Thomas, 128
Cooper, Robert, 120
Cooperative Movement, 35, 36
Cornhill Magazine, 13
Cornish, Samuel, 119
Countess of Huntingdon's Connexion. *See* Huntingdon's Connexion, Countess of
Covenanters, 93
Cowper, B. Harris, 131
Cox, E. W., 38, 39
Cox, Samuel, 132-33
Cox (printers), 100
Crimean War, 69, 125
Critic, 38
Crockford, John, 38, 39
Cruikshank, George, 119
Cudden, Ambrose, 99
Cullen, Paul Cardinal, 107, 108
Cunningham, J. W., 149n
Cunningham, William, 149n
Curnock, Nehemiah, 81
Cyclopedia of Biblical Literature, 131

Dale, R. W., 70
Dallas, Alexander, 21
Darby, John Nelson, 88
Darwin, Charles, 13, 151n
Darwinism, 28
Davies, Llewellyn, 153n
Davis, Israel, 112, 113
Dawn of Day, 40
Dearmer, Percy, 153n
Dell, Robert, 104
Democrat, 172n
Denison, G. S., 29-30
Denvir, John, 105
Diamond, Charles, 106
Dictionary of the Bible, 133
Diocesan journals, 43
Directories, 37, 39
Disestablishment movement, 41, 42, 43, 58, 59, 60-61, 94
Disruption of 1843 (Scotland), 91
Dissenters, 57, 71
Dodd, William, 9, 23, 37
Dods, Marcus, 90
Dolling, "Father" (Robert), 153n
Döllinger, Ignaz von, 167n
Dolman, Charles, 98
Dominicans, 108
Douglas, David, 93
Dream of Gerontius (Newman), 105
Driffield, W. E., 100
Driver, S. R., 113
Dropsie College, 113
Drummond, Henry, 96
Dublin, 95, 101, 106, 108
Dublin Evening Post, 106
Duffy, James, 106
Dunton, John, 8
Dutton, Ann, 9, 15

Eardley, Sir Culling, 62
East London Mission, 87
Ecclesiological Society, 27
Eckett, Robert, 163n
Eclectic Society, 16
Economic Review, 37
Economist, 28, 75
Edinburgh, 48, 49, 133
Edinburgh Review, 4, 11, 16, 33, 58, 60, 92, 99
Education Act of 1870, 55
Emerson, Ralph Waldo, 59
Encyclopedia of Religion and Ethics, 133
English Church Union, 29
English College, Rome, 99
Englishwoman's Domestic Magazine, 136
Episcopal Church of Scotland, 42

Essays and Reviews, 18, 29-30, 33, 34, 80, 132, 161n
Evangelical Alliance, 52
Evangelicals, 15, 21, 28, 45-56. *See also* Anglican evangelicals, Scottish evangelicals
Exeter Hall, 61
Eyre, John, 46

Family Herald, 137
Family periodicals, 48, 54, 137-38
Farm Street community (Jesuit), 105
Field, 39
Foote, G. W., 172n
Fortnightly Review, 13
Fox, William Johnson, 73
Franklin, Jacob, 110
Fraser, A. C., 92-93
Free Church Movement, 64-65
Free Church of England, 22
Free Church (Kirk) of Scotland, 91-93, 103. General Assembly, 92
Freeman, E. A., 60, 75
Freeman's Journal (Dublin), 107
Freethought, 117-22
French Revolution, 10, 57
Friends. *See* Quakers
Froude, R. Hurrell, 26
Fry, Roger, 152n

Gallwey, Peter, 105
Garbett, Edward, 18-19
Gaskell, Elizabeth, 77
Gaskell, William, 77
General Baptists, 70, 71
Gentleman's Magazine, 9
George, Henry, 153n
Gerard, John, 105
Germany, 89, 132
Gilbert, W. S., 139
Gladstone, W. E., 28, 31, 35, 60, 63, 103
Glasgow, 78
Good Templars, 129
Gore, Charles, 152n, 153n
Gosse, Edmund, 133
Graetz, Heinrich, 113
Grant, James, 158n
Grant Duff, M. E., 75
Gray, Sir John, 107
Greenberg, L. J., 113
Greg, W. R., 75
Guild of St. Matthew, 36
Gurney, Samuel, 173n
Guthrie, Dr., 91

Hackney Phalanx, 23, 24, 25
Haddan, T. H., 27
Haeckel, Ernst, 122
Haldane, Alexander, 18-19, 27, 69, 158n
Hamilton, Andrew, 18
Hampden, R. D., 27
Hansard's Parliamentary Debates, 39
Harrison, Frederic, 115
Hastings, James, 133
Hayes, Matthew P., 166n
Headlam, Arthur C., 31
Headlam, Stewart, 36
Heaton, John, 71
Hebrew periodicals, 114
Hedley, Cuthbert, 100
Henderson, John, 62
Henry, Michael, 112
Herford, Brooke, 77
Herzl, Theodor, 112
Hetherington, Henry, 119
Heymann, S. L., 113
High Anglicans, 3, 4, 21-32
Hincks, William, 76
Hine, Edwards, 130
Hobson, J. A., 121, 153n
Hodder and Stoughton (publishers), 63, 132
Holborn Review, 82, 84, 85
Holland, Henry Scott, 36, 37

Holyoake, George Jacob, 119-20, 121
Home Rule, 105
Hood, Edwin Paxton, 59
Hooker, Sir Joseph, 151n
Hopkins, Gerard Manley, 105
Horne, R. H., 73
Hort, F. J. A., 132
Houghton, Walter, 4
Hughes, Hugh Price, 13, 65, 82-83, 143
Hughes, Thomas, 34, 36
Hull, 84
Humanist, 122
Humanity, 115
Huntingdon's Connexion, Countess of, 22, 86
Hutchinson, G. A., 55
Hutton, Richard Holt, 28, 34-35, 74, 75, 76
Huxley, T. H., 122
Hyde, Douglas, 108

Iconoclastes (pseud.). *See* Charles Bradlaugh
Idea of a University (Newman), 169n
India, 5, 114, 115
Ireland, 5, 21, 42-43, 83, 90, 94-95, 101, 106-8
Irish Monthly, 108
Irish periodicals, 42-43, 83, 95, 106-8
Irish Temperance League, 128
Irving, Edward, 96

Jackson, Thomas, 80
Jews' Free School, 111
John Bull, 23, 38, 44
Johnson, Lionel, 168n
Johnson, William H., 120
Jowett, Benjamin, 33, 151n
Joynes, J. L., 36
Justice, 36

Keating, George, 98
Keating, Patrick, 98
Keating and Brown (publishers), 98
Keble, John, 26, 28
Kennedy, W. P., 92-93
Kilham, Alexander, 83
Kinder, Richard, 76
Kingsley, Charles, 34, 35, 139
Kitson Clark, G. *See* Clark, G. Kitson
Kitto, John, 131
Knowles, J. T., 34

Labour Church, 115-16; Union, 115
Lady's Magazine, 136
Lancashire, 115, 129
Lancashire Independent College, 59
Lancet, 39
Lane, Denis, 105
Lathbury, D. C., 28, 31-32, 167n
Law Times, 38, 39
League of the Cross, 128
Lee, F. G., 29
Leeds, 71, 114
Letter to Lord Brougham (Miller), 90
Lewes, G. H., 60
Ley, Frank Rooke, 104
Liberal Party, 60, 64, 71, 83
Lichfield, 43
Lightfoot, J. B., 132
Lingard, John, 99
Linwood, William, 59
Littledale, Richard F., 30
Liverpool, 1, 74, 81, 105, 109
Livesey, Joseph, 126
Lloyd George, David, 64
Lockhart, Mrs., 104, 105
Lockhart, William, 105
Lodge, Oliver, 115
London Female Mission, 47, 136
London Journal, 137
London Missionary Society (LMS), 46, 64
London Quarterly and Holborn Review, 152
Londonderry, 95

Louth, 84
Low Church, 3, 15
Lowe, Robert, 167n
Lower classes, periodicals for, 135-36
Lucas, Frederick, 100-1, 104
Lucas, Samuel, 125
Ludlow, John Malcolm, 34, 35-36
Lurgan, 95
Lyceum, 108
Lynch, T. T., 59
Lyon, G. L., 113
Lyra Apostolica, 26

Macaulay, J., 55
Macaulay, Thomas, 4, 16
Macaulay, Zachary, 16
MacCabe, William Bernard, 169n
MacDonald, George, 139
MacHale, Archbishop, 107
Macleod, Norman, 13, 90, 137
Macmillan's Magazine, 13, 34
MacNeill, Eoin, 108
Magazines, religious, 5, 9-10, 11, 12, 13
Maguire, Robert, 127
Maitland, S. R., 24, 26
Manchester, 56, 77, 84, 126
Manning, Henry Edward, 100, 101, 102, 104, 106, 128
Mark Rutherford (W. H. White), 133
Marmaduke, James, 97
Marsden, J. B., 149n
Marshall, Thomas Lethbridge, 77
Martineau, Harriet, 73
Martineau, James, 73, 74-75, 77
Marx, Karl, 36
Masson, David, 91
Maurice, F. D., 33, 35, 36
Mauriceans, 34, 75
Maynooth College, 52, 100
Mayor, J. E. B., 132
McDonnell, T. M., 99
Medical Missionary Association, 124
Meldola, David, 111
Mercurius Theologicus, 8
Merry England, 104
Messenger and Advocate, 110
Metaphysical Society, 34
Methodist New Connexion, 83-84
Methodists, 10, 15, 45, 57, 79-86, 87. *See also* Bible Christians; Calvinistic Methodists; Methodist New Connexion; Primitive Methodists; Protestant Methodists; Wesleyan Methodists
Metropolitan Tabernacle (London), 72
Meynell, Alice, 104
Meynell, Wilfrid, 104
Miall, Charles, 61
Miall, Edward, 4, 58, 60-61
Middleton, Bishop Thomas, 25
Mill, James, 58
Mill, John Stuart, 73, 115
Millar, Thomas, 95
Miller, Hugh, 90-91, 92
Milner, Bishop John, 97-98
Milner, Mary, 136
Missionary press, 10-11, 123-24
Mitchell, Joseph, 111
Mivart, St. George, 103
M'Kechnie, C. C., 84-85
Montefiore, Claude, 113
Monthly Register, 104
Moody, Dwight L., 49
Moore, George, 108
Moran, Patrick F., 108
Moravians (United Brethren), 86-87
More, Hannah, 16, 53, 134
Morgan, Richard Cope, 49
Morley, John, 36
Mormons (Church of Jesus Christ of Latter-Day Saints), 1, 109-10, 142
Morning Advertiser, 158n
Morris, William, 36
Moyes, James, 100
Mozley, J. B., 25

Mozley, Thomas, 24
Murray, Archbishop Daniel, 106
Musicians, church, 134
Myers, Asher, 112-13
Myers, F. W. H., 115

Nangle, Edward, 21
Napoleon III, 76
Napoleonic Wars, 125
Narrative of Events Connected with the Publication of Tracts for the Times (Palmer), 25
Nares, Robert, 23
National Council of the Evangelical Free Churches, 64-65
National Society for Promoting the Education of the Poor in the Principles of the Established Church, 40-41
National Sunday League, 122
National Temperance League, 126
National Temperance Publication Depot, 173n
National Temperance Society, 126
National University of Ireland, 108
Neale, John Mason, 26-27
New Chronicle of Christian Education, 157n
New Church (Church of the New Jerusalem), 109
New College, Edinburgh, 93
New Dissent, 57, 79-88
New Ireland Review, 108
Newbery, John, 31
Newman, Ernest, 121
Newman, Francis, 74, 122
Newman, John Henry, 24, 25, 26, 27, 28, 35, 37, 99, 102, 105, 107, 134, 175n
Newry, 95
Newspapers, religious, 7, 11-12, 13, 49-51
Nichols, James, 80
Nichols, John, 47
Nicoll, William Robertson, 13, 63-64, 133, 134, 143
Nightingale, Florence, 151n
Nineteenth Century, 34
Noetics, 37
Nonconformity, 3, 15, 46, 57-65, 67, 69, 79, 83, 86, 125
Norris, Henry, 24, 25
Norwich, 97
Notes & Queries, 8
Nugent, James, 105

Oakeley, Frederick, 24-25
O'Connell, Daniel, 99, 106
O'Curry, Eugene, 107
Old Dissent, 45, 58, 67-78, 131
Olivers, Thomas, 80
Oriel College, Oxford, 37
Original Secession Church, 94
O'Shea, Kitty, 83
Owen, David, 41
Owen, Robert, 119
Oxford Movement, 17, 23, 24-25, 26, 101
Oxford University, 133; Press, 39

Pacquet of Advice from Rome, 7
Paine, Thomas, 118
Palmer, Edward, 47
Palmer, George Josiah, 30
Palmer, William, 25
Parish periodicals, 43
Parken, Daniel, 58
Parker, John W., 38, 154n
Parkin, Thomas, 119
Parliament, 90, 91
Parnell, Charles S., 83, 107
Particular Baptists, 70, 71
Pastor's College (Spurgeon), 72
Patmore, Coventry, 60, 168n

Pattison, Mark, 34, 75
Paul and Bee (shorthand reporters), 154n
Peace movement, 125
Peace Society (Society for the Promotion of Permanent and Universal Peace), 125
Pearson, C. H., 75
Penny Magazine, 40, 46
Peter Parley (pseud.), 138
Philo-Israel (pseud.), 130
Pilot, 106
Pitman brothers, 2, 135
Plymouth Brethren, 88
Pollock, Sir Frederick, 152n
Porritt, Arthur, 63
Positivist Church, 115
Positivists, 115
Post-Angel, 8
Powell, Baden, 132
Pratt, Daniel, 70
Pratt, Josiah, 20
Pratt, Parley, 1, 109
Presbyterian Church in Ireland, 94; Mission Board, 95
Presbyterian Church of England, 95
Presbyterian Church of Wales. *See* Calvinistic Methodists
Presbyterians, 57, 72, 89-96, 131; English, 95-96; Irish, 94-95
Preston Temperance Society, 126
Price, Edward, 98-99
Price, Thomas, 58-59
Priestley, Joseph, 10, 72, 73
Primitive Methodists, 82, 84-85
Prince of Wales, 30
Proctor, Richard A., 172n
Professional journals, 131-34
Prophecy, journals of, 49
Protestant, 4, 7, 51
Protestant Alliance, 52
Protestant Association, 51, 52
Protestant Methodists, 85
Protestant Operative Societies, 51
Protestant Reformation Society, 52
Punshon, William Morley, 81
Pure Literature Society, 56
Puritanism, 15, 67
Purton, Walter, 149n
Pusey, Edward Bouverie, 19, 151n

Quakers (Society of Friends), 57, 78-79, 124, 125
Quarterly Review, 11, 58, 92, 153n
Queen, 39
Quin, Michael J., 99, 100

Ragged School Union, 55-56
Ranken, G. E., 101
Raphall, M. J., 110
Rationalist Press Association, 122
Rationalist Society, 120
Rechabites, 129
Reform Act of 1832, 68
Reformed Episcopal Church, 22
Reformed Presbytery, 93
Relief Church, 94
Religious Tract Society (RTS), 2, 48, 53-55, 122, 134, 135, 136, 137, 138, 139, 143
Renouf, Peter le Page, 107, 168n
Reviews, religious quarterly, 11
Reynolds, G. W. M., 128
Reynolds, H. R., 60
Reynolds' News, 128
Richard, Henry, 125
Rigg, James Harrison, 82
Ripon, 1st Marquess of, 168n
Ritualism, 22, 26, 28, 29
Rivington, publisher, 24, 25, 26
Rivulet (Lynch), 59, 69
Roberts, Ellis, 42
Roberts, Robert, 88
Robertson, John M., 121

Robertson Nicoll, William. *See* Nicoll, William Robertson
Robillard, E., 103
Rogers, Frederic (Lord Blatchford), 27, 28
Rogers, James Guinness, 70
Roman Catholic Church, 24, 29, 101
Roman Catholics, 4, 7, 18, 21, 28, 42, 46-47, 93, 95, 97-108; Cisalpine, 99; Liberal, 93, 100, 101-3, 104; Ultramontane, 97, 99, 100, 101, 102, 103, 105
Rome, 99, 102
Roscher, Wilhelm, 167n
Roscoe, W. L., 74, 75
Rose, Hugh James, 25-26
Ross, W. Stewart, 172n
Roth, Cecil, 170n
Rotunda, London, 118
Round World and they that dwell therein, 143
Rowntree family, 78
Rugby, 33
Ruskin, John, 36
Russell, Charles (Lord), 168n
Russell, Charles W., 100
Russell, Matthew, 108
Ryland, J. E., 59

St. Martin's-in-the-Fields, London, 30
St. Michael's Church, Derby, 43
St. Saviour's Priory, 108
St. Sepulchre's Church, Cambridge, 26
Saladin (pseud.). *See* Ross, W. Stewart
Salvation Army, 41, 87
Salvation Printing Office, 87
Samuel, S. M., 112
Sanford, J. L., 76
Sankey, Ira David, 49
Sanwith, Humphrey, 81
Sayce, A. H., 113
Scotland, 5, 18, 42, 48, 49, 89, 94, 108, 128
Scotsman, 91
Scott, William, 25
Scottish Church, Regent Square, 96
Scottish evangelicals, 18, 90
Scottish periodicals, 89-94, 108
Scottish Missionary Society, 94
Scottish Reformation Society, 52, 89
Scottish Temperance League, 128
Secret History of the Oxford Movement (Walsh), 53
Seebohm family, 78
Senior, Nassau, 37
Sermon periodicals, 2, 135
Shaftesbury, 7th Earl of (Lord Ashley), 55, 173n
Shaftesbury Magazine, 55
Sharp, Martin R., 27
Shaw, G. B., 36
Shebbear (Devon), 85
Sheffield, 129
Sidgwick, Henry, 152n
Simony press, 44
Simpson, Richard, 101-3
Sinclair, W. M., 149n
Smart, Christopher, 9
Smeal, Robert, 78
Smeal, William, 78
Smith, Goldwin, 75
Smith, James, 166n
Smith, Thomas, 71
Smith, William Robertson, 133
Smithies, T. B., 136
Snead-Cox, J. G., 101
Society for Improving the System of Church Patronage in Scotland, 90
Society for Irish Church Missions to Roman Catholics, 21
Society for Promoting Christian Knowledge (SPCK), 40, 132
Society for Physical Research, 115; *Journal*, 115; *Proceedings*, 115
Society for the Abolition of the Slave Trade, 124

Society for the Diffusion of Useful Knowledge, 46
Society for the Liberation of Religion from State Control, 61
Society for the Promotion of Female Education in China, Africa and the East, 137
Society for the Promotion of Permanent and Universal Peace. *See* Peace Society
Society for the Propagation of the Gospel (SPG), 20, 40
Society of Friends (Quakers), 57, 77-78
Society of Jesus (Jesuits), 105
Society of St. Vincent de Paul, 105
South Place Chapel, 73
South Place Ethical Society, 116
Southwell, Charles, 119
Spears, Robert, 77
Spectator, 8
Spencer, Herbert, 60
Spiritualists, 114-15
Spurgeon, C. H., 2, 49, 51, 63, 71, 72, 135
Spurrell, William, 42
Stamp tax, 11, 12, 51, 62, 68, 69, 118, 119
Stanley, A. P., 33, 34
Stark, W. Emery, 44
Stead, W. T., 115
Steele, Richard, 8
Stephens, J. F., 75
Stokes, Scott Nasmyth, 167
Story, George, 80
Strahan, Alexander, 34, 48, 90, 137
Stubbs, Bishop William, 153n
Sullivan, William K., 107
Sunday School Union, 56, 64, 138
Sunday schools, 129, 138
Sutton, H. S., 127
Suwalski, Isaac, 114
Swedenborg, Emmanuel, 109
Swedenborgians, 109
Synge, J. M., 108

Tarrant, W. G., 77
Tatler, 8
Tayler, J. J., 74, 75-76
Taylor, Adam, 71
Taylor, Daniel, 71
Taylor, Fanny Margaret (Mother Magdalen), 104, 105
Taylor, Robert, 118
Temperance movement, 125-29
Temperance press, 3, 4, 41, 83, 95, 126-29
Temple, Frederick, 33
1066 and All That (Sellar and Yeatman), 153n
Theosophical Society, 114
Theosophist, 114
Theosophists, 114
Thom, J. H., 74
Thomas, David, 134
Thomas, Urijah Rees, 134
Thompson, Andrew, 90
Thompson, Francis, 104
Times, 44
Tiverton, 71
Tonna, Charlotte Elizabeth Browne, 47, 136
Toplady, Augustus, 10, 16
Tories, 11, 27, 28, 101
Townsend, Meredith, 35
Tract periodicals, 134
Tractarians, 24-25, 26, 27, 166n
Tracts, 2, 53, 134
Tracts for the Times, 24, 26, 134
Tregelles, S. P., 131
Trevor, John, 115-16
Trimmer, Sarah, 10, 135
Trollope, Anthony, 175n
Tuam, 107
Tweedie, William, 126
Tyrrell, George, 105

Ulster, 49, 94, 95
Union List of Serials, 151n, 163n
Union Magazine, 94
Unitarians, 10, 57, 72-77, 131
United Brethren (Moravians), 86
United Kingdom Alliance, 126-27
United Presbyterian Church, 94
United Secession Church, 89, 94
United States of America, 5, 88, 89, 109-10, 114, 132, 133
l'Univers, 105
Universalism, 72
University College, 108

Vallentine, Isaac, 111
Vatican Council (1869-70), 101
Vaughan, Herbert, 100, 101
Vaughan, Robert, 58, 59-60
Vaux, James Edward, 30
Vidler, William, 72
Voluntary Church Association, 94

Wales, 5, 41, 86
Walker, Robert, 104
Wallis, John, 101, 104
Ward, William George, 24, 25, 100, 102
Waterloo Directory of Victorian Periodicals, 2, 154n, 156n, 171n
Watson, Christopher Knight, 31
Watson, Joshua, 41, 42
Watts, Charles Albert, 121-22
Watts, John, 121
Webb, Beatrice, 153n
Webster, William, 8
Weekly Miscellany, 8, 9
Weekly newspapers, 11, 49-51
Wellesley Index to Victorian Periodicals, 8, 160n
Welsh periodicals, 5, 41-42, 71, 86, 135
Wesley, Charles, 80
Wesley, John, 9, 10, 15, 45, 79-80, 126
Wesleyan Methodist Association, 85-86
Wesleyan Methodist Connexion, 79-80, 83
Wesleyan Methodists, 79-83, 84, 86
Wesleyan Reform Union, 86
Wesleyan Reformers, 85-86
Westcott, Bishop B. F., 36
Westlake, W. C., 78
Westminster, archdiocese of, 100, 101
Westminster Review, 11, 34, 74
Wetherell, Thomas F., 102, 103
Whately, Richard, 37
Whigs, 7, 68
White, Joseph Blanco, 37
Whitefield, George, 9
Whittemore, Jonathan, 62, 64
Wicksteed, Charles, 74
Wicksteed, Philip H., 116
Wigley, George J., 105
Wilberforce, Basil, 153n
Wilberforce, Henry, 104
Wilberforce, Samuel, 104, 153n
Wilks, Samuel C., 149n
Williams, Sir George, 56
Wilson, H. B., 34
Wilson, William Carus, 16, 138
Wiseman, Nicholas, 99-100, 101, 102, 104
Wolf, Lucien, 112, 113
Women's periodicals, 47, 136-37
Woodlock, Bartholomew, 169n
Worcester College, Oxford, 25
Workers Onward, 129
Working class, periodicals for, 51, 136
Working Men's College, 35
Wright, John, 77

Yeats, W. B., 108
Yiddish periodicals, 114
Yonge, Charlotte, 28, 138
Yorkshire, 115
Young Men's Christian Association (YMCA), 56

Young Women's Christian Association (YWCA), 56

Zangwill, Israel, 112
Zenana Bible and Medical Mission, 124
Zenana Missionary Society, 124
Zionism, 112

ABOUT THE AUTHOR

JOSEF L. ALTHOLZ is Professor of History at the University of Minnesota. He has written *The Liberal Catholic Movement in England*, *The Churches in the Nineteenth Century*, *Victorian England, 1837–1901*, has coedited *The Correspondence of Lord Acton and Richard Simpson*, and has edited *The Mind and Art of Victorian England.* He has also written several articles.